Barings Bank,
William Bingham
and the Rise of
the American Nation

Barings Bank, William Bingham and the Rise of the American Nation

A Transatlantic Relationship from the Revolutionary War through the Louisiana Purchase

DAVID TEARLE

McFarland & Company, Inc., Publishers
Jefferson, North Carolina, and London

LIBRARY OF CONGRESS CATALOGUING-IN-PUBLICATION DATA

Tearle, David, 1947–
    Barings Bank, William Bingham and the rise of the American nation : a transatlantic relationship from the Revolutionary War through the Louisiana Purchase / David Tearle.
        p.   cm.
    Includes bibliographical references and index.

    ISBN 978-0-7864-4437-3
    softcover : 50# alkaline paper

    1. Baring Brothers & Co.— History. 2. Merchant banks— Great Britain — History — 18th century. 3. Investments, British — United States — History — 18th century. 4. United States— History — Revolution, 1775–1783. 5. United States— History — 1783–1815. I. Title.
    HG2998.B36T43   2010
    332.1'22 — dc22   2009046463

British Library cataloguing data are available

©2010 David Tearle. All rights reserved

No part of this book may be reproduced or transmitted in any form or by any means, electronic or mechanical, including photocopying or recording, or by any information storage and retrieval system, without permission in writing from the publisher.

On the cover: Cheapside, London, circa 1800 (Papworth's *Select Views of London*, Westminster City archive photograph)

Manufactured in the United States of America

McFarland & Company, Inc., Publishers
  Box 611, Jefferson, North Carolina 28640
    www.mcfarlandpub.com

Acknowledgments

I would like to express my indebtedness to the authors of the few works that have been published on the early years of William Bingham, Francis Baring and Henry Hope.

In particular, without Robert Alberts' *Golden Voyage, The Life and Times of William Bingham*, I could not have contemplated this work. William Bingham was largely ignored by American historians, until Margaret L. Brown produced three substantial articles for the *Pennsylvania Magazine of History and Biography* in 1937.

Bingham's profile lapsed again, despite Frederick S. Allis' epic two-volume, 1,325 page *"William Bingham's Maine Lands, 1790–1820,"* published by the Colonial Society of Massachusetts in 1954.

In the 1960s Robert Alberts picked up the William Bingham story again in the exhaustive study, *Golden Voyage*. Alberts (and Allis, and Brown) started from the history of an American entrepreneur and politician and found Francis Baring. By contrast I was researching the early history of Barings Bank and found William Bingham.

Baring Brothers & Co. was a private family concern that remained in the ownership of the Baring family from 1762 until 1995, when "rogue trader" Nick Leeson brought it to its knees and it was sold to the Dutch Bank ING for £1. Its history was well recorded, privately in the company records, and in family records. The company employed the services of archivists, firstly T. L. Ingram (between 1959 and 1978) and subsequently Dr. John Orbell, who has recently retired from the archive (which continued under the ownership of ING).

The first published work on the Baring Brothers bank was by John Orbell, *Baring Brothers & Co. Ltd., A History to 1939*, published by Baring Brothers & Co. Ltd. in 1985. This was followed up shortly afterwards by a major work (commissioned by the bank itself) written by the celebrated historian Philip Ziegler and published in 1988 by Collins: *The Sixth Great Power, Barings, 1762–1929*.

My starting point for Barings was Ziegler's book, and this was followed by some time spent in Baring's archive in London, help from John Orbell (and his book) and in particular help from Moira Lovegrove, who provided the necessary permissions. John Orbell directed me to the history of Hope & Co., the Dutch bank, by Marten G. Buist. *At Spes Non Fracta, Hope & Co., 1770–1815*, was commissioned and published by the bank in 1974, another very comprehensive work.

The story took me to Philadelphia next, and help from the Historical Society of Pennsylvania, The Library Company of Philadelphia, the American Philosophical Society, the Library at Winterthur, Delaware, the University of Pennsylvania Archives (Nancy R. Miller), and the Independence National Historical Park (Andrea Ashby).

Back in Britain I have been helped with information and sourcing illustrations by the archivists and librarians at the Devon Record Office, the Hampshire Archives and Local Studies Centre at the Hampshire Record Office (Alys Blakeway and Sarah Lewin), the City of Westminster Archive Centre (Rory Lalwan), the Local History Centre at the Lewisham Library Service (John Coulter), and the Wiltshire Heritage Museum (Lorna Haycock).

Since so much research these days is done via the internet I must also acknowledge the wealth of information readily available from (amongst many others) the Lilly Library at the University of Indiana, the UK and U.S. National Archives, the Library of Congress, the Biographical Directory of the United States Congress, the University of Virginia Library, the National Parks Service and the University of Pennsylvania Archives.

I also owe a very special debt of gratitude to my wife Shelagh, who put up with a grumpy writer and unmangled the typescript.

Contents

Acknowledgments v
Preface 1

1. Early Days in England — 5
2. Early Days in Philadelphia — 14
3. Trouble Brewing — 23
4. City Tavern — The Eve of War — 32
5. The Secret War — A Parisian in America — 37
6. William Bingham's Martinico Odyssey — 41
7. Willing, Morris and Bingham, Supplying Washington's Army — 50
8. Benjamin Franklin, an American in Paris — 62
9. Barings, Hopes and the Triple Alliance — 68
10. Bingham Returns to Philadelphia — 77
11. Mr. and Mrs. Bingham — 82
12. The Grand Tour — 90
13. New Country, New Constitution — 101
14. Property Fever — 112
15. Sir Francis Baring, Bart. — 118
16. Bingham and Baring Strike a Deal — 125
17. Barings and Bingham, American Consolidation — 135
18. The Death of Anne Bingham and a Turning Point — 144
19. The Louisiana Purchase — 153
20. Finale, a Concluding Commentary — 164
21. Epilogue — 170

Appendix A—The Historical Value of Money	175
Appendix B—Genealogy	176
Appendix C—Heritage Locations	184
Appendix D—Anne Willing Bingham	187
Appendix E—Baring and Bingham's Aristocracy	192
Appendix F—William Bingham and the *Pilgrim* Affair	194
Chapter Notes	197
Bibliography	229
Index	235

Preface

Researching and writing this book was not triggered by an interest in the American Revolutionary War, but by a local story in Devon, England, where my wife and I have lived now for several years.

We were walking the South West coast path along a section that had been described to us as Lord Revelstoke's carriage drive. A passing interest in who Lord Revelstoke might have been and why he should build this splendid drive led to a series of connections which took me back in time to Philadelphia in 1774 and the first Continental Congress.

Lord Revelstoke, it turned out, was Edward Charles Baring, who had acquired the Membland Estate in 1876, while he was senior partner of Baring Brothers Bank. His fellow senior partner in the bank and cousin, Henry Bingham Mildmay, had also acquired the adjacent estate of Flete at much the same time. The two Baring men had married sisters who had grown up at Flete before the estate (and that of Membland) had been lost to their family through some distant financial disaster. The question of why the two London grandees would marry two Devon sisters was still hanging when I read of the Barings Bank crash of 1890 — the one that preceded the Nick Leeson affair by almost 100 years, and was of equal magnitude, if without quite such devastating results.

Barings Bank crashed in 1890 because of one speculative investment too many in Argentina — the partners seemed somehow distracted in Devon. Only reluctant but decisive action by the Bank of England with support from, amongst others, Rothschild saved a run on British and European banks. Barings, as was the custom at the time for merchant banks, was a partnership and the liabilities of the partners unlimited. The quid pro quo imposed by the Bank of England on the partners, in particular Edward Charles Baring and Henry Bingham Mildmay, was draconian — in effect putting both men into bankruptcy and requiring the disposal of the Devon estates and the Mayfair townhouses and the sale of their sumptuous contents.

I resolved to write that story as "To the Manors Born" and while researching that I felt that I needed to know more of the early history of Barings Bank and the Baring family. From relatively humble roots in the wool trade in Bremen the family created the world's most successful merchant bank. Baring family members were to go on to dominate British politics for 100 years.

Francis and John Baring established their merchant house in 1762 in London, one of many attempting to service the huge expansion of world trade at the end of the 18th century. They were finding their feet and just turning a profit in the years running up to the American War of Independence. By 1803 they had arranged the financing of the Louisiana Purchase, and were described later by Richelieu as the "sixth greatest power in Europe after Britain, France, Austria, Prussia and Russia." The change from just another merchant house to preeminence seemed to happen around the time of and just after the American War of Independence and the creation of the United States. Was it a coincidence? And who was this senator from Philadelphia, William Bingham, who appears in the Baring family tree in 1798 and whose descendent, Henry Bingham Mildmay, was so publicly involved in the crash of 1890?

Researching William Bingham led inevitably to his clandestine role in supplying Washington's army as agent for the Continental Congress in French Martinique and his connection with Philadelphia merchants Thomas Willing and Robert Morris. The firm of Willing & Morris was deeply involved in the financing and organization of the Revolutionary War. Barings Bank acquired the agency of the United States in 1804. President John Adams said (after his term of office) of William Bingham that "he, Washington and the country had really been governed by Bingham and his family connections."

My enquiries started with the definitive and scholarly history *The Sixth Great Power, Barings 1762–1929* by Philip Ziegler, to whom I am indebted. This led in turn to Robert C. Alberts' biography of William Bingham, *The Golden Voyage*, similarly acknowledged, and then to Marten G. Buist's history on Hopes Bank, *At Spes Non Fracta*.

Each of these works are exhaustive and detailed, but I could not help but think that they were telling the story from a particular standpoint, especially Ziegler and Buist, whose books were commissioned by the banks themselves. Not so Alberts' *The Golden Voyage*, but that is clearly written as the life and times of one man — in this case William Bingham.

I decided that these great works were like ships passing in the night, not seeing each other, so I set out to go back and write the story as it actually unfolded and in the wider context of the political and mercantile history of Great Britain and the United States of America.

I have used many other sources to get a broader perspective on this remarkable story. I have been allowed access to the Barings Archive in London and studied hundreds of documents from sources in Britain and America.

This book covers events that took place over 200 years ago that have shaped the modern world and in particular laid the foundations for a superpower, the United States of America, and forced Britain to create a vast empire elsewhere in the world. This history comes to an end in 1804 and opens the door for the next one, but that is for another day and another book.

1. Early Days in England

Consider the year 1762. Britain and her empire were on top of the world—the French had been soundly defeated in the Seven Years War and her American colonies were finally secure, or at least, so it seemed. The industrial age had already dawned. The merchants of London, Bristol, Liverpool, Amsterdam, Philadelphia, Boston and New York were prospering as never before. At the end of December that year a new merchant house appeared in Cheapside, in the City of London, and over the door was the name John and Francis Baring & Co.

But the Baring story did not start in London, or even in England. It started in Bremen, Germany, when in 1717 20-year-old Johann Baring was sent to Exeter to act for the Vogel family textile business. Johann's parents were Lutheran pastor and professor of theology Franz Baring and Rebecca Vogels, the daughter of one of Bremen's leading wool merchants. Unfortunately, Franz Baring died in 1697 when Johann was only a few weeks old, and the youngster was brought up by Rebecca and her parents. The boy's future was now to lie in the wool trade and not the cloth.[1]

At the time much of Bremen's wool came from the English West Country, finished and dyed in Exeter prior to shipment, rather than in the raw form because of punitive British export taxes. The reciprocal trade from Germany to England was of linen made from continental flax, wine, tobacco and sugar.

The colored serge for the Vogel business was imported from Edmund Cock, an Exeter merchant and fuller and it was to him that the 20-year-old Johann was sent by his mother to serve an apprenticeship to learn the skills of wool finishing.

Johann was clearly successful, helped no doubt by the £500[2] that was his share of his father's estate, and in due course he decided to set up business on his own account, rather than return to Germany. He became a British citizen in 1723, adopting the name John. His success in business was matched by an excellent marriage to Elizabeth Vowler, the daughter of one of Exeter's most successful merchants, then retired, known as John Vowler of Bellair,[3] trading in tea, coffee and sugar. Although described in contemporary trade directories as a "grocer," John Vowler was clearly a very wealthy man as Elizabeth's dowry and subsequent inheritance on his death produced the very substantial sum of £20,000.[4] This ability to make good marriages capable of enhancing business success, starting with Franz and Rebecca and continuing with John and Elizabeth, is a common theme in the growth of the Baring family.

John and Elizabeth Baring's business—it was clearly very much a joint effort—continued to prosper, and five children were born to them between 1730 and 1744. John was born in 1730, Thomas in 1733, Francis in 1740, Charles in 1742 and Elizabeth in 1744. The burgeoning financial success of the business was such that in 1736 they were able to move from the center of Exeter to the substantial estate of Larkbear on the outskirts of the city. John and Elizabeth Baring could now count themselves amongst the West Country's most wealthy families. They were, however, despite their growing affluence, still "trade" and not "landed gentry"—not yet aristocratic, but perhaps on the way to achieving this aspiration.

This social climb received a setback, however, when John, whose health had been poor for some time, died of consumption in 1748 at the age of 51. Elizabeth had become accustomed to running the business and bringing up the children towards the end of John's life. She not only continued to run the business but with the help of eldest son John, now 18, actually expanded the merchant and factory operations.

John Baring senior left an estate of £40,000, of which £17,000 went to Elizabeth, £15,000 to John and £2,000 each to the other children.[5] This was a great deal of money and Elizabeth could well have retired gracefully on her inheritance but clearly felt that there was unfinished business to which she should attend.

With long-term objectives for her family clearly in mind, Elizabeth made sure that her sons received the best possible education. John, the eldest, just 18 at the time of his father's death, was sent to Geneva and travelled widely through Europe, expanding not only his own horizons but acquiring contacts and correspondents that would later feature in the expansion of the Baring business.

John returned from his European travels in 1755, and the younger bothers Francis and Charles were sent to London to be schooled and apprenticed to leading merchants. This left John and Thomas to run the business in Exeter with the continuing involvement of their strong-minded mother. This was destined to be a brief arrangement, as Thomas died suddenly in 1758 at the age of 25 and tragically soon after his marriage to Elizabeth Parker.[6] Charles, now 16, was thus recalled to assist his elder brother in the Exeter factory. Charles may well have felt aggrieved at being sent back to Exeter while Francis remained in London to complete his education and apprenticeship. If this was the case it would perhaps provide some explanation for his later behaviour. It soon became apparent, perhaps not surprisingly given his tender age, that Charles was not yet equipped for the responsibilities of running the Exeter business, either in experience or temperament. Difficulties lay ahead for Charles that in the end led to a split with his siblings and the mainstream business.

Francis, on the other hand, showed exceptional ability at his studies, particularly with his mathematical skills at Mr. Hargue's French School at Hoxton, and later at Mr. Fuller's Academy in Lothbury. He was apprenticed to Samuel Touchet,[7] a distinguished if colorful merchant with strong connections in the West Indian and cotton trades. Young Francis watched Touchet's approach to business with interest, and as he became more involved forged relationships, with Touchet's help, that had a major impact on the development of the Barings merchant and banking enterprise. At the end of his indenture with Samuel Touchet, Francis Baring considered himself fully trained, and after seven years in London had no desire to return to Exeter. He decided instead to set up as a merchant on his own account.

Francis' desire to stay in London and set up on his own presumably found favor back in Exeter, probably with younger brother Charles. There would, however, be risks in establishing a completely new business that could

Cheapside, London, circa 1800, from Papworth's *Select Views of London* (City of Westminster Archives Centre).

put the family capital in jeopardy. Fortuitously some of the risk could be laid off when Baring's London agent and longtime friend Nathaniel Paice proposed that Francis take over his merchant business as he retired. Nathaniel Paice was very well established with trade in America and the West Indies, and a director of the South Sea Company.[8]

With the advice and assistance of Nathaniel Paice it was decided to reorganize the Baring family business into two linked partnerships, one in Devon and one in London. Charles Baring would run the Exeter-based John and Charles Baring & Co., while Francis would run John & Francis Baring & Co. in London. John Baring would nominally be at the head of both partnerships. Partnership agreements for these two houses were created on Christmas Day 1762. Francis was 22 years old, Charles 20 and John 32.[9]

John Baring was by now an accomplished and relatively wealthy businessman in his own right, and in 1755 he had acquired the Mount Radford estate in Exeter, where he continued the life of a country gentleman that his father was becoming accustomed to before his untimely death. His role in the expanded family enterprise was to supervise the activities of his younger brothers, but in reality while Charles probably needed attention, Francis was a long way off in London and would have to fend for himself.

From 1763 John and Francis Baring & Co. operated from Cheapside, London, nominally with £20,000 of the family's capital, and John and Charles Baring & Co. from Exeter with the remaining £30,000. Unfortunately for Francis the reality was somewhat different and he actually found himself working with as little as £4,200.[10]

Francis Baring in London involved himself in trading in manufactured wool products, mainly for the Exeter partnership, but also for other West Country manufacturers. Significantly he was also providing financial or banking services by collecting money due on sales and remitting the proceeds to the other agency clients as well as to the family business. While it was probably not obvious at the time, it was this banking activity that would make the Baring brothers' London business stand out from the multitude of other merchants and traders in the city at the time. The rapid growth of world trade at the end of the French wars offered many opportunities and the house soon had accounts throughout Europe, initially in the wool trade but soon in other commodities such as copper, indigo, cochineal and even diamonds. Unlike Samuel Touchet, though, he had not involved himself in any human cargoes, at least not at that stage.

This growth in international trade in the latter part of the eighteenth century was not matched, however, by the financial machinery to facilitate it. The bill of exchange was the usual instrument for making payments between international centers and had been widely used since the Middle Ages. This was, however, an agreement to receive payment after the delivery or even subsequent sale of goods and required trust between the parties to work. The system could break down when this trust faltered, or when no relationship at all existed between buyer and seller. What was needed in such circumstances was a third party, trusted by both parties and having confidence in the supplier to supply and the buyer to pay. This third party would "accept" the relevant bill — guarantee its payment when it fell due. The buyer, of course, would be expected to place the "accepter" in funds prior to the due date. The acceptor would take a commission from the sale consideration, typically 5 percent, to cover his risk and his time in facilitating the transaction.

While Francis Baring did not invent the "acceptance" business, he was without doubt an early and successful exponent of the procedure. There were particular benefits for John and Francis Baring & Co. since cash flow could be generated from commission without tying up capital in the transactions involved. On the down side, however the payment guarantee was absolute and the liability on acceptance required constant vigilance (there were no limited liability companies at this time, and all guarantees were personal). Funds had to be accessible somewhere to cover the risk, although in those days before financial regulation this was not a legal prerequisite.

Elizabeth Baring, Francis' mother, was still very much concerned for Francis' future and warned him in a letter she wrote (in 1766, shortly before her death) of the risks that he might be taking, citing "Mr Touchet's example of grasping at too much."[11]

Francis was fully aware of the risks that he was taking, and the eventual fate of his erstwhile patron Samuel Touchet.[12] His situation was not improved by the sudden demands that Charles would make on his working capital, and he admitted much later in life that his experience in the early days did not necessarily match his ambition. However, as he built on the business of Nathaniel Paice he decided that the secret of success, in addition to the traits of intelligence, reliability and honesty that he had already shown, was to have access to accurate and timely intelligence, or information. To that end he set about establishing a network of correspondents throughout the world. To interpret the information he was gathering, however, he needed a broad understanding of the world, politics, religion, mathematics, geography, indeed all the sciences. As it happened he had been given an education, which, coupled with his undoubted intellect, was to be up to the task.

He made mistakes, of course, and not all his correspondents were reliable. Although he turned a profit in his second year of trading, it was ten years before the business was in cumulative surplus.

While the London business had been allocated £20,000 of the family capital of £50,000, in reality Francis had just £4,200 to work with in 1763. He inherited £5,000 on the death of his mother in 1766 and drew £2,000 from his original inheritance from his father. His brother put in £7,810 in 1766,

Francis Baring (1740–1810) by Benjamin West (Baring Archive Ltd., reference #PT010).

£1,500 in 1767 and £3,000 in 1769. By 1777 his personal capital in John & Francis Baring & Co. was less than £2,500. He remarked towards the end of his life that he had started out with a fortune of £10,000 and had spent £9,000 and was well into the last £1,000 before he really understood the business he was in. He also suffered the demands of the Exeter business and in particular the bad management of Charles, whose wild speculations and partnerships were squandering the capital of both businesses.[13]

He was able to share some of the load when he married Harriet Herring (1750–1804) in 1767. Harriet Herring was from a well-to-do family; her father William was a noted patron of the arts, and brother to Thomas Herring, Archbishop of Canterbury from 1747 to 1757. Harriet was also, helpfully, the co-heiress to the Herring fortune and in due course she was able to bring a sizeable legacy into their partnership.[14]

Harriet's father William was wealthy, well travelled, and like many young aristocratic gentlemen of the time had completed the Grand Tour of Europe, during which it was customary to collect works of art. He continued to commission from a number of artists in Britain on his return. Young Harriet, born at Lambeth Palace in London, was just 17 years old when she married. How she met Francis Baring is not known but she (or maybe her father?) must have been impressed with his credentials. She was certainly not destined for a life of luxury, at least not in the early years of their marriage, but like Francis' mother before her she seemed totally committed to the task ahead and held a powerful belief in building for generations into the future. For two years Francis and Harriet "lived over the shop" in Cheapside, but in 1769 they moved to new premises and a new home at 6 Mincing Lane, in the city of London, where their ten children were born: Maria, Dorothy, Elizabeth, Lydia, Thomas (1772–1848), Alexander (1774–1848), Henry (1777–1848), William (1779–1820), George (1781–1854) and Frances (b. 1785).[15]

Despite his relatively precarious position in the early years, Francis soon came to believe that the benefits of the guaranteed business from John and Charles Baring & Co. in Exeter was more than outweighed by the risks indulged in by Charles, and he might do better entirely on his own, and free of the Exeter partnership.

The opportunity to sever the links finally came in the autumn of 1776 after yet another risky scheme from Exeter. This time Charles appeared unannounced in Francis Baring's offices at Cheapside, together with three "associates" who had proposed a plan for spinning wool by machinery.[16] They were all en route to Lancashire to examine the new cotton mills with a view to establishing mechanized wool spinning in Devonshire.[17] Charles assured Francis that perhaps 200 to 300 pounds would be required for a trial before any commitment would be made. Two weeks late they returned, Charles having already signed a binding agreement for partnership whereby he agreed to advance capital of £20,000. Francis and by now John were totally convinced that the enterprise would sink both houses and decided that while the Baring partnerships should continue, this new enterprise should entirely be at Charles' own risk and with his own capital. Charles refused and John and Francis proposed that the partnerships be dissolved. Charles, believing that

Descendants of John Baring

Descendants of Francis Baring

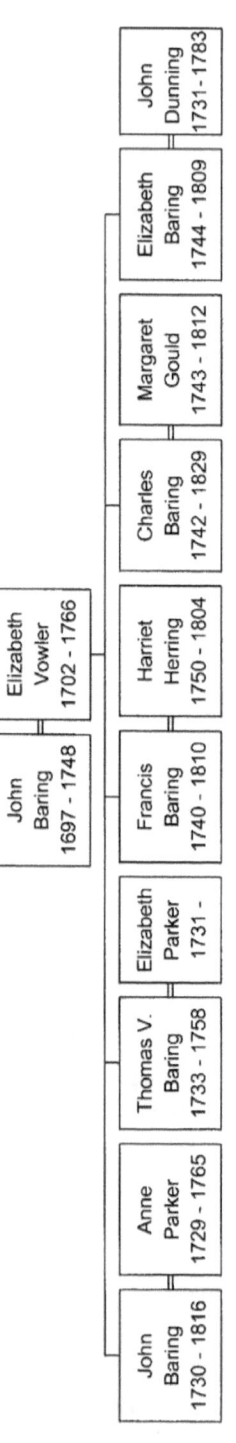

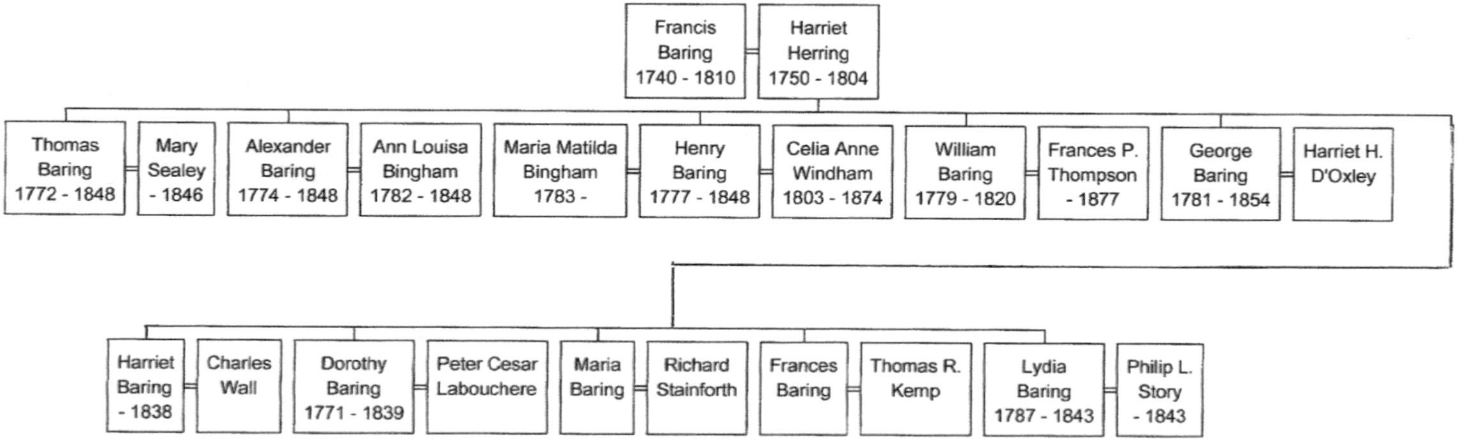

Ancestors of Francis Baring

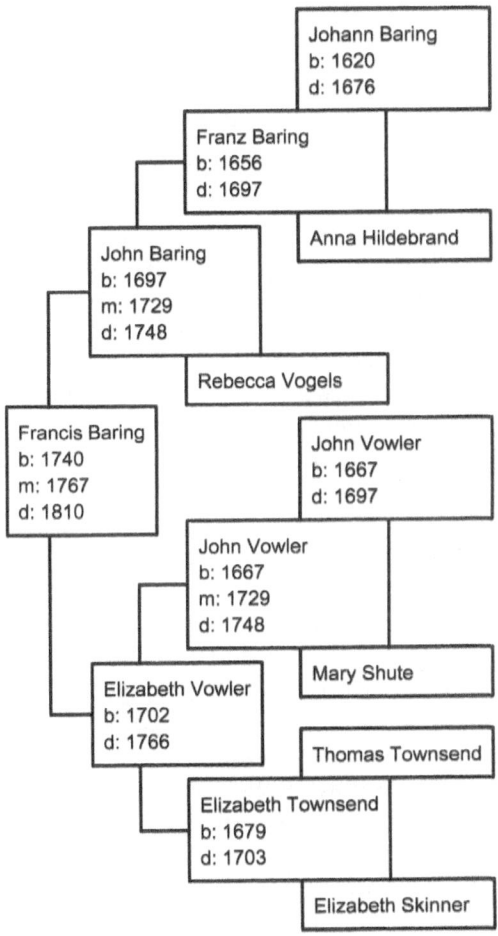

without Exeter's business London would not survive, (he may have been right) accepted. The partnership between Exeter and London was terminated at the end of December 1776.[18]

Francis Baring was a man with many original ideas. He had already decided that with correct and timely intelligence and the right connections, financing trade, rather than trade itself, had the potential for much greater rewards. In that respect Francis Baring was perhaps the world's first merchant banker.

The rise of the house of Baring had begun.

2. Early Days in Philadelphia

While Johann Baring had left his native Germany to make his mark in England, across the Atlantic in colonial America there were many families who had left Britain to pursue a future in the New World. Some of these families were also making significant progress, and over the next 50 years or so would be drawn together, intertwined, and become leading lights in the mercantile and political development of a new country.

In 1755, as Francis Baring was starting his apprenticeship in London with Samuel Touchet, a new merchant house was opening in Philadelphia. Robert Morris joined Thomas Willing in the partnership of Willing, Morris & Co., with its premises on Front Street, and adjacent wharves on the River Delaware.

This was not a new undertaking, however, as its origins go back to the business established by Thomas' uncle in 1726. This elder Thomas was born in Bristol, England, descended from a line of West Country merchants trading wheat, flour, sugar, tobacco, and molasses with the West Indies and the American colonies, and he was later joined by his brother, Charles, who in due course took over the running of the enterprise.[1]

In 1731 Charles (1710–1754) made an excellent marriage to Anne Shippen (1710–1791), daughter of Abigail Grosse and Joseph Shippen. The Shippen family were already one of Philadelphia's most prominent, having immigrated to Boston in 1668 from Yorkshire, England. Joseph's father, Edward had moved from Boston to Philadelphia, making a great success of his merchant business and his political career.[2]

This marriage of Charles Willing and Anne Shippen produced eleven children, ten of whom lived to maturity, leading to the establishment of yet another prolific and successful Philadelphia dynasty. Mary (Molly) married William Byrd III and inherited and lost one of the largest fortunes in Virginia, while Elizabeth married Samuel Powel, who later became mayor of Philadelphia.[3]

Charles Willing, as was now the custom in his circles, built for himself and his wife Anne one of the finest and most spacious houses in the city,

Statue of Robert Morris (1734–1806) in Independence National Historical Park.

occupying the block bordered by Third, Fourth, Spruce and Willing's Alley. He was active in public life; he assisted in the establishment of the Philadelphia Associators (a militia company) in 1744 and was a founder and trustee of the Academy and College of Philadelphia (now the University of Pennsylvania). Following in the steps of his father-in-law, he was elected mayor of Philadelphia in 1748 and again in 1754, the year of his death.[4]

The first child born to Charles and Abigail was Thomas Willing (1731–1821) who, growing up in the days before the Pennsylvania College, was sent back to the family home at Bath,

Thomas Willing (1731–1821) (Collections of the University of Pennsylvania Archive).

England, at the age of nine, for preparatory studies, in the care of his grandmother and uncle. He went on to London to study law at the Inner Temple and commerce at Watts Academy, before returning to Philadelphia in 1749 to join his father in the family business, where he was made a partner in 1751. Unfortunately Charles Willing died suddenly in 1754 at the age of 44 from ship fever contracted visiting one of his own ships. Thomas Willing, 23, the oldest of Charles and Anne's children, inherited the family home on Third Street, the warehouses and wharves and a fleet of shipping and business connections throughout Europe and the West Indies.

One of Charles Willings' key assistants had been a young Englishman, Robert Morris. Thomas Willing and Robert Morris had worked together for several years prior to Charles' death, and they established a strong working relationship and a friendship that would last, more or less, for the rest of their lives. When Thomas inherited the business he immediately took Robert Morris, just 20 years old, into junior partnership.

Robert Morris was born in Liverpool, England, in 1734. His grandfather Andrew Morris was a merchant sailor active in the trade with Chesapeake Bay from 1710, and his father, also Robert, had left England for Oxford, Maryland, to act as an agent for his employers, the Liverpool tobacco merchants Foster, Cunliffe and Sons. Robert Sr., who appears to have been a relatively well-educated man, owning a library (unusual for the time), married Elizabeth Murphet around 1732. Little is known of Elizabeth, who may well have died in childbirth, and she does not appear to have left Liverpool for America with her husband.[5]

Robert Morris Jr. left England to join his father in 1747, on one of Cunliffe's ships, at the age of 13.[6] His father entrusted his education to a Reverend Gordon. Robert was perhaps not impressed with his tutor, reporting to his father, "I have learned, Sir, all that the master could teach me."[7]

This modest schooling was brought to an abrupt end, however, just two years later, in July of 1750, when his father was accidentally shot during a welcoming ceremony on board a vessel that had been consigned to him. Robert Morris Sr. survived the wound inflicted by the shot but died a few days later from blood poisoning. In accordance with his father's wishes, Robert Jr. was sent to Robert Greenway, a Philadelphia merchant, a guardian charged with completing the boy's education and mercantile training. Greenway was able to place him in apprenticeship with fellow merchant Charles Willing, a most fortuitous opportunity.

Robert showed considerable aptitude in the countinghouse, and when Thomas Willing returned from England in 1749 they became a formidable team, and Willing, Morris and Co. was soon the foremost merchant house in America.

After his own father's untimely death four years later Thomas Willing found himself not only with a mercantile empire to run but also involved, inevitably, in public affairs, following on from his father. He was fortunate that he was able to leave much of the day-to-day running of Willing, Morris and Co. in Robert's increasingly capable hands, and was elected Common Councilman in 1755, and judge of Philadelphia's Orphan's Court in 1756. He followed his father to the office of mayor of Philadelphia in 1763, the year of his marriage to Anne McCall. This union of the Willings and the McCalls produced 13 children, and another dynasty.

Thomas Willing's political influence also continued to grow from the time of his father's death. He attended the 1754 Albany Congress as assistant secretary to the Pennsylvania delegation with Benjamin Franklin. He served as a Pennsylvania commissioner to oversee trade with the Indians and to survey the boundary between Pennsylvania and Maryland, and was a member of the Pennsylvania Assembly from 1764 to 1767. He was a justice of the Pennsylvania Supreme Court from 1767 to 1777. He was elected a trustee of the Philadelphia College in 1760 and a member of the American Philosophical Society in 1768.

Another family whose Quaker roots can be traced back to the West

Country of England was also making a mark in Philadelphia. John Bingham (a goldsmith by profession) and his wife Anne were early arrivals (sometime before 1680) to Burlington County, New Jersey, with a patent from John Fenwick for 1,000 acres in what was to become known as "Fenwick's Colony," the first permanent English-speaking colony in the Delaware Valley. His son James, born around 1668, moved to Philadelphia. Although he was described as a blacksmith, he accumulated considerable property and standing in Philadelphia before his death in 1714. He and his wife Anne are buried in Christ Church, where he had been a vestryman. They had one son, another James, his occupation being described as a saddler, who married Ann Budd.[8]

James Bingham inherited considerable property from his father and from the Budd family. His only surviving son, William, despite still being described as a saddler, married into yet another prosperous family. In 1745 he married Mary (Molly) Stamper, daughter of wealthy English merchant John Stamper, alderman, member of the Common Council and eventually the mayor of Philadelphia. Stamper was a contemporary of Benjamin Franklin and a founding investor of the Library Company of Philadelphia. In 1761 he bought from the Penn family the whole of the front of Pine Street from Second to Third for £1,200 sterling and built a number of fine houses, including one for himself at 224 Pine Street, known subsequently as the Stamper-Bingham-Blackwell Mansion. Like John Baring back in Exeter, Mayor John Stamper and Judge Thomas Willing at Spruce and Third were two of the very few in Philadelphia to own a carriage at that time.[9]

William Bingham joined his father-in-law John Stamper in partnership in the rum trade with the West Indies, and, like Stamper, Bingham became a member of the Common Council and a vestryman of St. Peter's Protestant Church.

William and Molly Bingham had five children, the fourth of whom was another William, born on April 8, 1752. Still only third-generation immigrants to colonial Pennsylvania, the Bingham family was now doing very well indeed — the young William Bingham would not need to make horseshoes or saddles for his living.

At six years old he was registered for the College of Philadelphia, which had been established by Benjamin Franklin, John Dickinson and others in 1755.[10]

Not much is recorded of William Bingham's early life, but we do know that his education at the College of Pennsylvania was thorough and probably the match of anything that he might have received in England. While the curriculum was classical, with emphasis on Greek and Latin, it also included geography, mathematics, logic, rhetoric, natural and moral philosophy, and of course the language of commerce in the eighteenth century, French. He matriculated from the College of Philadelphia in 1765, graduating with hon-

William Bingham (1752–1804) by Gilbert Stuart, 1797 (Baring Archive Ltd., reference #PT011).

Descendants of Thomas Willing

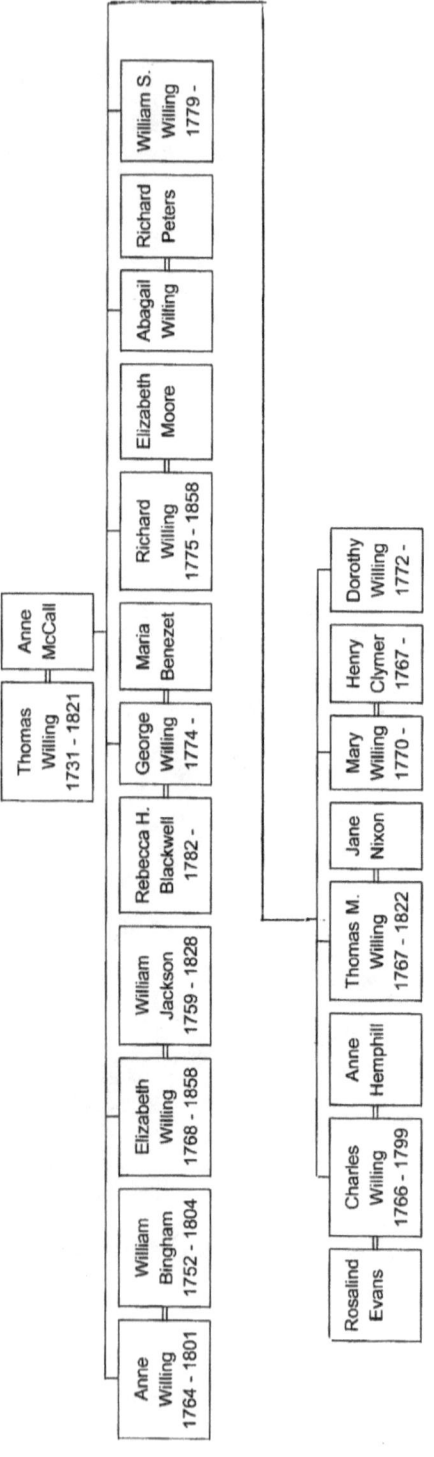

Early Days in Philadelphia 21

Ancestors of Thomas Willing   *Ancestors of William Bingham*

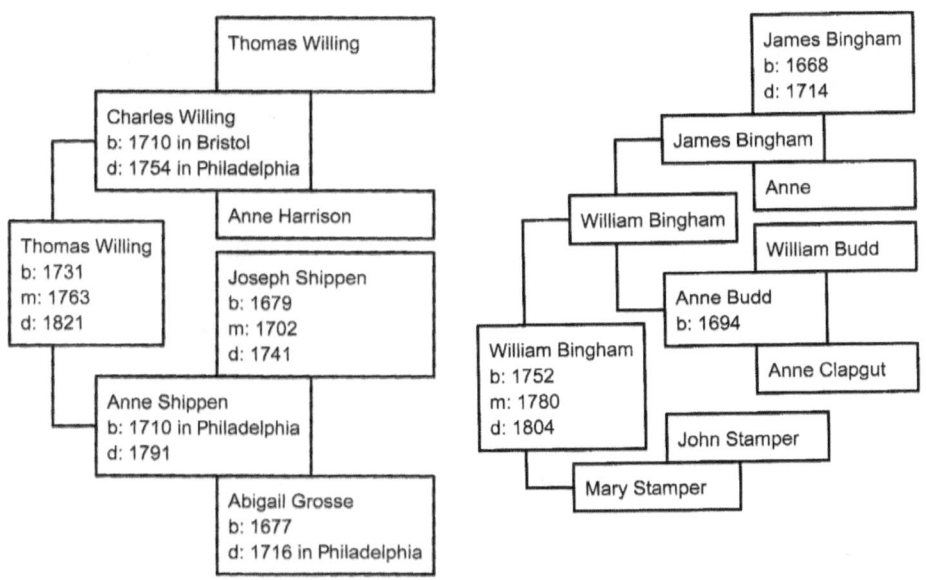

Descendants of William Bingham

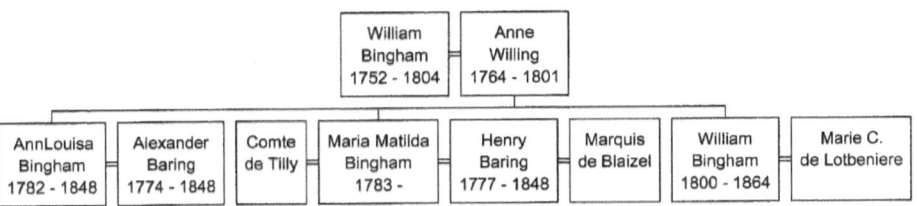

ors in 1768, following in the footsteps of his brothers James and John (of whom we know very little indeed).[11] At the college William Bingham had the good fortune to be taught Latin by James Wilson, who had emigrated from Scotland in 1766. While teaching at the college Wilson was also studying law in the practice of John Dickinson, and was awarded an honorary Masters degree and admitted to the bar in 1767. William Bingham and James Wilson would later become close business and political associates.

Bingham's father died in 1769 when William was only 17, but he was able to continue with his education, graduating with a Master of Arts degree from the college in 1771. His mother then introduced him to the influential Quaker merchant Thomas Wharton, who agreed to take him into his business to learn the skills of the countinghouse. Bingham used the opportunity to put the family fortune to work, and while still a clerk with Wharton had two ships at sea in his own right — the 20-ton brig *Sally*, and the 40-ton brig *Elizabeth*, owned in partnership with merchant master Robert Montgomery.[12]

Bingham did not spend much time with Thomas Wharton but the connection appears to be a critical link in the way his future was to develop. The Wharton family name appears in Pennsylvania around 1683, when another Thomas emigrated from Westmoreland, England. His son John served as coroner of Chester County, Pennsylvania, where his son, the aforementioned merchant, was born in 1735. He became a staunch opponent of the Stamp Act and one of the first to sign the non-importation agreement of 1765. In 1774 he became a member of the Committee of Correspondence and in 1775 the Committee of Safety. In 1777 he was elected governor of Pennsylvania, an office which he held until his death in 1778.[13]

William Bingham's short apprenticeship with Thomas Wharton came to an end early in 1773 when he set off for the Grand Tour of Europe. Such tours were popular among wealthy Philadelphia families at the time, as they were in England. With the storm clouds of a conflict with Britain growing, maybe it was a case of now or never. Few records of his trip have survived. He may well have made useful mercantile connections and perhaps seen the resentment between Britain and its American colonies from the other side. He toured Italy, France and England, returning not only with an eclectic collection of artwork, but with recent experience and knowledge of affairs in England.[14]

Bingham returned in 1774 to a country now incandescent about its treatment by the British government. The direction of his life was about to make sudden and quite unpredictable change.

3. Trouble Brewing

By the middle of the eighteenth century the American colonies had become powerful enough to demand a voice in the control of their own destiny. Unfortunately these demands were totally at odds with the British view of its empire. To the British government any relaxation in the handling of the colonies would result in the unravelling of its hard-won empire. We now know, of course, that the failure to hold onto the colonies would result in just that.

Around 1750 the British Empire in America comprised eight island colonies in the Atlantic and the Caribbean (Jamaica, the Leeward Islands, Antigua, Nevis, St. Kitts and Montserrat, Barbados, Bermuda and the Bahamas) and 15 provinces along almost 2,000 miles of the American eastern seaboard (Newfoundland, Nova Scotia, Massachusetts, New Hampshire, Rhode Island, Connecticut, New York, New Jersey, Pennsylvania, Delaware, Maryland, Virginia, North Carolina, South Carolina and Georgia).

Newfoundland and Nova Scotia were remote settlements taken from the French and little more than outposts. The remaining 13 colonies (who were to rebel against Britain and form the basis of the new nation) had a population of about 1.25 million plus a further 200,000 Negro slaves (most of whom were in Virginia). For comparison, the population of the British Isles was about 7 million at the same time.

The economies of the colonies showed much diversity. To the north, New England specialized in fishing, shipping and ship building. Boston was a major trading and shipping center, its American-owned and -built fleet playing a major role in the supply of the greater British Empire. Massachusetts was the center of a major rum-distilling trade, used to exchange for fur from the interior, and for slaves in West Africa, while New Hampshire's wealth lay in timber, particularly for ships' masts.

Upstate New York had a thriving Indian fur trade and Pennsylvania was developing an extensive iron industry.

To the south, in Maryland, Virginia and the Carolinas, tobacco was grown using Negro slave workers. To the extreme south rice and indigo were the staple crops.

The Caribbean Islands all had economies entirely based on sugar, dependent on the home (British) trade, and susceptible to French competition. Even then they were only marginally profitable.

Britain had developed a formidable empire through a structured mercantile system with control and the supply and re-export of goods from the center. As far back as 1660 the Navigation Acts barred foreign ships from the ports of British colonies and all trade was handled by British or colonial vessels. Britain's dominant Navy was matched by an equally dominant merchant marine.

By making its own ports the center of trade for the empire, Britain was able to gain advantage over its perceived competitors, mainly the French and Dutch. It obtained a first call on colonial supplies and could deny them to competitors if necessary; it provided British merchants a share of the profits on the import and re-export trade, particularly on very profitable commodities such as tobacco, rice and slaves. The Navigation and Trade Acts also prohibited the direct export to "foreign" countries of certain staple products, initially sugar from the islands, but later tobacco, rice, molasses, rum, naval supplies, copper and fur. Agricultural and timber products, however, were not proscribed and could be exported freely.

While these measures might appear excessively restrictive, the quid pro quo was a guaranteed home market for colonial commodities, and substantial profits for American merchants who were soon rivalling their British counterparts. They were also providing the environment to build up a substantial mercantile marine, American owned and manned, without which American independence, as we shall see, would not be possible.

The American colonies were at this time, therefore, more or less in equilibrium with the home nation, as well as their neighbors—Indians to the east, Spanish to the south and French to the north. This state of affairs may have continued indefinitely but for the eruption of the conflict between France and Britain in 1753, which was to become known as the Seven Years War, or the French and Indian War in America. The imperial titans squared up to establish which power was to be dominant, particularly in the east and on the American mainland. The efforts of Wolfe in America and Clive in India left Britain as the first world superpower, and in 1763 Parliament approved a peace treaty with France.

The effective disappearance of the French flag from North America lead the colonists to believe they no longer needed the protection of the mother country, thus fostering a feeling of self-sufficiency and independence. The mother country, Britain, on the other hand felt the need for closer organization and integration within the empire, and was coming to count the enormous cost of defending the colonies from the French and their Indian allies.

Financing the French war in North America was achieved by a loose arrangement of "requisition" whereby the British Crown demanded a contribution from each colony in rough proportion to its resources. The supply of these resources was dependent on the goodwill of the colonial assemblies, and incentives were used to encourage payment, by way of reimbursement. In addition the government undertook to supply the military hardware, ammunition, artillery, tents and other supplies, provided the colonies recruited and clothed and paid adequate numbers of men.

Some colonies were better than others and this added to pressure within the government to tighten its fiscal and political control. The British need to exert controls over trade with what it perceived as the enemy (in particular French settlements in the West Indies and in the St. Lawrence Valley) also caused mounting problems over this period. Direct trade with the French West Indies became illegal in 1756 but the colonists continued trading illicitly by using "neutral" ports such as St. Eustatius (Dutch), or Monte Christi, Hispaniola (Spanish).

The British government attempted to control this smuggling by the navy at sea and by the use of more customs officials on land. The effect of this, of course, was to create resentment among the colonists and irritation to the British, leading to even tighter controls.

In 1760 the British attempt to enforce the Molasses Act of 1733 lead to a campaign of defiance by merchants in Boston over writs of assistance, which empowered customs officers accompanied by a local peace officer to enter warehouses, stores or even homes, by force if necessary, to search for smuggled goods. Unlike a search warrant, no information had to be sworn, and the name of the informant could be concealed. Public resentment grew with the rhetoric of a young barrister, James Otis, who declared publicly that writs of assistance were "against the fundamental principles of law,"[1] and further that the acts of the British Parliament authorizing them were contrary to natural equity and therefore void. Although writs of assistance continued to be issued, they were no longer enforced. James Otis' speech reflected a growing resentment at central control *of any kind*, not only among the merchants but also in the wider population.

During this time and thereafter, the British government failed to grasp what being "an American," whether it was a "British American," a "German American" or a "Dutch American," was all about. The original immigrants had made difficult journeys and endured terrible hardships for a variety of reasons—to escape religious persecution, or to make money. They had several things in common, though; in particular a very strong work ethic and a determination to self-govern. By 1760, many families had six or more generations behind them and had accumulated real property by their own efforts. They saw intervention by the British government as a very serious affair.

George II had died in 1760 and he was succeeded to the throne by his son, the 22-year-old George III, who was determined to restore the influence of the Crown over the "Whig Oligarchy" that had prevailed during the reigns of his father and grandfather. This period was characterized by a shift of power away from the German Hanoverian monarchs towards a series of manipulative ministers, from Robert Walpole onwards. The politics of the period was essentially domestic, and the American colonies were fairly low on the agenda.

This position changed after the Seven Years War (1756–1763) when Britain and France attempted to settle the issue of "world supremacy," the outcome of which was in favor of the British. George III had been on the throne for three years and was keen to flex his muscles, and he and his ministers decided to set about what they considered to be "the American Problem," in particular how the new territories should be governed, how they should be defended and, most importantly, how this should all be funded.

The policy of the British government, the aspirations of King George, and the American colonial reaction to all of that would soon reshape the world.

Things got off to a bad start in 1763 with the British government's "Great Proclamation" limiting the boundary of American colonial activity to the Allegheny Mountains, effectively preventing westward expansion — seen by the colonists as destroying their future. In any case they could see no reason to replace the French by the Indians as the barrier to westward expansion. Particularly upset by the proclamation was the frontiersman, landowner and soldier George Washington, who had served in the British Army with great distinction in the French and Indian War. (His success as a military commander under the British flag enabled him to make a match with a wealthy young widow with 17,000 acres and a fortune to match, but the British Army still did not offer the regular commission that he felt he deserved, an irritation that was to stay with him for the next 20 years, and a decision that the British government would live to regret.)

"The Great Proclamation," seen from the British perspective, was an elegant solution that would prevent further conflict with the Indians, stop settlers escaping from British control, and make it easier for British troops to defend the colonies from further attack, particularly the French. The outbreak of the Indian War, the so-called "conspiracy of Pontiac" in May 1763, further re-enforced the British resolve to exert a firm grip over the colonies.

British Prime Minister Grenville now turned his attention to taxation. Britain's national debt before the war was £60 million and by 1764 stood at £133 million, with interest payments crippling the public finances.[2] He resolved that the Americans should pay the indirect taxes that they had hitherto largely evaded by introducing the Sugar Act in 1764 — a revision of the

Molasses Act but with the provision of custom officials to enforce payment. This not only initiated colonial resistance to trade regulation for raising revenues but it also cost more to administer than it raised in tax revenues. Grenville's government, however, pressed on with this approach, extending it in 1765 by a special "tax for America" called the Stamp Act, which taxed all licenses, playing cards, legal documents and papers. Opposition to these measures became increasingly vocal and for the first time the now famous cries of "no taxation without representation" were heard. Colonists took to describing themselves "sons of liberty"—an expression coined by Isaac Barré in Parliament in a speech opposing the Stamp Act.[3]

The Grenville administration never survived to face the crisis provoked by its measures, since it was no longer in office. Grenville resigned in July 1765 to be replaced by the Marquis of Rockingham.

In August 1765 Stamp Act riots broke out in Boston, and in October the Stamp Act Congress took place in New York. This was the first time that individual colonies had worked together, and it was agreed that until the Stamp Act was repealed they would impose a non-importation ban on British goods.

Rockingham's new administration was less enthusiastic about the Stamp Act and its consequences and was coming under pressure from merchants in London, Liverpool and Bristol who were being hurt by the boycott of British manufactures and the refusal of American merchants to settle their debts.

The Stamp Act was duly repealed in 1766, and the immediate crisis was over. Perhaps the most significant result of the affair was that the inhabitants of the various colonies who had achieved only modest unity in the French and Indian war a decade earlier were now managing to cooperate in a common cause and develop a sense of common identity in resisting the British encroachment on their constitutional rights. By 1765 James Otis was already asking the question "why trade, commerce, arts, sciences and manufactures should not be as free for an American as for a European?"[4] The events of 1765 to 1766 caused a hardening of attitudes on both sides which persisted over the remaining years before matters finally and inevitably came to a head.

Rockingham introduced the Revenue Act in 1766, reducing the duty on molasses to a level that the colonists said they could afford to pay, and by 1776 it had raised more than the Sugar Act, Stamp Act and the later Townshend's Duties put together.

Rockingham, if left to his own devices, would perhaps have let matters rest, but his administration failed in 1766, to be replaced by that of William Pitt, now Earl of Chatham. Faced by a massive budget shortfall, Chatham's Chancellor of the Exchequer, Charles Townshend, proposed a series of "external" duties (lead, paper, paint, glass—and tea!).[5] Townshend was also responsible for the establishment of the American Board of Customs, to tighten customs regulations, and the New York Restraining Act, requiring the colony to provide supplies and billets for British troops. The colony had previously refused on the grounds that it was covert taxation.

At this point the British cabinet was thrown into confusion and left rudderless by the sudden mental collapse of Chatham early in 1767, and in his absence the lead was taken by his erratic chancellor, Charles Townshend. Townshend himself lasted just a few months before he died in August of 1767, at which point Chatham resigned, to be replaced by the Duke of Grafton. Grafton was perhaps not the best appointment at the time as he was more concerned with domestic matters than what was going on across the Atlantic.

The reaction to the Townshend Duties, enacted in 1767, was, if anything, more defiant than two years previously, and led to prominent merchants and politicians organizing a non-consumption agreement followed a few months later by a second non-importation agreement. The driving force behind the colonial cooperation was the radical Boston lawyer Samuel Adams. Boston was increasingly becoming the center of resistance because the new Board of Customs was based there, and more British troops had been sent to support its activities.

In February of 1768 Adams drafted a manifesto denouncing the Townshend Duties as violating the principle of "no taxation without representation," rejecting the principle of colonial representation at Westminster, outlining plans for resistance in Boston and calling for joint action in defense of colonial liberties. This was circulated to other colonial legislatures, with the authorization of the Massachusetts House of Representatives, and received with approval by most, particularly Virginia. A flood of support for the resistance to the Townshend Acts poured from the colonial press, notably John Dickinson's *Letters from a Farmer in Pennsylvania*, arguing against Parliament's right to impose commercial regulation for the purpose of raising revenue.

Colonial resistance now took a more sinister turn, with organized acts of violence, particularly against customs officials—the newly established American Board of Customs was terrorized into withdrawing from Boston to the safety of a warship, and finally to the fortress of Castle William.

In New York and Philadelphia local merchant houses were establishing links in Holland, in breach of the Navigation and Trade Acts. Illicit trade was opened up through the Dutch West Indies at St. Eustatius, and the Portuguese Atlantic Islands. Dutch tea was illegally and openly imported in huge quantities. British imperial authority and its system of commercial regulation was unravelling. It was becoming increasingly clear in London that no appreciable revenue would be forthcoming from the Townshend Duties without military intervention, and the British government (now under the guidance of Frederick, Lord North (who took over as prime minister on the resignation of his cousin Grafton) decided on a tactical retreat and repealed the duties (other than on tea, in attempt to reserve their right to such taxation). In response the colonial non-consumption and non-importation agreements lapsed, at least temporarily. The retention of the tea duty had an immeasurable fiscal effect for the British Treasury, but henceforth would stand as a fatal stumbling block to the restoration of good relations between Great Britain and its American colonies.

On the very day in March 1770 that the Revenue Act repealed the Townshend Duties, what was soon described as "the Boston Massacre" took place, which was probably the point of no return in Anglo-American relations. America and Britain were sliding towards war.

Four regiments of British soldiers had been stationed in Boston since the fall of 1768 and had been subject to verbal and physical attacks. In February 1770 a mob attacked the home of a customs official who fired a gun from an upstairs window, wounding an 11-year-old. Troops were called out to keep the peace. On March 2 another fight broke out between soldiers and workmen. On March 5 a mob of 50 or 60 men surrounded the Customs House. Captain Preston sent seven soldiers to assist the sentry. The mob attacked the soldiers, who fired, killing five and wounding six, mostly bystanders.

It is debatable what actually happened, but the colonial press had a field-day; the following night a meeting was held in Boston's Old South Meeting House, and a crowd of over 1,000 people would not leave until the governor agreed to withdraw the soldiers to their barracks.

The British troops were withdrawn and did not return until after 1776. Preston and his soldiers were tried for murder. They were famously defended by John Adams, later president, and acquitted.

If the concept of revolution was seeded anywhere, it was on the floor of the Old South Meeting House, where James Otis inspired the setting up of Committees of Correspondence in each of the colonies. The first of these was set up in Boston by Samuel Adams in 1772, when the British government decided that the judges of the Massachusetts Court would be paid from custom-house receipts rather than by the colony itself. A town meeting expressed the view that judges would in future be biased, and that this was yet another infringement of their liberty. Sam Adams wrote from the Massachusetts Committee to the other colonies expressing his concern. The other colonies quickly followed suit with their own committees.

These developments did not go unnoticed either by the governors or by the British government in London, which continued to believe that dissent was largely restricted to Massachusetts, which could be dealt with in due course.

For a while the non-importation agreement started to break down and the momentum of the "sons of liberty" started to slow, but Lord North's Tea Act of 1773 changed all that.

The Tea Act was passed in May 1773, ironically in an attempt to assist the financial fortunes of the ailing East India Company, whose trading position had been badly affected by the colonial non-importation agreements and a general reduction in trade. Although Lord North had repealed four out of the five Townshend Duties, the import tax on East India Company tea, at three pence per pound, remained in place. The Americans declined to buy the tea in any great quantity, preferring to bring in smuggled Dutch tea, both on principle and because it was cheaper. The East India Company had made the simple pragmatic proposal that the three pence duty be removed, but the government was determined to demonstrate its right to tax.

The provisions of the Tea Act, in effect, were to tax the tea at source, in India, but allow it to be shipped direct to American ports, and thereby remove the previous re-export tax. This would make the tea nine pence cheaper, even when the three pence import duty was included. However, the East India Company would have the right sell using only merchants or agents affiliated with the company.

To the Americans, already outraged over the principles of taxation, this was perceived as a further oppression and it was decided through the Committees of Correspondence that the East India tea would not be landed. The activists saw an ideal opportunity to advance their political cause. In all the major ports steps were taken to intimidate those who had agreed to act as company tea agents.

The first public action was taken in Philadelphia in December 1773, where an assembly of several thousand people in the State House yard passed a series of resolutions denying the right of parliamentary taxation. The captain of the East Indiaman *Polly* was present at the meeting and he agreed to comply with the wishes of the assembly and left the following day, his entire cargo intact. In Charleston the tea was landed but held in a warehouse, from where it was later sold to finance the conflict with Britain.

However, in Boston, there was no such peaceful outcome. The popular leaders met and demanded that the consignees of the tea resign, which they refused to do. The first tea ship, the *Dartmouth*, arrived in Boston Harbor on November 27, 1773, followed by two more a few days later. As in Philadelphia mass meetings demanded that the tea be returned. Governor Hutchinson stepped in and insisted that it be landed. By this time the consignee was prepared to return the cargo to Britain but Hutchinson refused a permit and ordered warships to prevent *Dartmouth* from sailing. Meanwhile the cargo, upon which duty was payable after 20 days, had been registered at the customs house. On the twentieth day, December 16, with customs men about to land the cargo, the mob took over and men disguised as Indians dumped the tea chests into the harbor.

News of what became known as "The Boston Tea Party" reached London in January 1774. The reaction of the press and the public was angry and unequivocal; Massachusetts should be punished, as an example to the other colonies.

Unfortunately the death of George Grenville in 1771 had removed the most strident opposition leaders (i.e., supporters of American conciliation) and his followers had been absorbed into the North administration. Those who supported Chatham's conciliatory approach to the Americans had withdrawn or been removed from the cabinet, which was now dominated by North's imperialist henchmen. The King himself, now extremely concerned about the patriots, was prepared to support firm action. The British government's response was to pass a series of bills through Parliament, known in Britain as the Coercive Acts, and by the Americans as the Intolerable Acts.

The first act was the Boston Port Act, passed in March 1774, effectively closing the port of Boston to all shipping until such time as the East India Company was recompensed by the citizens of Massachusetts for its lost tea, to be enforced by the Royal Navy.

The Massachusetts Bay Regulating Act was passed in May 1774, passing effective control of the colony to the British Crown (in the form of General Gage).

The Administration of Justice Act, May 1774, empowered the (British) governor of Massachusetts to remove trials of capital offenses to some other colony or to Great Britain.

The Quartering Act of June 1774 gave the British Army the power to billet its troops in any location, including the dwellings of private individuals.

Finally, and although not intended as a punitive measure, the Quebec Act was passed later in the year. The Quebec Act was essentially a housekeeping measure, but was seen as yet another intolerable act.

General Gage was dispatched to Boston to enforce the new measures, arriving in May of 1774. News of the succession of acts passed by the British government and the arrival of General Gage and his troops spread rapidly along the Atlantic seaboard of the colonies, stirring up massive support for Massachusetts. Town meetings were called and held in defiance of colonial governors, with motions carried to cease trade with Britain and call a Continental Congress of all the states.

There would be no turning back.

4. City Tavern — The Eve of War

News that the British were to close the port of Boston reached Philadelphia in May of 1774. Paul Revere rode into the city with a request from the citizens of Massachusetts for support. On June 1 Philadelphia's shops and businesses were closed as a token of solidarity, and two weeks later John Dickinson and Thomas Willing presided over a general meeting of citizens held in the State House yard. Eight resolutions were passed. The Boston Port Bill was declared to be illegal and it was agreed that the colonies should convene a Continental Congress to decide what further action should be taken. A committee of 43 members was formed which would meet in July at Carpenters Hall, chaired by Thomas Willing. This convention issued a declaration of colonial rights and pledged Pennsylvania's support in any united action.[1]

The reports of Boston's plight were met with equal alarm in Virginia, already on the verge of revolt, and instigated by Thomas Jefferson and Patrick Henry, a Provincial Convention was formed — in effect a revolutionary legislature.

The venue of the First Continental Congress (first proposed by Samuel Adams) was chosen by the Massachusetts Assembly to be Philadelphia and the date to be September 1, 1774. British General (and now Governor) Gage immediately dissolved the assembly. The other royal governors also acted to prevent their assemblies from choosing delegates, but one way or another every colony except Georgia had a delegation ready to attend the Congress before the end of August.

The delegates included Patrick Henry, George Washington and Richard Henry Lee from Virginia, John and Sam Adams from Massachusetts, John Jay from New York, Silas Deane from Connecticut, Joseph Galloway, Thomas Mifflin and John Dickinson from Pennsylvania, William Livingston from New Jersey and Thomas McKean from Delaware. The new Congress sat for six weeks in Carpenters Hall, Philadelphia, "to deliberate and determine upon

City Tavern, Philadelphia, William Russell Birch, circa 1800. "The City of Philadelphia in the State of Pennsylvania."

wise and proper measures..." against the mother country to restore the "union and harmony most ardently desired by all good men."

The delegates agreed to reconvene the following May, adjourned and returned to their homes, having pledged to defy the Coercive Acts and support Massachusetts with a trade embargo against Great Britain, adopted a declaration of rights, and finally drafted letters to the British people and to King George III. Thomas Jefferson summarized the view of the delegates: "Our cause is just, our union is perfect ... if necessary foreign assistance is undoubtedly available."[2]

While the intention of most delegates, considering themselves as they did "British Americans," was to try to bring Britain to its senses and cut a better deal, the public view polarized inevitably into "patriots" and "loyalists." Loyalists were hounded down and the fabric of royal colonial government disintegrated as local committees of association assumed executive powers and took over the role of the colonial legislatures. By the end of 1774 revolutionary committees were active, encouraging the drilling of militia and endeavoring to acquire military equipment and gunpowder by seizure or by arrangements to purchase abroad.

By imposition of the Coercive Acts, described as the "Intolerable Acts" by the rebels, George III's government had thrown down the gauntlet — the Continental Congress picked it up with determination, and the news of this was soon back in London.

In the afternoon of April 24, 1775, an express rider from Trenton clattered into Philadelphia and went straight to the City Tavern, carrying dispatches addressed "To all friends of American Liberty," and declaring that on the previous Wednesday night a brigade of British regulars "without any provocation" had fired on and killed six New England militiamen at Lexington. The dispatches went on to confirm that in the ensuing confused engagements the British suffered 73 dead, 200 wounded and 5 missing, while American casualties were 49 dead, 39 wounded and 5 missing.[3]

The Second Continental Congress duly assembled as agreed on May 10, 1775, in the Assembly Chamber of the State House in Philadelphia, with a total of 64 delegates, this time representing all 13 colonies. Notable additions were John Hancock from Massachusetts, Robert Livingston from New York, Benjamin Franklin (recently arrived from London and from a last-minute and unsuccessful appeal to the British Parliament for a peaceful outcome), Thomas Willing, James Wilson and Edward Biddle from Pennsylvania and Thomas Jefferson from Virginia.

Since hostilities with Britain had now already broken out at Lexington and Concord, Congress, like it or not, was no longer a "talking shop" but a revolutionary government, and at least for the time being had to combine the responsibilities of executive, legislative and judicial administration.

The delegates agreed that a proper united army (rather than just the state militias), and someone to lead it would be essential to bring Britain to the negotiating table. From the time of the first skirmish with the British at Lexington, Virginia's delegate General George Washington had taken to arriving at Congress wearing the uniform of an officer of the Fairfax militia.[4] Since there were no other viable candidates, Washington was elected unanimously as commander-in-chief of the new army. Washington was not only a very experienced officer in the British Army but had for a while been committed to a military response to the British strictures. He had been passed over for senior appointment within the British Army at the end of the Seven Years War. He had been vocal in his opposition to the Stamp Act and blamed the British government for falling tobacco prices; he found the "Intolerable Acts" intolerable and was incensed when generous land grants offered to officers serving in the Seven Years War were restricted to regulars only. There is no doubt that Congress felt they had the right man — even if he was the only man.

On June 14 (the day that rebel militiamen were defeated at Bunker Hill) Congress resolved to raise six companies on the Pennsylvania, Maryland and Virginia border to be funded centrally (rather than by individual states); this force would be known as the American Continental Army. Washington was instructed to draw up the necessary regulations, and by July 3 he was in Cambridge, Massachusetts, as commander. Congress issued a "Declaration of the Causes and Necessity for Taking Up Arms," which stopped just short of a "Declaration of Independence."

Congress hoped that this document would be sufficient to encourage Britain to negotiate, but (under advice from General Gage to London that Congress was already set on its freedom), George III proclaimed the colonies to be in a state of rebellion, with the result that all-out war was now the only likely outcome.[5]

Through the summer and fall of 1775, the colonies prepared themselves for war by setting up committees of public safety and committees of correspondence. Militias were drilled, and firearms and gunpowder were collected. Within days of his return from London and his attendance at the Congress, Benjamin Franklin was appointed chairman of the Philadelphia Committee of Public Safety. Thomas Wharton was also appointed to the Philadelphia committees of safety and correspondence.

On November 8, 1775, the Continental Congress created a national Secret Committee (renamed the Committee of Commerce in 1777, and the forerunner of the Department of Commerce) to procure arms and manage imports and exports. On November 29 Congress created the Committee of Secret Correspondence (later known as the Committee of Foreign Affairs, and eventually to become the Department of State).[6]

Thomas Willing became the first chairman of the Secret Committee (later replaced by Robert Morris), and its members included Benjamin Franklin, Robert Morris, Philip Livingston, John Dickinson, Thomas McKean, John Langdon, Silas Deane and Samuel Ward.

Benjamin Franklin was appointed chairman of the Committee of Secret

Correspondence, its members at that time being John Dickinson, John Jay and Benjamin Harrison (of Virginia), Thomas Johnson (of Maryland) and Robert Morris (of Pennsylvania). James Lovell was later appointed and became its expert on ciphers and codes. The committee named a young merchant from Philadelphia who had recently returned from Europe as its secretary — William Bingham.[7]

The situation with Britain was further inflamed by the publication of Thomas Paine's *Common Sense* in January 1776, and on June 7 the Virginia Assembly instructed Richard Henry Lee to prepare a resolution at Congress, seconded by John Adams from Massachusetts, "that these United Colonies are and of right ought to be free and independent states."

Pennsylvania, New York, South Carolina and New Jersey were still opposed to independence at this stage, but Congress went ahead anyway and set up a committee consisting of Franklin, Adams, Roger Sherman, Robert Livingston and Thomas Jefferson to draft the Declaration of Independence.[8]

On July 4, 1776, Congress adopted the measured language of Thomas Jefferson's Declaration of Independence from the British Crown: "We hold these truths to be self evident, that all men are created equal, that they are endowed by their Creator with certain unalienable rights, that these are life, liberty and the pursuit of happiness. That to secure these rights, governments are instituted among men, deriving their powers from the consent of the governed. That whenever any form of government becomes destructive of these ends, it is the right of the people to alter or abolish it, and to institute new government, laying its foundation on such principles and organising powers in such form, as to them shall seem most likely to effect their safety and happiness."

In 27 sentences the declaration listed the impositions made by the British government from the Revenue Act of 1764 to the most recent Coercive (or Intolerable) Acts of 1774, and concluded:

> We, therefore, the Representatives of the United States of America, in General Congress Assembled, appealing to the Supreme Judge of the world for the rectitude of our intentions, do in the name, and by the authority of the good people of these colonies, solemnly publish and declare, that these United Colonies are, and of right ought to be Free and Independent States; that they are absolved from all allegiance to the British Crown, and that all political connection between them and the State of Great Britain is and ought to be totally dissolved.... And for the support of this declaration, with a firm reliance on the protection of Divine Providence, we mutually pledge to each other our lives, our fortunes, and our sacred honour.[9]

5. The Secret War — A Parisian in America

The creation of both the Secret Committee and the Committee of Secret Correspondence by the Continental Congress was a critical step towards independence from Britain, firstly by recognizing the need to act quickly and secondly by appointing men of intelligence, ability and influence.

The activities of the two committees were often intertwined — not surprising since they had several members in common, in particular Benjamin Franklin, Robert Morris and John Dickinson.

Congress was by now acutely aware of just how inadequate its preparations to defeat the British were: it had no standing army, very limited supplies of military hardware and supplies (in particular gunpowder) and no factories to make weapons, no navy, no federal organization structure (although most states had, or were drafting, constitutions of sorts), no treasury or banks ... the list was endless.

The Secret Committee was charged with the physical objectives of obtaining the supplies and military equipment that would be required to sustain the Continental Army and defeat the British.

The purpose of the Committee of Secret Correspondence under Franklin's leadership was political, to sound out sentiment abroad towards the American Revolution and establish any alliances and trade links that would further the cause. In reality, as Franklin was fully aware, only the French were likely to have the inclination and the resources to assist, motivated by their antipathy to Britain as much as a desire to help to create the United States. Franklin was personally opposed to seeking such alliances, preferring to wait for an approach to be made, but time was not on his side and so he contacted his own network of correspondents in Europe. In particular he wrote to Charles Dumas at The Hague in December of 1775 to establish the likelihood of any state or power in Europe forming an alliance with the rebels in exchange for the benefit of its substantial and growing trade, "if, as it seems likely to happen we should be obliged to break off all connection with Britain."[1]

As it happens, Franklin's letter may have been redundant since before Dumas could have received it, a mysterious stranger appeared in Philadelphia asking to meet with the Committee of Secret Correspondence. He described himself as a Flemish merchant acting on his own account but insisted that any meeting should be at a secret rendezvous of his choosing and that each member should arrive alone, each by a different route and in the middle of the night!

The mysterious stranger was called Julien Archard de Bonvouloir (in French literally "goodwill," but the aptness of the family name is just a happy coincidence); in fact he was a distinguished soldier sent by the French secretary of state, the Comte de Vergennes, to establish the extent of American resistance to Britain. Bonvouloir would admit none of this however, merely hinting at the possibility of a connection with the French government. He did, however, suggest that, "As long as you are subjects of Great Britain, we can not, and must not do anything for you. The only means that you have of obtaining our support is by declaring yourselves independent."

In fact, Vergennes had decided as early as the summer of 1775 that the increasing difficulties Britain was having with its recalcitrant colonies might be used to enhance the power and prestige of France and already had agents in London to ascertain the British position.

At much the same time as the Committee of Secret Correspondence was meeting Bonvouloir in Philadelphia, Arthur Lee was meeting a Frenchman with aristocratic bearing named Pierre-Augustin Caron de Beaumarchais, in London.

Dr. Arthur Lee (a physician) had been acting as agent for Massachusetts (at the same time deputizing for Benjamin Franklin in his similar role for Pennsylvania). After Franklin's petition to the British government for a peaceful resolution was rejected, he was summarily dismissed from his longstanding position as deputy postmaster general for America. However, he stayed on for a while in England "to give what assistance I could as a private man."[2]

Lee, an irascible Virginian, was officially appointed by the Secret Committee to act as its first secret agent in London on November 30, 1775, and Benjamin Franklin was recalled to Philadelphia.

Caron de Beaumarchais,[3] dramatist and courtier to Louis XVI, had been acting as a secret agent for the French government in London and espoused himself to the cause of the American rebels. Lee had convinced him (using inflated reports of patriot strength—fabricated by himself or furnished by his correspondent Samuel Adams) of the value to France of a long-term treaty of commerce in exchange for immediate assistance.

Beaumarchais wrote a memorial to Louis XVI proposing a policy of secret assistance to the colonial rebels on February 29, 1776. Vergennes supported this proposal in another memorial dated March 12, 1776, to the King, and royal assent was granted in May 1776.

Meanwhile, encouraged by the clandestine visit of Bonvouloir, the Committee of Secret Correspondence dispatched Silas Deane (who had been a delegate to the Continental Congress from Connecticut) to France on March 3 (arriving in Paris July 7, 1776) "in the character of a merchant" (specifically as a Bermuda merchant dealing in West Indian goods) "to obtain a supply of clothing and arms for 25,000 men, ammunition and 100 brass field pieces."[4]

On May 2, 1776, 1 million livres was furnished by the French Treasury to Beaumarchais to provide secret military supplies under the guise of legitimate commerce. Spain contributed an equal amount.[5] Silas Deane eventually reached Paris on July 7, 1776, with instructions to acquire munitions on favorable credit terms for eventual settlement in exchange for American produce.[6]

By the time Deane arrived in Paris, Beaumarchais had arranged a "front" in the form of the fictitious trading company Roderique Hortalez & Co. (Roderigue Hortalez et Cie). Arthur Lee was kept informed of these developments and was also advised that while the French government would assist in supply, it would not at that stage enter into war with Britain. Lee sent this information to Congress by agent and courier Thomas Story.

Before the news of the French position reached Congress, Deane had already agreed to terms with Beaumarchais and the latter engaged himself in procuring supplies, most of which came direct from stocks at French arsenals. Deane was able to send word to Congress in late 1776 that he was dispatching vessels carrying "200 brass cannon, 30 mortars, 30,000 fusils, 200 tons of gunpowder, 4000 tents and clothing for 30,000 men."[7]

The French government immediately set about commissioning and arming 20 vessels. Unfortunately when news of this filtered back to the Secret Committee in Philadelphia it was misinterpreted as evidence of early French involvement in the war — in fact these vessels were actually being prepared as armed escorts for the Hortalez shipments, for which Deane was now claiming much of the credit.

Meanwhile, Congress had empowered the Secret Committee to organize supplies for the Continental Army. Robert Morris succeeded Thomas Willing (his business partner) as chairman of the Committee on December 13, 1775, and the firm of Willing, Morris & Co. was instructed to use its diverse mercantile contacts to establish a supply chain centered on French Martinique with links in Cape Francois, Curacao and St. Eustatius. Willing, Morris & Co. was probably the only merchant house with the financial strength and credit to be able to set up and maintain the process. It was understood, however, that Willing and Morris would continue to trade on their own behalf as well as for Congress. Congress instructed the Secret Committee to draw on the Continental Treasury (such as it was) for cash funds initially, but continued supply could only be sustained by payment in American goods (flour, grain, lumber, indigo, rice, tobacco, skins, furs, ships' masts, etc.) for exchange in the West Indies for gunpowder and arms. How these American goods were to be made available to Congress was a different matter, however.

Franklin, Morris and their committees decided that an agent would be needed in Martinique to organize military supplies in conjunction with Willing, Morris & Co. and act as a conduit for information to and from Deane in Paris. The committee needed to place someone in whom they had complete trust, not only in his loyalty to the cause but also in his ability as an agent. Robert Morris needed a man with mercantile experience and Benjamin Franklin wanted someone to represent the colonies, act as intelligence agent and communicate with Silas Deane in Paris.

William Bingham came highly recommended (most likely by Thomas Wharton), with all the right qualifications, not the least of which was his fluent French and recent experience in Europe. He was also in the right place at the right time, and on June 3, 1776, the Committee of Secret Correspondence appointed him to this vital role as its agent in St. Pierre, Martinique (and his position as secretary to the committee was taken temporarily by Thomas Paine).

In September Congress, now yet more hopeful of support from France, drafted a treaty of Amity and Commerce and dispatched it with agent William Hodge to Paris (via William Bingham at Martinique). On September 26 Congress secretly elected three commissioners to the court of France, Benjamin Franklin, Thomas Jefferson and Silas Deane (who was to be promoted from his role as agent). On account of his wife's illness, Jefferson was unable to take up this appointment, and Arthur Lee, who was already in Europe, was appointed in his place.

Benjamin Franklin arrived in Paris on December 3, 1776.

6. William Bingham's Martinico Odyssey

It was clear to Congress that the Continental Army would have to import nearly all its ordnance and supplies to conduct a war with Britain, and on September 18, 1775, it authorized the Secret Committee "to import 500 tons of gunpowder, and if that proved impossible to make up any deficiency with saltpetre and sulphur, 40 brass 6-pounder fieldpieces, 20,000 musket locks and 10,000 stand of good arms."[1]

By the end of December Thomas Willing, as chairman of the committee, reported that the requirement had now become "20,000 stand of arms, 300 tons of lead, 1 million flints, 1500 boxes of tin and assorted hardware, 500 sheets of assorted copper, 60,000 blankets, 130,000 yards of cloth for uniforms, 160,000 sewing needles, iron wire, medicines and surgeons instruments."[2]

The Secret Committee, in turn, authorized the firm of Willing, Morris & Co. to take overall charge of commissioning supply contracts, meaning of course that Robert Morris would effectively be in sole charge of equipping and supplying Washington's fledgling Continental Army. In the same way that only George Washington could organize the colonial army, only Robert Morris could supply it.

As we have seen, Morris and Franklin, probably with advice from Thomas Wharton (who had come to know him well), chose the 24-year-old secretary to the Committee of Secret Correspondence, William Bingham, to be their agent in Martinique. He was well educated—at Franklin's College (The College of Philadelphia)—and of course, well connected, with recent experience in France and a good command of French. He was appointed on June 3, 1776.

Bingham was briefed separately by Morris and Franklin as to his role and objectives.[3]

He was instructed to make his way to St. Pierre, Martinique, where he would appear "as a private merchant" interested in the supply of goods to and from the West Indies. He was to make connections with French or Dutch merchant houses prepared to ship West Indies goods on credit until such time as Willing, Morris & Co. could arrange the supply of private produce from the mainland as payment.

Robert Morris was uniquely qualified to manage this massive foreign procurement. He combined the private trade of Willing, Morris & Co. with that of Congress, and while risking his own credit and personal fortune on many occasions, there is no doubt that he, Thomas Willing and William Bingham in Martinique were able to make or add to their fortunes as agents of Congress. Even if Congress had taken a dim view of this, there was, in fact, no alternative available.

Bingham's instructions, after his arrival at St. Pierre, initially were to await a private shipload of gunpowder that was already in passage from Europe to St. Eustatius or Martinique (in the charge of Captain Beall). Bingham was already an investor of £500 sterling in this adventure.[4]

Secondly, once in St. Pierre he was to make connection with "good French or Dutch houses" that would be prepared to ship West Indies goods to Willing, Morris & Co., for which shipments he would personally receive 5 percent commission.

Thirdly, he was to buy goods on credit up to a value of £1,500 sterling, to the account of Willing, Morris & Co., until such time as colonial produce could be shipped in for exchange or payment. Bingham himself would have a 50 percent concern in these adventures. He was also specifically instructed to buy linen or other European goods that could be conveyed back in the ship in which he had arrived.

On June 3, 1776, Robert Morris committed his objectives for William Bingham to paper in a letter written on behalf of Willing, Morris & Co. On the same day Bingham received his instructions from Benjamin Franklin on behalf of the Committee of Secret Correspondence.[5]

By the time that Bingham received his instructions from Morris and Franklin, the Secret Committee (or more likely Benjamin Franklin) had put together a strategy to supply Washington's Continental Army at home, and to seek out assistance from friendly countries, both financially in terms of loan, gifts or credit, and militarily, either with troops or with the supply of munitions.

The British Navy was immensely powerful and its ships were already cruising the waters of the Caribbean. There was no question of American vessels, such as they were, engaging British warships in any strategic sense. However, for decades American (and British) merchants had been circumventing the Navigation Acts and smuggling goods from the West Indies to the eastern seaboard, by using fast-sailing vessels with limited draft which were able, with experienced masters, to negotiate the coves, inlets and bays of the coast. Morris' plan was to use the same technique to bring in the supplies that would be essential to sustain a campaign against the British.

This was the age of the "privateer" and the Secret Committee had high expectations of being able to turn private merchant vessels to work for the American cause.[6] To this end Congress issued letters of marque and reprisal, which when completed and approved licensed the captain of a vessel *to* "fit out and set forth" in the name of Congress to "subdue, seize and take all other vessels, goods, wares and merchandizes belonging to Great Britain."

Good, timely intelligence was vital to determine what support might be available and to ascertain the likely British response, particularly in respect to France. Congress and the Committee of Secret Correspondence needed trustworthy agents in the right places, and they also needed a mechanism to transmit information quickly and reliably. The merchants of America and Europe already had well-established networks of correspondents, and Congress accepted that Willing, Morris & Co. was better placed than any other firm to provide the necessary confidential and secure connections. Franklin himself had established his own network of correspondents and political agents while in England. He was also aware that the British government had become expert in the field of intelligence and the world of spies and that he should be circumspect in his written communication.

This was the background to the missions of the first agents of Congress, Silas Deane in France, and William Bingham in Martinique. Deane's role was likely to have more political significance, but Bingham was vital in gathering the supplies that were essential for the Continental Army to pose a significant threat to Britain.[7]

Robert Morris and Benjamin Franklin spelled out the detail of Bingham's mission in the letters of June 3, 1776.

Sir,

You are immediately to repair on board the sloop *Hornet*, Wm Hallock Esq Comr. Bound to Martinico; — On your arrival deliver this letter you are entrusted with to the General there and show him your credentials.

You are earnestly to endeavour to procure from him 10,000 good musquets, well fitted with bayonets; if he cannot or will not supply them, you are to request his favour and influence in procuring them in that or any other island, if to be had. We propose to pay for them by remitting the produce of this country with all possible dispatch to any island that may be agreed on. You are to take especial care that the musquets you send are good. We direct you to send 2500 of them by the Hornet on her return & the remainder in parcels not exceeding 1000 in swift sailing, well appointed vessels, with directions to the masters to put into the first port within the united colonies, where they can safely land. We desire you to obtain from the General if possible a French Man of War or frigate to convoy these vessels so far that they may be out of the course of the British ships that are cruising in the West Indies. You are carefully to publish all the papers delivered to you by us for that purpose & disperse them as much as you can throughout the Dutch, English and French West Indies, having first obtained the General's permission to do in the latter.

You must with the greatest prudence endeavour to discover either by conversation with the General or others the design of the French in assembling so large a fleet with great number of troops in the West Indies & whether they mean to act for or against America....

You are to continue at Martinico until we recall you & are to cultivate an intimate and friendly correspondence with the General & other persons of distinction there, that you may be enabled to procure all the useful intelligence you can. You are immediately on your arrival to inform Silas Deane Esq. of it & desire him to address to you his dispatches for us.

"Whenever you obtain intelligence which you think of such importance that it ought to be immediately conveyed to us, you are to charter a fast sailing vessel, if no other opportunity offers & send her to this continent....

You are to observe the strictest secrecy & not to discover any part of the business you are sent upon to any persons, but those to whom you are under an absolute necessity of communicating it, in the transaction thereof. It will readily occur to you that an appearance of commercial views will effectually cover the political; therefore you will make frequent enquiries amongst their merchants what articles of this country produce are most wanted in the islands & you must consider yourself as authorised by the United Colonies to engage for the payment of the 10,000 musquets in such articles deliver'd at Martinico (or any other island they may fix on) as fast as they can be introduced...

When you write to Mr Deane desire him to put his current dispatched addressed to you, under cover to the General, but when he has any particular matters to communicate either to Congress, yourself or to us, that he thinks should not be risqued through that channel for fear of inspection let him procure a merchant in France to put such dispatches directed for you under cover to a merchant in Martinico with an express injunction to deliver them into your hands; and when you have made acquaintance with an established merchant of good reputation in Martinico, you had best name him to Mr Deane, that he may so address his dispatches without the intervention of a merchant of France. We shall from time to time furnish you with intelligence of what is passing on this Continent in order that you may not only make good use thereof in the West Indies, but also transmit the same to Mr Deane. It is of great importance that he should be fully and frequently advised of what passes & as you may often have earlier & fuller intelligence by means of news papers and private letters, than our avocations will permit us to give, you will be on the watch; send all the advices forward to Mr Deane marking what you receive from us, what private letters, from what public papers & what from hearsay and always distinguishing what can be depended on & what is doubtfull. In short, sir, you are to be constantly on the watch & to give to Mr Deane & us every information that you think connected with the interest or that can be improved to the advantage of the United Colonies.

You may possibly find it necessary or usefull to visit Guadeloupe, St. Eustatia or other foreign island. If you do, always take passage in foreign vessels and don't be long absent from Martinico at any one time, as our dispatches will be directed thither.

Should you at any time during your stay in the West Indies have an opportunity to contract on reasonable terms for arms, ammunition or other articles wanted here, give us information thereof & you shall be instructed on that head; in the meantime you will encourage as many private Adventurers as you can, by holding up the high prices we give, the low price of our produce, & as we have cruisers on this coast to watch the enemies tenders, cutters, etc, small vessels have a good chance of getting safe in & out of the bays, rivers and inlets on our coast.

As we have already many cruisers & are daily adding to the number, you will take proper opportunities of sounding the General & learn from him whither he could admit Prizes made by our cruisers to be sent in & protected there until proper opportunities offered for bringing them to the Continent. But this being a matter of great delicacy you must introduce it as a thing of your own & not as any part of your instructions.

Dated at Philadelphia, this 3rd Day of June 1776
Signed:
B. Franklin, John Dickinson
Benj. Harrison, Robt. Morris[8]

William Bingham was to establish himself firstly as a private merchant acting with Willing, Morris & Co. At the same time, armed with a letter to the governor general of the island, he was to introduce himself and establish the official French government position in relation to his activities and to the rebel American colonies. From this response, should there be one, he was then to determine the actual assistance (if any) that might be available. Franklin was already aware that the French were increasing their naval fleet in the West Indies. But was it the intention of the French government to use these ships and troops for or against America?

Regardless of this official response, he was to maintain the appearance and activity of a private merchant and acquire and ship the armaments, powder and all the other material on Thomas Willing's list of "what articles are necessary for the army."[9] In the first instance he would need to establish credit for this, awaiting shipments of American produce for sale or exchange. He did not know in advance what goods to expect, or when they might arrive, and nor in fact did anyone else, since at this early stage Congress had no agreed rights to commandeer or requisition supplies from individuals or colonies.

Bingham was also to act as a conduit in the supply of information to and from Silas Deane in France and acquire whatever intelligence he could on his own account, this to be sent back in the vessels returning to America with cargo, or, if of vital importance, by chartering a fast vessel for the purpose. He was to further the American cause using the printed or spoken word and attempt to win friends, particularly with the governor and his staff. He was to convince them, if they were not already convinced, that France should join with America in a common cause. It is not clear how he was to square all that with his guise of a private and adventurous merchant.

Finally, and most riskily, he was instructed to encourage privateers, by whatever means at his disposal, to espouse the American cause, for which he would need a very good story, or the possibility of healthy returns.

Once in Martinique William Bingham would be on his own. He was 24 years old and his adventure did not start well. He found the sloop *Hornet* at anchor in the River Delaware. She was recently back from the New Providence expedition, her stern badly damaged and taking on water. She was clearly going nowhere and Bingham sent a message to the committee for further instructions. It was to be a long week aboard *Hornet* and with its sickly crew before new orders arrived. He was now to find the ship *Reprisal*, commanded by Captain Lambert Wickes. Wickes received his orders on June 10 and welcomed the opportunity for an adventure rather than the convoy escort duty to which he had been assigned.[10] Wickes, a former Willing, Morris and Co. master, saw opportunities for himself in the new American navy. He received William Bingham on board on June 13 and wrote to the committee on June 16: —

> To the Honourable Committee of Secret Correspondence,
> Philadelphia.
> Gentlemen:
> I have received your orders and instructions by Mr Bingham, the 13th instant, but the shallop with the provisions did not arrive till this day.... You may depend on my best endeavours in your service to prosecute this voyage with the most expedition and advantage in my power. My people, all but two are in good health, and the officers are well satisfied with this cruise, and hope thereby to render their country an essential service, as well as themselves. There is now one two-decker, two frigates, one twenty gun ship, and a sloop of war lying in Old Kiln Road, and we are waiting an opportunity to get out by them with impatience; so you may depend upon our embracing the first favourable opportunity of getting out and proceeding on our intended cruise.
> From, gentlemen, your most obliged humble servant,
> Lambert Wickes[11]

Reprisal[12] was in the company of *Lexington* and *Wasp*, who, having escorted a convoy of merchant vessels down the Delaware, were now pinned down by British frigates, either in the bay or standing off. By now Bingham had spent a week aboard *Hornet* and two weeks on *Reprisal*, but on June 28 the fine weather broke, giving Wickes the opportunity to slip out of the bay and into the haze.

However, later in the day a ship was sighted heading into the bay in full sail, and identified as the armed brig *Nancy* inbound from the West Indies with ammunition and military stores for the Pennsylvania Safety Committee, commanded by James Montgomery. He was being pursued by British frigates and in desperation turned northwards at Cape May rather than enter the bay as a sitting target. As darkness fell he ran *Nancy* close in with the aim of getting as much of the cargo off as possible. The British frigates, unable to follow, launched their tenders and started a search of the shallows.

This was the opportunity that Wickes needed to break out but the plight of *Nancy* and its cargo was considered paramount. Boats were lowered from *Reprisal*, *Lexington* and *Wasp* and rowed off around the Cape to provide what assistance they could.[13]

Meanwhile Montgomery was transferring his cargo of rum, sugar, gunpowder and muskets in the ship's boats to Turtle Gut Inlet. Guided by the sound of the activity, the British boats loomed out of the murk. *Nancy* engaged two boats while the unloading continued. The third British boat disappeared into the gloom to guide the frigates closer.

Around midnight the boat from *Reprisal* arrived, with Lieutenant Richard Wickes (brother of Lambert Wickes) in command, followed by *Lexington*'s tender with Captain John Barry, and a boat from *Wasp*. As the senior officer present, Captain Barry took charge and boarded *Nancy*, and with Montgomery's approval he ordered her to be grounded at Turtle Gut inlet where all hands would remove as much of the cargo as possible before first light.

By this time a crowd of locals, hearing the commotion, had gathered, and were put to work hauling the gunpowder and guns to safety. A cannon was found and fired into the darkness in the general direction of the British boats.

Daybreak revealed two British frigates and by early morning *Nancy* was within range of their heavy cannon. After two ranging shots they found their target. All the muskets and 286 kegs of gunpowder were safely ashore, leaving the remainder of the rum and 100 kegs of powder still aboard. The frigates lowered five boats, each with its compliment of marines, to capture *Nancy*.

With great presence of mind Barry ordered the men back into the boats while Montgomery laid a trail of powder from the hold to the companionway, where he wrapped the last few pounds into the remains of the mainsail. He put a baulk of burning timber on the mainsail as a makeshift time-fuse and hurriedly joined his men in the boats, just ahead of the advancing marines.

The six men plus the mate of the first boat to arrive boarded *Nancy* in triumph, at which point the sail burnt through. The explosion from the powder, the rum and the sugar was heard 40 miles north of Philadelphia. The remains of *Nancy*, her cargo and seven British sailors were still falling several minutes later.

The remaining British boats, their oars shattered by the blast, made their way back to the ships. After a short pause, in revenge, the frigates opened fire on the single cannon on the beach and sailed away. The unfortunate Lieutenant Wickes was hit by a cannonball and killed, the only American fatality of the encounter. He was buried two days later at Cape May.

As an important agent for Congress, William Bingham was confined on board *Reprisal*, concerned no doubt about the consequences of the massive explosion he had heard on the morning of June 29.

The weather on Wednesday July 3 was clear, as was the horizon, the British ships having been recalled to New York for General Howe's attack on New York.

Reprisal sailed out of Delaware Bay escorting 13 merchant ships. At dusk and once well out to sea Wickes left his charges and headed south for Martinique. Despite the action a few days earlier the crew of *Reprisal* were largely raw recruits and the first days of the journey were the first opportunity for Wickes and his officers to ready the men for the tasks ahead.

The first week at sea was uneventful, but, on July 11, *Reprisal*, south of Bermuda, came across a merchant vessel flying the Union Jack, the 240-ton *Friendship*, Captain Charles Mackay commanding, bound for London out of Grenada. She was carrying a valuable cargo of rum, cocoa, coffee and sugar, and was to become *Reprisal*'s very first "prize." If William Bingham was in any doubt what was in store for him, he was now about to find out.[14]

Friendship was instructed to lie to while Wickes' crew boarded. Captain Mackay was given the opportunity to surrender his vessel in exchange for his freedom once in Martinique, an offer which he accepted. Wickes then addressed the remainder of the crew, extolling the virtues of joining the American cause. They were more likely impressed by better conditions and the generous prize money that was on offer. To a man (officers included) they agreed to serve for the Americans on board *Reprisal*.

Wickes assigned warrant officer John Parks and a small crew to the *Friendship* with instructions to return to Philadelphia. Parks was given letters from Wickes to the Committee of Secret Correspondence confirming Bingham's progress.

During the following week *Reprisal* encountered and took a further two prizes. A fourth ship was allowed on its way for the lack of enough trained men to take her back.

On the afternoon of Saturday July 27, almost four weeks out of Delaware Bay, *Reprisal* was off St. Pierre, Martinique, with the town silhouetted against Mont Pelee. St. Pierre, a safe haven in the evening sun, must have been a welcome sight for Wickes and his crew. William Bingham was no doubt relieved to have reached Martinique, but apprehensive of what the future might hold for him.

Wickes, however, had a more immediate problem to resolve. A warship could be seen riding at anchor and dominating the harbor. Wickes raised his glass and passed the news to Bingham that it was the British sloop-of-war HMS *Shark*,[15] showing 16 guns. Bingham and Wickes would have no way of knowing the motives of the British ship, and why it was in a French harbor — events could have moved quickly since leaving America. Was it possible that France had somehow allied with Britain?

Wickes was uncertain of engaging a British warship with his makeshift and largely British crew, but he was in command of an American man-of-war.[16] He ordered the bosun to put *Reprisal* at readiness to engage HMS *Shark*.

7. Willing, Morris and Bingham, Supplying Washington's Army

The British warship lying at anchor at St. Pierre was not expected. *Reprisal* would perhaps have had an element of surprise in an engagement, but Wickes had only 87 of his original crew of 130, the others were on their way back to Philadelphia with the prizes. He had the 36 men from the *Friendship* and the other prizes but their loyalty was as yet untested, and many of his American crew had no experience of naval battle.[1]

Wickes' primary orders from the Committee of Secret Correspondence were to deliver William Bingham safely to Martinique, but as an American warship he would be expected to engage the enemy once that task was completed. Wickes decided that he would have Bingham and his baggage rowed ashore in one of the boats, and with that safely accomplished he could reasonably set about attacking *Shark*.

Word of a possible naval engagement quickly spread through the town of St. Pierre and the quays were soon packed with eager spectators.

Bingham, now safely ashore and surrounded by his baggage, watched as *Shark* slipped her cables and followed *Reprisal* across the harbor entrance. *Shark* closed in, hailing twice in French then once in English for *Reprisal* to heave to, and followed this up with a warning shot across her bow. Wickes turned across the wind towards the British ship, firing a broadside as soon as she was in range, *Shark* returning fire immediately. The fire-fight continued for half an hour or so, *Shark* being hit several times with some damage and two casualties, one of which was fatal. *Reprisal* burst a cannon, wounding one sailor. Then, without warning, one of the huge guns of the shore battery fired a shot across *Shark*'s bow, followed by a second that took out the main topmast stay sail. At this *Shark* withdrew, and stood off to sea. *Reprisal* returned to harbor, where Bingham was able to greet Captain Wickes as he came ashore, together with applause from the assembled crowd.

The evening was now drawing in and Bingham went at once to the governor's residence to introduce himself and present his credentials, identifying him as agent from the Continental Congress. He was well received by Governor de Courcy, who explained the presence of the British warship — *Shark* had appeared the same afternoon to present a letter of complaint (concerning French naval activities) from the British admiral of the fleet in the West Indies to the military commander General le Comte d'Argout.

General d'Argout was actually in Fort Royal, 30 miles away, so Captain John Chapman of *Shark* had presented his letter to Governor de Courcy. The governor may well have relished the opportunity that *Reprisal*'s arrival presented to take a potshot at the troublesome British warship.

The governor explained to Bingham that the French battery had fired on *Shark* because of what he described as "hostile activities within French territorial waters." Bingham then explained to de Courcy the details of his assignment to Martinique, and the discussions continued when General d'Argout arrived from Fort Royal, around midnight. D'Argout also formally received Captain Wickes, who requested protection for *Reprisal*, leave to stay for repairs, and time ashore for his crew; all three requests were granted.[2]

In the morning the British Captain, John Chapman, apparently undaunted by the previous day's events, returned to the shore to complain about his treatment and to request permission to seize *Reprisal*. The unfortunate Chapman was then jostled by a crowd of angry local inhabitants, necessitating an armed guard to enable him to reach the governor's residence.[3]

Governor de Courcy kept Chapman waiting two days before declining his request and reminding him that any further hostile activity would meet with the same fate as the first.

Within a few days Bingham had found his feet and started to acclimatize to the oppressive Caribbean climate. General d'Argout requested that he attend a briefing on the official position of the French government in relation to the American rebels, where the reasons for his warm welcome became apparent. He explained to Bingham that he had received dispatches from the French Court (which had arrived into St. Pierre the previous Sunday), in which the governors of all French possessions were instructed (as Bingham later reported to Congress) "to favour the Americans throughout all their ports and protect their commerce at sea, whenever and wherever they should find the opportunity."

D'Argout also confirmed to Bingham that he should remit this to Congress as not only official French policy, but also as his own personal position.[4]

D'Argout went on to agree that he would provide some measure of convoy protection from American vessels and assist in the communication of confidential dispatches between America and France. Bingham must have been genuinely astonished at the support he was being offered, particularly when d'Argout further agreed to allow American prizes (captures) into port for selling or disposal. The general regretted, however, that he was unable (or instructed not) to offer help in the procurement of arms or gunpowder.

Bingham passed this encouraging news back to Lambert Wickes and prepared his first report for the Committee of Secret Correspondence. The freedom to use French ports was of the utmost significance. American prizes could now be condemned and sold or turned into American privateers in Martinique and possibly in other French islands without the need to run the gauntlet of their return to an American port.

With his immediate diplomatic tasks completed, William Bingham turned his attention to the mercantile assignments outlined in his instructions from Robert Morris, and made contact with Richard Harrison and Adrien Le Maitre.

Harrison was a young merchant from Virginia, already established as an agent for Virginia, and he had just been joined by Le Maitre, who left for Martinique at the same time as Bingham. Harrison assisted Bingham in finding accommodation and premises to establish the cover for his new venture.

Bingham delivered the letters from the Secret Committee instructing Harrison to turn over the proceeds of the cargoes of the *Fanny* and *Peggy* which had been dispatched to provide working capital for his first task, the "procurement of ten thousand stand of arms and as much powder as could be had." All that could be had on Martinique were 500 muskets, some cavalry sabres and very little powder, all of which Bingham acquired ready for shipment back to Philadelphia on *Reprisal*, which Wickes was refitting at Fort Royal. Bingham also bought as much in the way of dry goods and linens as his initial capital would allow to return with *Reprisal*, and then turned his attention to establishing communications with the Secret Committees and Willing, Morris & Co. in Philadelphia, and Silas Deane in Paris.[5]

He reported the detail of his activities so far in letters written on August 4, 15 and 26. General d'Argout had offered the use of his own official pouch for correspondence destined for Silas Deane in Paris. Bingham accepted but assumed (rightly) that such correspondence would probably be intercepted and read by more senior French diplomats, so decided to "enhance" the strength of the American position (as he knew it) and the benefits the French would derive from a commercial and political relationship.[6]

The following day he wrote Silas Deane another, more realistic review of affairs, including confirmation of the Declaration of Independence, official news of which had arrived that day. This letter was dispatched to Deane via a merchant ship where interception was less likely.

Bingham passed the package of letters, public and private, destined for Philadelphia to Captain Wickes, who set sail on August 26 together with his meagre cargo of arms; it was, however, the first consignment of a supply line that would be critical for General Washington's success.

Nineteen days later, *Reprisal* sailed up the River Delaware after a voyage without major incident or prizes to its credit. Bingham's first letter describing the sea battle with HMS *Shark* had preceded him and by the time of his arrival had been published in newspapers across all 13 colonies. Lambert Wickes disembarked to find himself a hero for this first naval "victory" and for the safe arrival of the three prizes taken on the voyage to Martinique. *Reprisal*'s cargo of arms was immediately consigned to Robert Morris, as were the letters for the Committee of Secret Correspondence. Bingham's linens and dry goods, however, were to the private account of Bingham, Willing and Morris and were sold on directly to merchants Mease and Caldwell for a substantial profit, the start of a very lucrative enterprise indeed.

Robert Morris had already decided that the "(Continental) Congress consisted of too many members to keep secrets" and that the Committee of Secret Correspondence should be just that — secret from all but a few trusted friends, including of course Benjamin Franklin (who had just arrived from New York after more unsuccessful peace negotiations, this time with General Howe).[7]

With Deane now established in Paris and Bingham in Martinique, Franklin and Morris set about creating a physical supply chain for Washington's Continental Army and the intelligence network for an unprecedented diplomatic mission. Once this was in place Congress decided the best place for Benjamin Franklin was in Paris as one of three commissioners to France, and he left Philadelphia for Paris in October of 1776, and henceforth his involvement would be from there.

During the fall of 1776 ships arrived from America with goods for Bingham to sell to raise cash needed to buy arms, but the news of progress in the war was not good, with reports of General Washington's defeats at Brooklyn Heights and White Plains and his retreat through New Jersey to the Pennsylvania side of the Delaware River.

Bingham heard that Washington's army was now down to 6,000 battered and poorly provisioned troops, and that Philadelphia was in turmoil with its government close to collapse. Undaunted Bingham wrote to Silas Deane: "To say that the affairs of America are in a desperate situation, while we keep united, is an absurdity."[8]

Bingham received a letter from Robert Morris on behalf of the Secret Committee via the Continental sloop *Sachem*, which had been "dispatched for the sole purpose of bringing back such a supply of blankets, coarse cloth, coatings, flannels and other woollen goods suitable for winter wear as you can procure in Martinico. They are already much wanted and will be more so. Therefore we earnestly entreat you to exert your utmost interest to procure ... a large supply of the above articles.... We must not be disappointed of these goods, therefore you must pledge the credit of the United States pretty freely."[9]

Bingham had tried to pledge the credit of the United States but with little success; credit was only possible against his own personal guarantees and he had already pledged that to a total of 250,000 livres by November 1776.

Events in America had reached a low point when Morris wrote Bingham: "Our American Affairs have not at this time so pleasing an aspect as we would wish, and that should they grow much worse, it may not be a desirable thing to bring property hither.... It is possible our affairs may go so wrong that the property will be safer with you than with us.... If such event is likely to happen we will contrive you the earliest notice of it to prevent you shipping goods either on your or our account at any time when they might likely to come into the jaws of the enemy."[10]

At this time the Continental sloop *Independence* arrived in St. Pierre loaded with American goods and with a young man from Philadelphia, William Hodge. Hodge was carrying the Treaty of Amity and Commerce between America and France, which had been drafted by Congress following encouraging news brought by Captain Wickes in Bingham's reports of the position of the French government (as described to him by General d'Argout).[11]

Bingham was instructed to show Mr Hodge "proper attention, assist him in procuring an immediate passage to France in a good ship, and supply him any money he needed. You will serve your country by forwarding Mr Hodge without delay; but you need not mention to the General how urgent we are on this point, unless you find it will promote his dispatch...."[12]

So important were the letters that Hodge was carrying that duplicate and triplicate sets were dispatched to Bingham via St. Eustatia and Cap Francois, for onward transmission to Silas Deane.[13]

In the same bundle of documents that Hodge was carrying was the first reference to a Monsieur Hortalez. Bingham was required to ask of General d'Argout and Governor de Courcey if they had been advised of any shipment of arms from this gentleman, and if so to confirm that he, Bingham, was authorized by Congress to receive them on behalf of the United States. General d'Argout and Governor de Courcy were unaware of any such shipment but agreed to advise Bingham should they arrive. Bingham would have been in no doubt about the significance of M. Hortalez and his shipment when he was instructed to sail to St. Eustatia and ask the same questions of Johann de Graaf (the Dutch governor) concerning its possible arrival there.[14]

Silas Deane had already advised Robert Morris what could be expected from the first Hortalez shipment, "clothing for 20,000 men, thirty thousand fusils. One hundred tons of powder, two hundred brass canon, twenty four brass mortars, with shells, shot, lead, etc., in proportion." To get the shipments to America, the unfortunate Caron de Beaumarchais had already spent the 1 million livres from the French treasury plus the 1 million from Spain and in the end added another 2.6 million of his own — for which he was never repaid by the French or the Americans.[15]

For various logistical reasons the Hortalez shipments were agonizingly slow in coming, not helped by disagreements about the route they should take — direct to American ports with the risk of capture or via Martinique and St. Eustatia, where the merchandise could be transferred to American vessels capable of running into small inlets and harbors.

American vessels were now arriving from America expecting to collect the Hortalez munitions, but because of the delay were only able to return with rum and molasses, which were in ready supply and the only goods that Bingham could acquire on credit. Good for business but unlikely to win a war. Bingham had expected these incoming vessels to be loaded with the tobacco, flour or rice that he could sell to improve his liquidity but little appeared until finally in January 1777 when the brig *Cornelia and Molly* sailed into St. Pierre. She had a cargo of flour and tobacco, one third on account of the Secret Committee, one third on account of Willing, Morris & Co. and one third on the account of other merchants.

At long last, the tide was now beginning to turn for Bingham, as it was for George Washington with his victory over the Hessians at Trenton and another successful encounter at Princeton. Robert Morris was clearly also more relaxed: "Our publick affairs wear a better aspect than when we wrote you last."[16]

Bingham was now able to attend to his private business, shipping whatever he could back to Willing, Morris & Co., where his share of the proceeds was handled by his brother-in-law and attorney in Philadelphia, John Benezet.

Eventually, Beaumarchais' French vessels began appearing in early 1777, not a moment too soon. The *Amphitrite*, *Mercure*, *Flammand*, *Mère Bobie*, *Thérèse*, *Amélia* and *Marie Catherine* went directly to Portsmouth, New Hampshire. The *Seine*, however, arrived in Martinique, en route, where Bingham had the bulk of its huge cargo transferred to smaller vessels for the final leg of the journey, where she was lost to the British in unfortunate circumstances.[17]

With the supply of military hardware underway Bingham turned his attention the next part of his original brief — the arming and fitting out of privateers and the acquisition of prizes. This was an expensive business, requiring cash, not credit, so Bingham's liquidity must have improved by this time.

In partnership firstly with Richard Harrison and then with Morris, Willing and others, Bingham engaged the captain of a merchantman, posting a bond of up to $20,000 and filling out blank letters of marque and reprisal authorizing the captain to engage and seize British shipping as prizes. The crew were then given an advance, which would be deducted from their prize money once their captures were returned to port, condemned by an Admiralty court and sold. Bingham had already established, of course, with General d'Argout that St. Pierre could be used for this purpose.[18]

Bingham's privateers, as was the custom, carried multiple sets of papers and flags, so that they could appear to be French if boarded by a British warship, but unequivocally American while bearing down on a British merchant vessel.[19]

Bingham's privateering enterprises were spectacularly successful, with over 200 British merchant ships captured in early 1777 with cargoes worth $10 million. The British government and British merchants, not surprisingly, were incandescent. Insurance rates rocketed as did the price of West Indian goods in London.

Two ships fitted out by Bingham, *Retaliation* and *Rattlesnake*, brought in to St. Pierre a total of 9 merchantmen and slave ships. Bingham's share of this adventure included 498 African slaves and a cargo of ivory.[20]

Bingham and Morris encouraged one particular sea captain, Coctiny de Prejent, to buy and fit out a brig, the *Esperance*, in Philadelphia, with a considerable amount of Morris, Bingham and government money. Unfortunately for the other investors, Prejent promptly sold the vessel and its cargo in Basseterre and used the cash to go into privateering on his own account, at which he became extremely successful. He never settled with Willing and Morris for the half share in *Esperance,* leading Robert Morris to blame Bingham for allowing Prejent to outfit privateers before clearing his debts with them first, which caused one of very few rifts between the two men.

In Paris, British Minister Stormont brought Prejent's activities to the attention of French Foreign Minister Vergennes on a number of occasions. complaining bitterly about the open use of French Martinique for the disposal of British prizes. Vergennes, playing for time and not wishing to worsen relations for the time being, suggested that General d'Argout's actions were not sanctioned by the French government and that he would soon be replaced in Martinique by a new governor, the Marquis de Bouillé.[21]

Bingham welcomed de Bouillé on his arrival in Martinique, anxious to ascertain if there would be changes to official French policy. Bouillé confirmed the bad news; France would now permit British vessels to stop and search her vessels and remove any American goods. American ships would no longer be allowed to load in French ports, and in particular sale of prizes in French ports was now prohibited. From the upbeat tenor of Bingham's letters to Morris it would appear that he felt that this change was temporary and designed to mollify the British for the time being. Clearly France was not yet ready for war with Britain, delayed perhaps by the downturn in American fortunes after the defeat at Brandywine and the British occupation of Philadelphia.

Despite the apparent hardening of the French position, Bingham's relationship with Bouillé seems to have been as comfortable as the previous one with d'Argout, and he was soon in his confidence.

The pendulum of fortune swung back to the Americans with the eventual arrival of the Hortalez shipments to Washington's army and the surrender of General Burgoyne at Saratoga, at the end of December 1777. When news of these events reached Martinique, Bouillé reversed the restrictions on Bingham's privateering activities, allowing prizes back into St. Pierre. Within a few weeks the French were ready to enter into a formal alliance with the United States. In Paris Vergennes and Franklin drew up the terms of two treaties between France and the United States, one of friendship and commerce (as carried by William Hodge), the other, of much more significance, a defensive military alliance.[22]

The British left Philadelphia for good in June 1778, and on June 17 British and French warships exchanged fire for the first time — they were now at war. A major part of William Bingham's original mission was complete, and in August of 1778 he made his first request to be recalled. He had already endured two difficult and exhilarating years in an oppressive climate and his future role was likely to be more consular. He was no longer needed in the critical exchange of information and he was more likely to derive his intelligence from shipmasters than from the Secret Committee in Philadelphia or Franklin and Deane in Paris.

On the other hand his private trade in association with Robert Morris continued to flourish and he was now a very successful merchant indeed with his profits accruing in Philadelphia. His financial arrangements on the public account were, however, much less secure. Congress owed him a great deal of money, and he could be excused for wishing to return to redeem his affairs.

He wrote to Franklin on March 5, 1778: "The General (Bouillé) regarding the interests of France and America as altogether inseparable, has thrown off all reserve, and constantly communicates to me the nature and purport of such of his dispatches as have regard to the situation of our affairs.... He expects an equal return of political information on my side, which from my limited and confined knowledge of what passes in Europe, I am unhappily deprived of an opportunity of giving him."[23]

He wrote again on June 16:

> It is a long time since I have had the honour of receiving any of your commands, and am the more surprised at it, as a packet boat has arrived with dispatches for the General, informing him of a treaty of alliance and commerce being concluded betwixt the Court of Versailles and the United States of America.

> I humbly think that I should be made acquainted with its contents, that I might act in conformity thereto, and as far as my small influence will reach, cooperate accordingly.
>
> As Agent for the United States of America in the West Indies, every circumstance that regards the country that I represent, and that forms a subject of controversy, immediately falls under my notice and attention; but how shall I govern myself with any degree of prudence or precision, or according to the terms that Treaty prescribes, when I am entirely ignorant of what it contains?[24]

The Committee of Foreign Affairs did write to Bingham on May 14, 1778, concerning the treaty, but it would appear that he never received the letter.

Not only was he being sidelined, he was increasingly in debt personally (in Martinique) to maintain supplies on the public account since Congress was still unable or unwilling to provide sufficient American goods for him to sell for cash. His difficulties were such that court judgments were being made against him in the islands, although they were, so far, being suspended, but only by the personal intervention of his friend de Bouillé.

He was reluctant, or unauthorized, to draw on Franklin in Paris and he suggested that funds could be generated from the many Americans now making money from the capture of British prizes. Bingham heard nothing in response to this proposal, but the long drought of correspondence from Congress was finally broken in March 1778 when James Lovell, as chairman of the Committee of Foreign Affairs, wrote with the first of four letters in three months. Lovell apologized profusely and sympathized with Bingham's financial embarrassment and in April 1778 he wrote again authorizing Bingham to draw on the commissioners in Paris the sum of 100,000 livres tournois (approx $15,000).[25]

Bingham's solvency was short-lived, however, as vessels from the Continental Navy started appearing in Martinique with authority from the Naval Committee to draw on him for the costs of re-fit and pay for officers and crew. At this stage Congress was clearly either taking advantage of Bingham's position or saw him as a very capable fixer.

In desperation, on April 13, 1779, Bingham took matters in to his own hands and drew on Franklin for another 100,000 livres tournois. He apologized but made it clear that he had been left with no alternative. Unfortunately for Franklin, Bingham's drafts were just part of an almost overwhelming tide of demand for cash over which the Committee of Finance in Congress had absolutely no control, and they were not well received.

William Bingham's discomfiture was relieved, at least for a while, when another key figure in American history appeared literally out of the blue in December 1779, when the Continental frigate *Confederacy* limped into St. Pierre, carrying John Jay, his wife Sarah (Livingston), her brother Colonel H.

Brochholst Livingston, and William Carmichael, who would be acting as Jay's secretary. Also on board was French minister Chevalier Gerard, returning to Paris.[26]

John Jay had resigned as president of Congress (and a host of other positions), to undertake a mission to draw Spain (and substantial financial support) into the alliance with America and France, since the French Treasury was struggling to support Franklin's continuous drain on its resources.

Confederacy had set sail, Captain Seth Harding commanding, on October 26, 1779. After ten days at sea, 1,100 miles out of the Delaware Bay, *Confederacy*'s mainmast broke, bringing down almost the entire rigging, killing one sailor and injuring another. Unable to maneuvre in the gale that blew up the night the rudder shaft broke, the ship was completely helpless and at the mercy of any passing British warship or privateer.[27]

Captain Harding made what repairs were possible at sea. French Minister Gerard insisted that they make for the Azores, 900 miles to the east. Captain Harding suggested that the safer (if longer) option was to sail south to Martinique, where another vessel could be taken while *Confederacy* was repaired. Gerard was overruled.[28]

Bingham and Jay would have known each other from the early days of the Committee of Secret Correspondence, and mutual respect soon turned into a firm and lifelong friendship.

Bingham put up John and Sarah Jay in his own residence; General Bouillé and the admiral of the French fleet were obliging and helpful. *Confederacy* was be taken to Fort Royal to be re-fitted, while her important passengers would be taken to France aboard the French frigate *Aurora*, which was due to sail on December 28, 1779.[29]

Ten days in Martinique in December must have been a very welcome distraction for the Jays after their ordeal in the north Atlantic; they were welcomed into St. Pierre society, toured the island and reviewed the troops assembled in their honor. John Jay bought "a very fine Negro boy of fifteen years old."

Jay was dismayed, but probably not surprised, to learn that Harding's officers had no money or the means of obtaining any for their unexpected sojourn in Martinique, which was creating difficulties in their brief relationships with their French counterparts. (The officers and men were presumably expected to be paid on arrival in France.)[30]

Jay resolved the issue by drawing a bill on Franklin for 100 guineas as an advance on his own salary, to be shared amongst the officers. Jay would like to have extended his generosity to the crew, but that was his beyond his resources. Bingham, therefore, not to be outdone, stepped in and also offered 100 guineas, again to be paid for by adding to the ever-mounting bills on Dr. Franklin in Paris.

Jay's arrival gave Bingham the opportunity for the first time to explain his financial plight in person to a senior member of government, so he took it. Jay was appalled to learn of the debt owed by Congress to Bingham, and therefore to creditors across the islands, and the resulting court judgments against him.[31] He was also unaware that Bingham had received no communications from Paris or Philadelphia for many months, and when he learnt that Franklin had refused to honor the drafts for the re-fit of the *General Gates* and the *Deane* he decided that something must be done. (Bingham had first learned of the dishonored drafts on October 9 when M. de Vaivre summoned him and demanded a promissory note for 150,000 livres, to be discharged within six months.)

However the issue that was troubling Bingham most, and the one that he most wanted to share with Jay, was a lawsuit that later became known as the *Pilgrim* Affair. Earlier in the year, on January 29, 1779, the Massachusetts privateer *Pilgrim* had brought the *Hope* into St. Pierre as a British prize. The vessel and its cargo had Danish papers and its crew spoke only Danish. Bingham intervened, believing that the seizure was illegal, and returned the vessel to its captain. Its cargo of flour, with Bouillé's approval, was sold and the proceeds returned in part to the captain, the remainder being held until such time as Congress could determine the lawful owner of the vessel and its cargo.[32] Bingham had assumed that that was the end of the matter, but learned subsequently that the American owners of the *Pilgrim* were suing him personally for the lost prize and that they had already had a judgment against him and his property.

Bingham had tried but was unable to get Congress to intervene on his behalf. His attorney in Boston, William Tudor, had written to him and confirmed that the *Hope* was carrying two sets of papers (perhaps Bingham should have suspected this—after all, that was what he had been doing), and probably was British and therefore a legitimate prize.

John Jay took all these issues to heart, and on December 22 he wrote to Congress: "the agent here tells me he is without cash and in debt on the public account. I fear he has been neglected. I shall, however, defer saying any more on this subject until I am better informed."[33]

On December 26, having been better informed (by Bingham), Jay wrote a glowing tribute to Bingham and his achievements to his successor as president of Congress, Samuel Huntington: "This leads me to take the liberty of remarking that it would probably be much for the public interest if Congress were to pay off all private debts due from them to subjects in France, and have none but national engagements with that Kingdom. The debts unavoidably contracted here for the outfit of the Deane, etc ought certainly be paid. Our credit and reputation suffer from such delay."[34]

John Jay and his entourage finally resumed their journey on *Aurore* on December 28, and arrived in France en route to Spain on January 22, 1780.

(John Jay endured two years of rejection in Spain. Meanwhile Congress spent £100,000 of the loans they anticipated from Spain and sent the drafts for payment, which not surprisingly were refused.)

Bingham, encouraged by Jay's visit, turned his attention to repairing the *Confederacy* and sailing home on her whether he had been officially recalled or not. He was still short of funds but managed to convince the French Navy to supply masts, against his personal assurances that these would be replaced by the Marine Committee, in due course.

On March 12, 1780, *Confederacy* left Fort Royal for St. Pierre, while Bingham prepared for Congress a detailed account of his work in Martinique.

"Whether my agency has been interesting to America, by promoting the glorious cause she is engaged in, is left to your august body to determine;- for my own part, I claim no merit but from the purity & rectitude of my intentions, my activity, & my zeal for your service;- The public interest alone has always been my guide — but if I have undertaken a task beyond my abilities to accomplish I cannot expect to be honoured with the public approbation, which invariable in its decisions, never consults any thing but its own advantage;- in that case, I shall be more afflicted, than surprised."[35]

In the absence of any other directive to choose a replacement for him in the islands, Captain Bingham nominated the merchant firm of Parson, Alston & Co. to act on behalf of Congress and issued them a set of instructions.

On Tuesday, March 28, Captain Harding loaded a cargo of cocoa (supplied by Bingham), Bingham's baggage and his mulatto servant boy. On Thursday, March 30, William Bingham boarded *Confederacy* complete with a testimony written by the Marquis de Bouillé and addressed to the president of Congress: "I have the pleasure to assure your Excellency that no one could have taken more interest than he in the subjects of the United States ... the position that he leaves could not be filled more worthily."[36]

Confederacy left St. Pierre on the morning of March 30, 1780, accompanied by a convoy of two American and two French vessels. Captain Harding fired a salute of 13 guns; 11 guns replied from the battery that had dismasted HMS *Shark* almost four years earlier.[37]

For William Bingham one episode in his life was drawing to a close, and another was about to open.

8. Benjamin Franklin, an American in Paris

By the time William Bingham had arrived in Martinique in 1776, Congress was sufficiently confident of French support to draft a treaty of Amity and Commerce (which had been carried by agent William Hodge to Paris via William Bingham), and secretly elected three commissioners to the court of France: Benjamin Franklin, Thomas Jefferson and Silas Deane.[1]

Silas Deane was already established in Paris and he was promoted from agent to commissioner. Thomas Jefferson declined to serve because of his wife's illness, and the destructive and troublesome Arthur Lee (who was already in London) was given the job.

Franklin was appointed October 22, 1776, and by October 29 he was leaving America together with his two grandsons. (William Temple Franklin, aged 16, was the son of Franklin's illegitimate son William, and Benjamin Franklin Bache, six years old, was his daughter Sally's son.) They sailed in *Reprisal*, recently returned from Martinique and still under the command of Lambert Wickes, with a cargo of indigo. Wickes captured another two prizes along the way and discharged Franklin, his entourage and his prizes at Nantes, on the west coast of France, to avoid British vessels in the English Channel. From there Benjamin Franklin travelled overland and arrived in Paris on December 3, 1776, where he joined his friend and former Secret Committee colleague Silas Deane.

Franklin's objective, with the help of Deane and the hindrance of Lee, was to continue to draw France into the war with Britain, to acquire whatever arms and military supplies that could be had, and to beg or borrow as much money as possible with the most favorable terms.

That Franklin achieved so much in such a short space of time appears to be despite his fellow commissioners, in particular Arthur Lee (of the Virginia Lees and brother to Richard Henry Lee, who had introduced the resolution for American independence before Congress). Franklin had already worked with Lee in England while they were respectively agents for Pennsylvania and Massachusetts and had not enjoyed the experience. He now had Thomas Jefferson to blame (for turning down the role of commissioner) for the additional burden of having Lee as an associate.

French diplomats admired and respected Franklin for his knowledge and scientific contribution, but they despised Lee in equal measure. While Franklin was achieving success by subtle negotiation, Lee's belief that the French had no alternative but to help the Americans in order to defeat the British was getting him nowhere. Franklin was acutely aware that other options were available to France—for example France and Spain could well join forces with England to suppress the American rebellion in return for the restoration of Canada to France and Florida to Spain. The fact that France committed itself so strongly to America had as much to do with Franklin himself as any long term strategy by Vergennes— in fact the ever-increasing demands on the French treasury contributed to the weakness that would eventually propel France to its own revolution.

Silas Deane, on the other hand, had a more practical approach, and a great respect for Franklin. While Lee may have helped to convince Beaumarchais to persuade Vergennes and Louis XVI to support the American cause through the 1-million-livres Hortalez & Co. plan, it was Deane on his arrival in France in July of 1776 who actually set up the first shipment of arms with Beaumarchais. In fact, by this time Beaumarchais would deal only with Deane, causing a split that threatened to derail the entire supply process, salvaged only by Deane's diplomacy.

Silas Deane had informed Congress correctly that the Beaumarchais contribution should be considered a loan that would need to be repaid in due course. Lee, on the other hand, had told Congress that he had personally negotiated the money as a gift from the King, and that Deane (and Robert Morris, his partner) were attempting to line their own pockets by charging Congress for goods that were being acquired for nothing.

Congress, not surprisingly, was confused by the conflicting information, which was not eased by ambivalent letters from Beaumarchais himself, and divided itself into two opposing factions.[2] Firstly, the anti–Deane camp was led by the Lee family of Virginia (Arthur, Richard Henry, and Francis Lightfoot), Thomas Paine, John Adams and Samuel Adams from Boston. The pro–Deane, pro–French lobby was led by Robert Morris, James Madison and John Jay, and for months this became the dominant topic in Congress, to the exclusion of almost everything else. Its effects would rumble on for years.

Fortunately for Franklin, Lee spent the early months of 1777 touring the capitals of Europe looking for support from other countries, at which he failed completely. Franklin was able to use the time to convince Vergennes that France should openly join the Americans and declare war on Britain.

Unfortunately for Franklin, Lee arrived back in Paris in July of 1777, and matters deteriorated further when Congress saw fit to appoint Lee's brother, William Lee, as minister to Berlin, and Ralph Izard as minister to Tuscany — a reflection of the bizarre influence the Lee family was able to exert over Congress. William Lee and Izard, in due course and having made no progress whatsoever, returned to Paris and decided unilaterally that they should now become part of the commission to France.

By this time, Franklin's subtle approach with Vergennes was starting to pay off. By December 1777 the French were also becoming concerned that the Americans might be negotiating terms with Britain which would leave them in a dangerous position. Vergennes responded by announcing that the French government would recognize the independent United States and provide an annual subsidy of two million francs.[3]

Franklin, having lost the useful and respectful Deane (who had been recalled to Congress to defend the charges of fraud made against him by Arthur Lee), now found himself surrounded by egocentric and troublesome colleagues, each of whom was capable of sinking any deal that he might be able to strike. He was, however, able to exclude William Lee and Izard and negotiations continued satisfactorily, and as result the Treaty of Amity and Commerce was duly signed on February 6, 1778.

Congress, probably too distracted to notice the progress that Franklin was making, decided that he needed some heavyweight support to replace Silas Deane, and decided that John Adams should join the commissioners in Paris. On February 15, 1778, John Adams and his eldest son, John Quincy, embarked on the Continental frigate *Boston* for France. Their journey was delayed by the excitement of a naval encounter with the British, but they arrived safely in Paris in July.

John Adams, although he considered himself the more senior politician, clearly felt overshadowed by Franklin and his undoubted popularity with the French public and court, and immediately took the side of Arthur Lee and the other self-styled commissioners. He instructed Vergennes to deal with him alone and no longer with Franklin. Vergennes responded by refusing to meet or correspond with him ever again, instructing the French minister in Philadelphia to advise Congress that Adams expressed "a rigidity, a pedantry, an arrogance and a self-love that render him incapable of dealing with political subjects."[4]

John Adams' demeanor was not improved when he learned that Franklin was appointed sole minister plenipotentiary in 1778, and he set about making preparations to return to America. His initial fondness and respect for Franklin had long since worn off and he was incensed by the adulation received by his former colleague. By the time he left he had decided that Franklin was conspiring to make his life difficult, and the remaining respect flickered and died.

Later Congress recalled William Lee and Ralph Izard, and Arthur Lee was appointed as minister to Spain but did not leave Paris for another year, continuing to make life difficult for Franklin.

Adams finally arrived back in America, but within a few months Congress decided he should return as envoy to negotiate a peace with Britain, although at the time of his dispatch such an arrangement seemed distinctly premature. Not surprisingly, when he arrived back in Paris in February 1780 there was little for him to do but renew his vendetta with Franklin and alienate the long-suffering Vergennes. To Franklin's great relief Adams was sent to Holland to negotiate recognition for American independence and pursue loans with the Dutch banks.

Franklin's job was not over since there was still the continuing need to negotiate money from France, and lots of it. While individual states had empowered themselves in their own constitutions to raise taxes, and might even be trusted to repay loans by foreign states, the *Articles of Confederation* (giving Congress tax-raising powers) were not ratified until 1781. Franklin therefore found himself not only trying to convince the French that Congress could be trusted to repay loans, but also in competition with individual states doing the same, with better credit ratings.

Franklin was instructed to raise loan after loan to pursue the war with Britain, and by the time each loan was approved by Vergennes the demand came from Congress for more. The Congressional Finance Committee lacked experience or accountability and Franklin was inundated by bills for expenditures over which he had no knowledge or control. He was saved from having to default only by Vergennes' repeated and helpful intervention, mainly because Vergennes was aware that default by the United States would ruin its credit in Europe and his own reputation.

To add insult to injury Franklin now had the Lee contingent sniping at him back in Congress, claiming that he was "the worst of men in the worst of times."[5]

In November 1780 Congress voted to request yet another French loan, this time of 25 million livres, and, believing that this may be beyond Franklin's ability, decided to send an envoy to negotiate the new funds. Congress appointed 26-year-old John Laurens from South Carolina (son of former president of Congress Henry Laurens), a colonel in the Continental Army and a former aide-de-camp to General Washington. Laurens brought with him as his secretary another Washington aide, 22-year-old Major William Jackson.[6]

Franklin was advised of these decisions in February of 1781 and by the time Laurens had arrived in March he had already persuaded Vergennes to convince King Louis XVI to provide an outright gift of six million livres. Vergennes got agreement to this final gift but on the clear and absolute understanding that no further funds were available for the simple reason that France itself now had to borrow to fund the war with Britain.

Vergennes took a dislike to Laurens, who continued to push for the balance of the 25 million livres as instructed. After a period of negotiation, Vergennes reluctantly offered Laurens a loan guarantee of ten million livres, provided that the loan itself could be obtained in Holland.

Rather than attempting to raise money in Holland, Laurens turned his attention to spending Franklin's six-million-livre gift on military supplies in Holland. Franklin believed that Laurens had been successful in raising the Dutch loan and was spending that. Laurens and Jackson put together three shiploads of arms and Laurens sailed for Philadelphia, together with two million livres of the gift in specie. Jackson was instructed by Laurens to find another vessel, load it and return as quickly as possible with yet more of the six million cash.

The vessel lying in Amsterdam chosen by Jackson for the return trip belonged to South Carolinian Alexander Gillon,[7] who had brought his ship around from Lorient to Amsterdam, sold its contents to Jackson and then offered to load two more ships and convoy them directly to Philadelphia, together with 1.5 million livres in specie, to which his attention had been drawn.[8]

Major William Jackson (1759–1828), by an unidentified artist, a miniature from life, later retouched by Henry Brown, circa 1795 (Independence National Historic Park).

Franklin, of course, was quite unaware of this activity and was incandescent to discover, eventually, that the money being spent was in fact his, money which he had already earmarked to settle the tide of bills that were engulfing him. Franklin stepped in and had the remaining 1.5 million livres seized while attempting to pacify an equally indignant Vergennes. Major Jackson was also furious, but with Franklin, since he had been led to understand by Laurens that the money they were spending had been raised by him to spend as he thought fit. Jackson continued to believe this rather than Franklin's version of events and demanded that the money be returned, a move which probably did not enhance his career, and which he subsequently regretted.

Jackson's belief in Laurens persisted until "Admiral" Gillon slipped his cables on August 12 and left Amsterdam, with the unsuspecting Jackson and several other Americans imprisoned on board, leaving behind the other two ships of the proposed convoy and a host of unpaid bills.[9]

Jackson and the others were now effectively captives, but at least they expected a nonstop voyage to America. The reality of their situation finally dawned when Gillon put in to Corunna to re-fit for a privateering adventure on his own account. Seizing the opportunity and after a struggle with Gillon, Jackson was able to escape from the ship in Corunna, from where he was eventually able to make his way back to Philadelphia.

Gillon himself arrived in Philadelphia, unabashed, in May 1782 after his privateering adventure in the West Indies.

On his return to Philadelphia, Jackson immediately wrote an abject apology to Franklin. Laurens arrived in September 1781, maintaining his story to the end and receiving a commendation from Congress. When Congress finally became aware of the truth of the situation Franklin received no thanks or apology — indeed a Committee of Enquiry in October 1782 recommended that Franklin be censured for recovering the final tranche of the French gift before it disappeared with Gillon. The recommendation was not passed, however.[10]

Franklin by now had had enough and asked Congress to be recalled to Philadelphia — he was, after all, 75 years old and in worsening health.

In October 1781 General Cornwallis surrendered to George Washington at Yorktown, Virginia. But before allowing Franklin to return to America, Congress had just one more job for him.

9. Barings, Hopes and the Triple Alliance

While Benjamin Franklin was coming to grips with his new role as American commissioner to the French court, Francis Baring was severing the links with John and Charles Baring & Co. in Exeter. Although he may not have realized it at the time, the foundations that he had laid from 1762 to 1776 resulted in his business being uniquely poised to take advantage of a world that would change dramatically after 1776.

These early years of Francis Baring's business, the 1760s and early 1770s, coincided of course with the increasing difficulties between Britain and its American colonies, which were being viewed with growing concern by the merchant community, if for no other reason than they were affecting transatlantic trade. The bulk of Baring's business at this time was in Europe, but he was also looking eastward with a growing involvement in the British East India Company. He was later to become a director and eventually its chairman. As his interest in insurances as a means of commission income grew, his influence led to his being appointed to the board of the Royal Exchange Assurance. He was building for the future.

While the early fortunes of John and Francis Baring & Co. were not outstanding, the standing of Francis Baring certainly was. He was becoming very well connected. Harriet Baring's sister Maria married Richard Stone of the bankers Martin & Co. in 1766. Richard Stone had been Baring's banker since 1764, and as events unfolded, a very useful business contact.

He also started to make political connections, the first probably being John Dunning (later Lord Ashburton), who also had family roots in Devon. Through John Dunning Francis Baring was introduced to Isaac Barré and more importantly to William Petty Fitzmaurice, second Earl of Shelburne, and in due course this unlikely triple alliance became very well informed and very influential.

As a result of the triple alliance, Francis Baring's new circle of friends and correspondents now included radical thinkers like Jeremy Bentham,

Henry Hope (1735-1811) after Joshua Reynolds (Baring Archive Ltd., reference #PR041).

Edmund Burke, Benjamin Vaughan, the scientist Joseph Priestley and other liberals whose views were not at all in line with the establishment; a surprising choice, perhaps, for a young merchant with great ambition.[1]

Francis Baring was also making commercial connections that would have far-reaching consequences, in particular with the Dutch banking firm of Hope & Co., whose family roots were close to the German Barings in Groningen, on the border of Holland and Germany.[2]

Now based in Amsterdam, Hope & Co. was a much older institution, going back as far as 1720 but was restructured in 1762 (just 12 months before John and Charles Baring started their partnership in London) when partners Thomas and Adrian Hope were joined in the firm by Thomas' son John and their American nephew Henry Hope.

Hope & Co. was very successful in a broad range of merchant and banking activities and had seen tremendous growth during the Seven Years War, particularly in the West Indies. With France at war with Britain there were opportunities to trade with the French colonies via the Dutch colonies of St. Eustatius and Curacao, which British naval power had previously prevented. The trade was profitable but also risky, with the ever-present possibility of capture by the British Navy or privateers. Ironically Hope had gained a second time from the conflict with its involvement in raising loans for the British government to finance its fight with France. Over time these loans totalled £50,000, a substantial proportion of which was handled by Hope, which was now rapidly cornering the market in international government finance. Holland was the financial center of Europe, and Hope was now the most powerful house in Holland.

When peace was restored in Europe in 1763 the need for finance for the recovery of trade led to an acute demand for credit just as many merchant houses were holding large stocks of colonial produce bought expensively, and now impacting adversely profitability and liquidity. The resulting credit crisis prompted a major collapse in July 1763 and many houses went to the wall. Fortunately Hope's years of experience had engendered a cautious and balanced approach to risk, and it emerged from the 1763 crisis more or less unscathed.

The first commercial contact between Hope and Baring appears to have come sometime after the 1763 crisis, when Francis Baring was offered the opportunity to negotiate a number of bills in London and the markets were in trouble in Holland. Francis Baring's success at this activity impressed Henry Hope and he a sent a further £15,000 of bills to liquidate. Barings was not a bank at this stage, but Francis agreed to negotiate them in the market.

Francis Baring approached his own banker (and future brother-in-law) Richard Stone, who had the bills discounted and remitted the proceeds to Baring to send on to Amsterdam. Unaware that Baring had used one of London's major banks to complete the transaction, Hope was immediately impressed with the resources of the Baring company and this cemented a relationship that would have far-reaching significance, possibly the most important single influence on the future of John and Francis Baring & Co.[3]

Although the relationship with Hope was now established, they were still just one of many correspondents in Europe, and Baring's trade continued to be dominated by woollen and textile goods, still mainly from Exeter. Most of this business was for John and Charles Baring & Co. and other west-country houses, whose bills, once accepted, could be made payable in London.

The end of the 1760s saw the first industrialization of textiles, leading to massive growth in the "Manchester Trade," and this business was added from the contacts Francis Baring had made during his time with Samuel Touchet. Touchet had gone dramatically bust in 1763 (after claims of fraudulent activity from a House of Commons Committee were made against him), and Baring may well have gained business from the failure.

Through the late 1760s the relationship between the British government and the American colonies continued its steady decline, and although it was still not having a major impact on Baring's still largely European business, it was increasingly becoming a matter for concern. Of more immediate importance, however, was the financial crisis of 1771 which had been precipitated, ironically, by the East India Company itself. Its influence had grown so quickly during the Seven Years War that it now found itself in difficulty controlling its vast empire, while at the same time the downturn in European demand and the effects of the first American non-importation agreements were sapping its liquidity. As the company's situation worsened, the Bank of England had no option but to step in to provide the capital to keep it trading, but then lost its nerve and summarily withheld further credit. As news of this spread in the city its share price collapsed, bringing the rest of the markets down with it. In the turmoil, one of London's major banking houses, Neale & Co., failed, triggering a wave of merchant house collapses in England and Holland.[4] Francis Baring, by luck, good judgment or timely information emerged shaken but intact.

In Amsterdam, Hope & Co. had been heavily involved with Neale & Co., with £50,000 at risk when the collapse came, but by good fortune they were holding other Neale & Co. assets that they were able to liquidate, which covered most of their exposure. Like Baring, Hope & Co. itself survived this crisis, but others were not so lucky and the cumulative effect of the 1763 and 1772 financial crises had fatally undermined Amsterdam's position as the financial center of Europe. London now became the financial center of Europe, at least for the negotiation and discounting of bills of exchange. Hope & Co. was down but not out and responded by switching the emphasis of its business towards the issue of more foreign government loans, an area of business that Baring was watching with increasing interest.

The failure of the East India Company was unacceptable to the British government, and a major contributor to its difficulties was the effect of American colonial non-importation agreements, which had been imposed in response to the Stamp Act in 1765. In 1768 Lord North's government had actually repealed the Townshend Duties other than the tax on tea, but the damage was already done, and as turned out it was too little, too late.

The Tea Act, passed in 1772, was not intended hurt American merchants, but was a pragmatic approach to generating East India Company revenues. By this time, however, the trust between the British government and the colonies was already gone. To the colonial rebels this was a further and intolerable infringement of civil liberties. The Boston Tea Party followed in December 1773, and the British government responded with the Coercive Acts of 1774, to which the colonists responded in turn, by calling the first Continental Congress in Philadelphia in November of the same year.[5]

Despite the efforts of Edmund Burke, Barré and the other radicals in Parliament to bring King George's government to its senses, Britain and America continued the inexorable slide to war, which came finally in May of 1775, when the first shots were fired at Lexington. The first casualties in Britain of course were the merchants in the Atlantic and Caribbean trade, who were now unable to trade and were owed a fortune by American merchants, and the factories in Lancashire which were forced to close when the imports of cotton dried up.

There can be no doubt that the events and political upheavals of 1775 and 1776 were the turning point for Francis Baring. In addition to the political and intellectual allies he had been developing, and his friends in Amsterdam, he had also made several other contacts, which would turn out to have great significance.[6] A study of the Francis Baring's ledgers for the period shows that as well as the established accounts for John and Charles Baring, the Devonshire Bank and merchants in Cadiz, Lisbon, etc., new names started to appear. In particular, Philadelphia's leading merchant house, Willing, Morris & Co., appears for the first time in December 1774. Then in September 1776, intriguingly, we see the name of Caron de Beaumarchais (as agent of King Louis XVI), who was in the middle of putting together, with Silas Deane, the first military shipments to America, via Martinique and William Bingham, under the guise of Hortalez & Co.

Direct trade with the American colonies by British merchants was difficult during the Revolutionary War, and in 1776 Francis Baring made his first speculative investment in East India Company stock. Opportunities for the East India Company in the Americas had now gone and the emphasis was on restructuring the organization, but Baring had seen an opportunity for himself and his business. By 1779 he was a director of the East India Company as well as the Royal Exchange Assurance Company.

As Britain's prospects in the war were diminishing, Francis Baring's political allies were gaining ground, in particular the Earl of Shelburne, who was now one of the most prominent opponents of the North ministry, as it stumbled over its policy towards America. Parliament became increasingly concerned about its inability to curb what it thought of as "the madness of King George"; in April of 1780 Parliament voted in favor of John Dunning's motion that "The Crown has increased, is increasing, and ought to be diminished."[7]

But it was not John Dunning and his Parliamentary motion that defeated Lord North and King George, it was another George — Washington — at Yorktown in 1781 and the surrender of Cornwallis. The British Parliament voted, without division, to bring to an end the war against America. Government by the monarch and a coterie of ministers in defiance of Parliament was now over, with the ignominious resignation of Lord North. The surrender by Cornwallis at Yorktown may well have saved Britain from its own republican revolution.[8]

As the dust settled, of the "triple alliance" Shelburne had become foreign secretary (and was eventually to become prime minister) and John Dunning (who in 1780 had married Baring's sister Elizabeth) was appointed to the position of chancellor of the Duchy of Lancaster (1782) and ennobled as Lord Ashburton. Isaac Barré, not to be outdone, was appointed treasurer of the Navy and then paymaster general (1782). Francis Baring had just become Britain's most influential merchant.

With Lord North gone the Rockingham Ministry took over in 1782, proposing a more liberal agenda, but Rockingham died a few months later and was replaced by Shelburne as prime minister. Francis Baring remained advisor to Shelburne during his brief tenure, before he gave way to William Pitt's revitalized Conservative Party in 1783, and Francis Baring now found himself advisor to (but not friend of) William Pitt the younger. Earl Shelburne was created the first Marquis of Lansdowne in 1784. Shelburne and Francis Baring remained close friends and very powerful political allies for the rest of their lives. Through their mutual associates, past and future, they were to have a quite remarkable effect on the future of Britain and the United States of America.

As Francis Baring's influence was growing so now was the business itself. Lansdowne had urged Baring to enter the House of Commons to elevate his position beyond that of just a man of commerce. Baring was acutely aware of the benefits that membership of Parliament might bestow on the reputation of the business (as it had in the case of Samuel Touchet), but he left the move until he was confident that he had the resources available to him. With the business in profit (returning over £10,000 per annum from 1780 to 1782)

Top: Lansdowne House (formerly Shelburne House), Berkeley Square, London, from Papworth's *Select Views of London* (City of Westminster Archives Centre). *Bottom:* Bowood House, Wiltshire, country estate of 2nd Earl Shelburne (1737–1805), later 1st Lord Lansdowne, from a painting by Buckler, 1806 (Wiltshire Archaeological and History Society).

and his new partners Charles Wall and James Mesturas taking some of the strain, the time was right, and in 1784 Francis Baring took the Parliamentary seat of Grampound in Cornwall (a "rotten borough" that could be purchased from its "owner" in those pre-parliamentary reform days). Grampound cost him £3,000. In 1790 he switched to Ilchester, costing him £1,500, and in 1794 Lord Lansdowne offered him the seat of Calne.[9]

For the next few years Francis Baring juggled his public and commercial activities adroitly; the American War of Independence had blunted trade but now new opportunities presented themselves, in particular the supply contract for the British Army which Baring acquired by offering to supply on a 1 percent commission rather than the higher profit margin made by previous contractors. Ironically the war also brought Baring into provision of public loans for the British government in the manner of the Dutch houses. Baring was able to sell the loans on for a profit (£19,000 between 1780 and 1784) to raise the money for the government to give back to him to supply the Army.

It was now no surprise that in 1786 Francis Baring was able to write to Lord Lansdowne:

> My time and attention is chiefly employed by three great objects, my Commercial Concerns, the public, and the East India Company. The first is the sole object to which I look for a pecuniary provision for my family; at present I am well supported, the business is in a very flourishing situation ... totally divested of moonshine, and the attention which I bestow is fully sufficient, but if that support should fail, I should not hesitate a moment about renouncing every other consideration to my duty to my family. The public requires time and I am fully possessed with a hope of doing some good, but the time which is employed is not embarrassing to my mind. I have men of sense and conversant with business to work with and I am under no apprehension about discharging my duty satisfactorily.[10]

The "good" that Baring wished to do formed the basis of Baring corporate and political philosophy for more than a hundred years, that trade should be unfettered by regulation or artificial constraint. To that end he argued vigorously for free trade with the United States and against limitation on the use of American shipping.

The house of John and Francis Baring & Co. had made a giant leap forward. Francis Baring may have been very shrewd or very lucky. He was certainly assiduous and very bright. He was very well educated. He became, or perhaps made himself very well connected. He had acquired a burning desire to succeed in a society in which he was a second generation immigrant. It is hard to establish at this distance which of these elements was predominant, but there is no doubt this man had come a long way and had absolutely no intention of stopping.

From this time, the merchant house of John and Francis Baring & Co.

now entered a phase of steady and sometimes dramatic growth, mirroring William Pitt and the new British Empire. Francis Baring, and Baring's Bank, as it had now become (but not yet in name), was being observed with interest by counting houses and governments in the Old World and the New World.

10. Bingham Returns to Philadelphia

Confederacy with William Bingham on board arrived in Philadelphia on April 30, 1780. It had been the coldest winter that anyone could remember. Conditions for Washington's army camped at Morristown were as bleak as they had been the year before at Valley Forge. Philadelphia itself had not recovered from the privations of the British occupation. Bingham returned to the family home on Pine Street and his mother Molly, whom he had last seen in June of 1776.

Bingham was shocked to observe Philadelphia after his four years' duty in Martinique. The effects of war with Britain were being felt in a number of ways, notably the economic and political situation. Congress had issued its own currency before the outbreak of war in 1775, denominated in Spanish dollars and valued variously in individual states, but inflation resulted from overprinting and to avoid bankruptcy Congress had devalued the paper Continental dollar from parity to one in forty.[1]

In addition to this turmoil the war was not going well; the victory at Saratoga was a distant memory and there was a real risk, likelihood in fact, of failure and capitulation to the British. France had joined the conflict but through 1778 and 1779 had concerned itself mainly with naval campaigns in the West Indies. The pressure on the Americans may have reduced, but what was needed was direct support on American soil. Washington's neglected and poorly equipped army had now been stuck for nearly two years, with morale at its lowest ebb. The collapse of Continental currency brought Robert Morris' supply chain to a halt, and the troops were now on the verge of mutiny.[2] The breaking point was reached in May 1780 with the fall of Charleston in South Carolina, a worse defeat than Saratoga had been a victory, with a catastrophic loss of equipment and over 5,000 men captured. Shortly afterwards General Gates was defeated at Camden, South Carolina, and in September the heroic Major General Benedict Arnold was revealed suing for peace with the British.

This was clearly a difficult time for Bingham to return. By contrast to the privations at home, the war had actually been good for William Bingham so far — he was returning from Martinique a very wealthy man indeed. However, a very substantial proportion of this money was tied up in the debt owed to him personally by Congress. This was not a good time to be extracting large sums of money from the government, but he wasted no time and the very day after his return he started the process of unraveling his unfinished business with Congress and recovering the debt. He presented his letter of commendation from Bouillé, together with a statement of affairs on the *Pilgrim* lawsuit (which was still unresolved) and a claim for salary and expenses in addition to the amounts owed to him on the public account.[3]

As Bingham was about to discover, Congress had actually authorized his return home, and prompted by John Jay's intervention had already instructed the Board of Treasury to advance £5,000 sterling (paid to his agent John Benezet) as part payment against his claims.[4] James Lovell and George Clymer were appointed to review Bingham's situation. So far so good.

Not surprisingly, no records had survived (if any existed in the first place) of the terms of Bingham's remuneration, and as Benjamin Franklin was in Paris, Lovell and Clymer asked Robert Morris for his recollections, but since he was too busy to be of any help, a further £7,000 advance to Bingham was proposed, which left the balance of Bingham's claims on Congress at 507,641 livres Martinique for commercial transactions and 110,324 livres for salary and expenses.[5]

Given the worsening situation with the war Bingham must have wondered whether his work in Martinique had been in vain or if he would ever see his money again; the American revolutionary experiment appeared to be at an end. Fearing the worst William Bingham enlisted as a private in the Second Company of the Fourth Battalion of the Philadelphia Association Militia.

There was no question that the will to fight on was still there, but Congress was effectively powerless to continue to raise cash to sustain Washington's military campaign. In desperation, a group of Philadelphia merchants and lawyers (many of whom had met at the same place in 1774 in support of Boston's plight) convened a meeting at the City Tavern, notably including Robert Morris, Thomas Willing and William Bingham. At the meeting James Wilson read from the prospectus he had been asked to prepare: "The greatest and most vigorous exertions are necessary for the successful management of the just and necessary war in which we are engaged with Great Britain."

Wilson's proposals called for the pooling of personal resources to raise £300,000 for the purposes of buying provisions and rum for the army. Ten percent of each subscriber's pledge would be payable at once, and the balance to be available on demand.

Wilson's proposals were accepted. Tench Francis Jr. was elected as a paid executive, and Robert Morris appointed chairman of the inspectors of the Bank of Pennsylvania. The directors were authorized to borrow money against the assets pledged for a period up to six months and issue banks notes bearing interest at 6 percent.[6]

At the meeting £270,000 was pledged, rising to £315,000 within few days. There were 92 subscribers; Robert Morris and two others subscribed £10,000 each. A further 27, including Bingham, Wilson and John Benezet, pledged £5,000, and Dr. Benjamin Rush £2,000.[7]

William Bingham in a letter to John Jay wrote: "At an alarming moment when the treasury was exhausted and the army suffering and threatening to disband for the want of provisions, the virtue of individuals was roused, which warded off the impending blow. A bank was established on private credit under the auspices of gentlemen of the first fortune in this city.... The subscription was filled up in a few days and much larger sums might have procured.... If the same public-spirited establishments take place in every State, we shall derive the greatest and most essential advantages from them."[8]

Congress was advised of the creation of the Bank of Pennsylvania, and further told that once approved by Congress it would be able to ship three million rations and 300 hogsheads of rum. Congress authorized the charter of the bank unanimously and Tench Francis opened for business on July 17, 1780.

Following Philadelphia's example, similar banks were up and running in Baltimore, Boston and New York within weeks.

To paraphrase Winston Churchill, it was not the beginning of the end, but it was the end of the beginning for the American Revolution.

Congress appears to have been wildly optimistic about the possibilities of a settlement with Britain, and while William Bingham and *Confederacy* were returning to Philadelphia in early 1780, John Adams had been sent back to Paris as a peace commissioner. Adams arrived in France with Britain far from ready to negotiate terms and took it upon himself to become commissioner to Holland instead. He stayed there for two years, securing first recognition of the United States, and eventually a loan of five million guilders from the Dutch bankers Staphorst and Willink.

As the tide of the war turned in June of 1781, and aware of the brittle relationship between Adams and Vergennes (and indeed Franklin), Congress decided to appoint a peace commission of Franklin, Thomas Jefferson, Henry Laurens and John Jay in addition to the absent Adams.

Of the three new appointments to the new peace commission, only Franklin was in Paris, and had agreed with some reluctance to stay on, poor Henry Laurens was captured at sea by the British and imprisoned in the Tower of London, John Jay was still in Spain still failing to secure Spanish loans, John Adams was in Holland raising finance and Thomas Jefferson had turned down a role in Paris for the second time.

The stage was set for negotiations to begin after the humiliating resignation of Lord North and his ministry in London. The Earl of Shelburne was appointed prime minister in a new administration, and he immediately sent agents to France to test the water in April of 1782.

Shelburne was a man that Franklin could do business with. He knew him well — apart from Shelburne's steadfast support for colonial Americans he was a patron and close friend to many of Franklin's own circle of friends, notably Joseph Priestley, Jeremy Bentham and Richard Price. Shelburne and Franklin also had a shared interest in philosophical and scientific matters. Their backgrounds were totally different, but they were now the right men in the right place at the right time.

Shelburne sent Richard Oswald to be his envoy in Paris to deal with Franklin, who would be on his own until the arrival of John Jay in July. The substantive issues for agreement were to be the recognition of the 13 colonies, Canada and the northern border, the western boundary and the Mississippi and the southern boundary (the 31st parallel), and the question of reparations and losses on both sides.

Franklin kept his host, Vergennes, and John Adams (still in Holland) appraised of his progress with Oswald, such as it was. John Jay returned from Madrid unwell with flu and was unable to participate in the talks until July, at which point Franklin contracted kidney stones and was himself unable to attend. John Jay, finding himself on his own, attempted to improve the terms by opening another strand of secret negotiation in which he suggested that America might be prepared to separate itself from the French. Jay's diplomacy may have been successful, since by the time Franklin had recovered and John Adams had returned from Holland the bones of an agreement were starting to emerge which were acceptable to them, John Jay and Henry Laurens (who by now had been released by the British and just arrived in Paris).

Franklin felt able to withdraw from the negotiations at this stage to concentrate on the question of money, or the lack of it, to cover the continual flow of bills that he was receiving for payment. Robert Morris (who was now superintendent of finance) and Robert Livingston (secretary of foreign affairs) had no choice but to instruct Franklin yet again to request another loan from Vergennes, which he achieved in February 1783, for six million livres.[9] For Vergennes this would turn out to be one loan too many.

Despite progress on the peace treaty and on Congress' finances the relationship between Adams and Franklin, now together again, continued to deteriorate. Adams claimed that if he had not been opposed, obstructed, neglected and slighted " the negotiation for peace would have been quicker and on better terms."[10]

Adams was by now convinced that Franklin was determined to sink any minister that might be sent by Congress to replace him in Paris, and that the addition of Franklin, Jay and Laurens to his original commission as peace commissioner was a personal slight. Adams sent these views officially to Congress, prompting James Madison to report to Thomas Jefferson that "Congress yesterday received from Mr Adams several letters dated September not remarkable for anything unless it be a display of his vanity, his prejudice against the French court and his venom against Dr Franklin."[11]

Franklin, exasperated by the damage that Adams was doing, particularly during the time he was trying to raise finance from Vergennes, wrote to Congress with his concerns, closing his letter: "I am persuaded, however, that he means well for his country, is always an Honest Man, often a Wise One, but sometimes and in some things absolutely out of his senses."[12]

To Franklin's immense relief Adams decided to travel to London, where he stayed for two months. (John Adams got his wish and was appointed American minister to the court of St. James in 1785, before finally returning to the United States in 1788.)

Despite all these difficulties, the Treaty of Paris was signed on September 3, 1783, but perhaps because of the lack of cohesion between them, Franklin and Adams had failed to make a commercial treaty with Britain part of the agreements. This omission would blight the relationship with Britain for years to come — the privileges of British colonial status were now gone and a strong trade relationship with the old country was vital for the economy of the newly independent United States.

Franklin felt that all that could be done had been done and set his thoughts to convincing Congress of the need of a minister in London, and his suitability for such a position, despite his earlier concern to return home. He waited but the appointment never came, going instead to his nemesis John Adams. Once Benjamin Franklin received word that his services were no longer required, in May of 1785, he started to make arrangements for his return to America.

Franklin was finally replaced as American minister to France by Thomas Jefferson, who arrived in Paris in 1785.

William and Anne Bingham were already there.

11. Mr. and Mrs. Bingham

In 1780 Robert Morris and Thomas Willing were partners in the creation of the Bank of Pennsylvania, but they were temporarily no longer partners in their merchant house. Thomas Willing had stayed on in Philadelphia during the British occupation, but Robert Morris had no choice but to leave the city to be able to organize military supplies without the risk of his own capture. By this time Morris had become the dominant partner in Willing, Morris & Co. and his commercial talents were being missed. Willing's credit in Europe started to come under pressure as a result of Morris' absence, to the extent that his bills were being protested. The very real possibility of ruin for Thomas Willing was only averted when Robert Morris instructed his agents to extend the necessary guarantees.[1]

Thomas Willing now also found himself under pressure from his political opponents, who criticized his continued presence in Philadelphia during the occupation and his earlier refusal to sign the Declaration of Independence (in fact Willing was in favor of independence but had felt the timing was not right in July of 1776). Fortunately his doubters were soon silenced by the success of the new Bank of Pennsylvania and his untiring activities in fund-raising and congressional duty. Thomas Willing and his family were now flourishing again. Thomas and his wife Anne had ten children, whose ages in 1780 ranged from the eldest, Anne (known as Nancy to the family), who was 16, to William Shippen, who was just one. The last of Anne's children was not yet born. They all grew up in the mansion built by Charles Willing on the block bounded by Third, Fourth, Spruce and Willing's Alley.[2]

During the summer of 1780, and among all the other distractions, including his continuing negotiations with Congress, uncertainties over the war and the creation of the new bank, William Bingham "noticed" Thomas Willing's daughter Anne (Nancy), not the 12-year-old girl that he knew before he left for Martinique, but the startlingly good-looking young lady that she had become. William's mother Molly (Stamper Bingham) and Nancy's mother Anne were friends and neighbors, William was eligible and now very wealthy and Nancy was described as quite simply the most beautiful girl in Philadelphia, if not all of America. Both families were probably delighted (and probably not surprised) by the turn of events, and after a short courtship William Bingham asked his former business partner and mentor Thomas for his eldest daughter's hand in marriage.[3]

William Bingham and Anne Willing were married at Christ Church, Philadelphia, on October 26, 1780. Their union forged yet another link in the chain of influential families of Philadelphia, with their relatives, the Willings, Powells, Benezets, Stampers, Byrds, Hares, Francises, Coxes, McCalls and Shippens, all present to witness the event.

If the creation of the Bank of Pennsylvania was one of the first real indications of the change in American fortunes, the arrival of French soldiers in the colonies was probably the next. French troops were now in Rhode Island preparing to attack the British, and unlike Washington's poorly equipped forces they were well trained, well equipped and well paid.

In command of the French expeditionary forces was Lieutenant General Comte de Rochambeau, and third in command was a Major General Marquis de Chastellux, philosopher, liberal and correspondent of George Washington. Apparently with time to spare before the British were to be engaged, the aristocratic Chastellux decided he would make a tour of the country, which he planned to end in Philadelphia and a stay with the French minister Chevalier de La Luzerne. Chastellux had a natural curiosity for the world around him and kept detailed notes of his travels. These eventually appeared in print as *Travels in America in 1780, 1781 and 1782* and became one of the first descriptions of travel and society in postcolonial America to be published in Europe.[4]

On his arrival in Philadelphia Chastellux was taken for a tour of Congress in the State House, where he was introduced to James Wilson — "a celebrated lawyer and author of several pamphlets on current affairs." In the evening he dined with Minister Luzerne, and later was taken to meet the recently married and celebrated Mrs. Bingham. "I went to see Mrs Bingham, only seventeen: her husband who was there, according to the American custom, is only five and twenty years — he was agent of Congress at Martinico, from where he is returned with a tolerable knowledge of French and much attachment to the Marquis de Bouillé." Chastellux called later on Mrs. Powel (Elizabeth Powel nee Willing, Anne Bingham's aunt).[5]

Why Chastellux would wish to meet the Binghams ahead of anyone else (he later met Samuel Adams and president of Congress Samuel Huntington) can probably be explained by the glowing commendation of William Bingham that General Bouillé had sent to his superiors in France as well as to Congress. Or more likely, perhaps, it was because of the reports of the beauty of Mrs. Anne Bingham.

Chastellux was also making an impact on Philadelphia and he was invited

Anne Willing Bingham (1764–1801), engraving from original portrait by Gilbert Stuart, circa 1796 (Print Collection, Miriam and Ira D. Wallach Division of Art, Prints and Photographs, New York Public Library, Astor, Lenox and Tilden Foundations).

to a ball, "for a select society, on the occasion of a marriage." Apparently there was only one notable marriage at the end of 1780 in Philadelphia, that of William Bingham and Anne Willing. John and Sarah Jay sent their congratulations from Madrid.[6]

Chastellux was joined in Philadelphia by more noble Frenchmen during his stay, including the Marquis de Lafayette, the Vicomte de Noailles (Lafayette's brother-in-law) and the Comte de Damas, aide to the Comte de Rochambeau, and they were all invited to the social event of the year. The Frenchmen were assigned dancing partners for "Bingham's Ball." The Comte de Damas was partnered with Mrs. Anne Bingham, and Vicomte de Noailles with Miss Nancy Shippen.

These happy times were not to last, however, and the next few months were difficult for both the Bingham and Willing families. Anne Willing (Anne Bingham's mother) died in childbirth in December. Her 13th child, Henry, survived, but only for a few months. A few months later John Benezet, William Bingham's agent throughout his time in Martinique (and husband of his sister Hannah) sailed to Europe on an extended business trip. His ship was lost and nothing more was heard from him. This was followed by the death of John Stamper, Bingham's grandfather (and his father's partner). By this time William Bingham's brother John had died, and as there are no records of James either, William presumably inherited much of the Stamper fortune at this time.

Despite the intervention of Rochambeau's army, in early 1781 the war with Britain was certainly not yet won, and the French involvement not decisive. Washington's underpaid and still ill-equipped troops were mutinous, this time over extensions to their enlistments. There was a general nervousness in government about its inability to control its own destiny, and the more conservative political element in Congress resolved to tighten its grip, particularly over fiscal matters, and to centralize authority in the national government. This "federalist" approach signaled a fundamental change in how Congress was to manage its affairs in the future. The endless and often ineffective committees were to be replaced with administrative departments, elements of executive government that exist to this day. These departments of state were Foreign Affairs, War, Naval Affairs and of course Finance.

There could only be one candidate for superintendent of finance, but Robert Morris accepted only with reluctance and on the clear understanding that he would be permitted to continue his own mercantile activities and that he would have sole discretion in the appointment of his staff. Congress acceded to these terms, and his first appointment was Gouverneur Morris as his assistant.[7]

Robert Morris took a firm, almost autocratic grip on his new department. To restore the credit that was lost, or never existed in the colonial government, he created a parallel currency—"Morris Notes"—that could be drawn against his own personal credit. He started to unravel the mountain of claims against Congress. He lifted the embargoes that had been placed on exported goods to encourage trade and placed army supply contracts with private businesses of substance and reputation in which he had personal trust.[8]

William Bingham, now approaching 30, wealthy and well connected, decided that this was the time to make his political mark by putting himself forward for the new post of minister for foreign affairs, but in the end lost out to Robert R. Livingston (the reason he was given was that there were too many officers being appointed from Pennsylvania already). William Bingham would try again for political office.

More than 12 months had passed since Bingham's return to Philadelphia and Congress had still failed to make any real progress on repaying his debts, but since Robert Morris had yet to supply the information on his terms of employment, that was perhaps hardly surprising. Bingham wrote again to Congress requesting that another part-payment be made at least towards the £34,000 ($150,960) that he owed himself to others on behalf of the American government. This was a very considerable sum of money, and also much needed by Congress elsewhere, but Robert Morris arranged with Benjamin Franklin in Paris to provide a credit of 100,000 livres ($20,000) in Europe. Shortly afterwards Congress agreed that Bingham's expense account of 110,324 livres would now be paid, and the remainder should accrue interest at 6 percent from June 1781. The balance of his account was eventually settled two years later in 1783. Robert Morris was subsequently criticized for favoring his friend and partner over other claims on Congress, in particular by Arthur Lee, who was outraged that Bingham had been paid in specie while other creditors (including the army) were being paid in Continental paper. Morris and Bingham survived the attacks, and with his political ambitions thwarted, at least for the time being, and his financial affairs more or less recovered, William Bingham turned his attention again to his mercantile adventures.[9]

Robert Morris, as superintendent of finance, set about establishing an effective financial structure for the newly independent nation, as part of which he would need a permanent commercial national bank. The Bank of Pennsylvania of 1780 and the others elsewhere had fulfilled a need, but in Morris' words they were "in fact nothing more than a patriotic subscription of continental money, for the purpose of purchasing provisions for a starving army."

Morris' new central bank would be chartered by Congress and have the power to borrow, issue government-backed stocks, issue paper money backed by currency reserves, and hold deposits and generally regulate the financial affairs of the nation, in the manner of the Bank of England or the Exchange Bank in Amsterdam.[10] Morris put forward a proposal to Congress for "a plan for establishing a national bank for the United States of North America," and to do this he enlisted two able colleagues—James Wilson would advise on legal matters and act as political advocate, and Thomas Willing would become chairman. And as an indication of the respect that Bingham by now engendered he was asked to establish the laws and protocols of this first central bank. Congress passed a resolution approving, in principle at least, the establishment of the Bank of North America (as it was to be called) on May 26, 1781, but only by the narrowest of majorities—by one state, in fact, which was probably an indicator of the problems that lay ahead in establishing a central government and a constitution.

Robert Morris was thinking ahead, as there was, however, a war still to be won. The final battleground was destined to be Yorktown, Virginia. General Washington and Rochambeau devised a final high-risk strategy to converge the American and French armies and the French fleet on General Cornwallis' military stronghold at Yorktown. The allied French and American armies assembled at White Plains, New York, on July 6, 1781, before starting the march to Virginia. General Washington, General Rochambeau and General Chastellux (for the second time) arrived at the outskirts of Philadelphia on August 30. They were escorted to the City Tavern, where George Washington met Robert Morris and other senior figures, before briefly attending Congress, and returning to stay at the Morris residence.[11]

For several days the American and French troops continued to march into the city, where they were saluted by the ships in the Delaware and the crowds in the streets.

The French soldiers marched past the State House to be reviewed by their own generals and, of course, representatives from Congress, President Thomas McKean and one delegate for each state. This was the first occasion for the independent United States to consider its protocol for such events. If the president of Congress were to return the salute of the French Army and distinguished generals (normally reserved for a king) would he be styling himself in the manner of the despised monarch from whom they had just separated?

The compromise adopted by Congress was to lift their hats and bow at the appropriate moment.

By September 5 the troops were gone, but not without giving Robert Morris yet another headache when the American troops refused to march any further unless they received one month's pay. When Morris managed to raise $40,000 from his fellow merchants and French general Rochambeau, the crisis was averted and the march southwards continued, leaving Philadelphia to wait and pray for victory.

News of the siege of Yorktown made its way back to Congress, but it was not until October 22 that a rider appeared at the home of the president of

Congress, Thomas McKean, in the middle of the night, declaring that Cornwallis had surrendered. Official dispatches from Washington followed two days later and the city erupted in celebration. General Washington (and his wife) arrived ten days later to a hero's reception.

Within days of the victory, on November 1 Robert Morris convened a meeting of the shareholders of the Bank of North America. Subscriptions for the target of 1,000 shares at $400 each had been slow, perhaps not surprisingly. However, 2.5 million livres in specie, part of the monies raised by Franklin from Vergennes, had now arrived in Boston from France. Morris sent the bank's future chief cashier, Tench Francis Jr., to collect it. Francis earned his spurs by negotiating the 14 wagons and 28 teams of oxen that Morris had supplied for two months and 500 miles, evading the still hostile British army along the way.

Tench Francis and his bullion had arrived at the end of October; at the same time dispelling any lingering suspicions of loyalist sympathy associated with the Francis name (the Francis family had a long association with the governing Penn family). Morris invested a substantial proportion of the French money into 633 shares of the bank, bringing its capital to $325,000, and now just $75,000 short of the $400,000 target.

At the City Tavern meeting Thomas Willing was duly elected president and 12 directors were appointed, including William Bingham, who had invested $42,800 in 107 shares, 95 for himself, 5 for his wife Anne, and 7 for his mother Mary (Molly) Stamper Bingham. Although still short of the projected subscription, the directors resolved to apply to Congress for a charter anyway, and against significant opposition the bill was approved on December 31, 1781.[12]

The Bank of North America opened from a shopfront (leased from Tench Francis) on the Market Street side of Chestnut Street just west of Third on January 7, 1782. Benjamin Franklin's house was across the yard to the rear. William Bingham appears not have been present for the opening, but he was probably otherwise engaged as Ann had given birth to their first child, Ann Louisa Bingham, the previous day.

Morris was now able to lend the money in the bank back to the government at 6 percent in the form of its own bank notes, which he then used to pay war supply contractors. To guarantee confidence in these new government notes, they were redeemable on demand in specie, as specified in the terms of the charter. Unfortunately, but not surprisingly, the contractors did just that, for a while badly depleting the bank's reserves of silver and gold, causing those notes that were in circulation to be discounted heavily, by as much as 15 percent in the southern states.

However confidence recovered; after this faltering start, the notes soon becoming accepted at par throughout the states. Morris even managed to sell

$50,000 of shares in the new Bank of America to Dutch houses, and the bank's share price finally started to rise.[13]

By March 1782 Lord North's ministry had fallen and Britain had determined to seek terms with America, but well before the ink was dry on the Treaty of Paris, Robert Morris was already turning his attention to winning the mercantile peace that was about to follow.

12. The Grand Tour

During the summer of 1782 Philadelphia was emerging from the gloom of the previous few years. Commissioners Franklin, Adams, Jay and Henry Laurens (Franklin at any rate) were negotiating peace with Shelburne's envoy. The French had been popular on their march through the city the previous year, and now with victory they could do no wrong. The French fascination with America was now mutual. French Minister Luzerne announced that Queen Marie Antoinette had given birth, and to celebrate arranged a party at the residence at Sixth and Chestnut. More than a thousand guests attended, including General and Mrs. Washington and, of course, Philadelphia's most popular socialites, William and Anne Bingham. Bingham's wealth and Anne's beauty were becoming irresistible.[1]

Even before the peace treaty with Britain was signed, William Bingham had recognized the commercial opportunities that would soon be presenting themselves, and in October of 1782 he established with Samuel Inglis and Robert Gilmor the new merchant house of Bingham, Inglis and Gilmor. Bingham had already done business with Baltimore merchant Gilmor and Inglis had been a partner of Robert Morris and was now a fellow director in the Bank of North America. Bingham and Inglis put up four-fifths of the capital, and Gilmor the rest. In anticipation of the peace treaty with Britain, the partnership lost no time and it was agreed that Gilmor should go to Amsterdam to set up in business there as their European agent, carrying with him letters of recommendation from Robert Morris.[2]

Bingham's next business venture was to join in land speculation with his friend and former tutor, James Wilson, who appears to have had a head start, buying up whatever land his limited resources would run to over the previous year. With his own money soon exhausted, he looked for loans in Holland for a proposed industrial development along the Delaware River. The Dutch banks declined Wilson's plan and he turned to William Bingham for financial assistance.

Bingham considered Wilson's project, but came up with a counterproposal, suggesting that he abandon the Delaware plan in favor of a partnership to acquire land in New York, to be managed by Wilson, who would also be an investor. Bingham and Wilson agreed terms and the business was established as the Canaan Company, with the intent to acquire 100,000 acres on the Susquehanna in south New York. The first acquisition comprised over 30,000 acres, including a site which was later to be established as the town of Binghamton.[3]

With his financial confidence growing rapidly Bingham had started to make money in various speculations, including wagers on the outcome of military and political events, and with spectacular success in devalued paper currency.[4]

Bingham was not embarrassed to flaunt his new wealth and doubts were being raised about its legitimacy. He was ostentatious and viewed by many in Congress as being too close to and certainly favored by Robert Morris. Despite the tireless efforts by Morris, in particular to finance the Revolutionary War, both were now being regarded in some quarters as profiteers. The reality is, of course, that they were profiteers, and those were, in essence, the terms that Congress had agreed to seven years earlier.[5] But there was considerable asymmetry in the rewards that the war had brought, and Bingham was now being viewed with suspicion, and his next political attempt to become a candidate for Pennsylvania in Congress failed as a result. Bingham had been passed over for minister for foreign affairs, and now he was passed over for Congress.

Bingham now took stock of his affairs; Robert Morris, his friend, mentor and protector, was about leave government to return to commerce and land speculation. Morris was already urging Bingham to work to recover American trade with Britain and there may have been other reasons, but we do know that William Bingham decided early in 1783 that he, Anne and the infant Ann Louisa would travel to Europe for an extended trip mixing business and pleasure. It would be William Bingham's second Grand Tour and Anne Bingham's first.

He was confident that the Bank of North America and other business interests were secure in the hands of his father-in-law Thomas Willing and partner Samuel Inglis. It was now safe to travel to Britain, in fact unusually, and for a very short time all of the countries of Europe were at peace with each other.

Apart from William, Anne and Ann Louisa Bingham, the entourage for the grand European tour included Anne's aunt Margaret and her husband Robert Hare, the brewing tycoon, and their son. The vessel chosen was a Willing, Morris & Co. ship, the aptly named *Commerce*, which departed in May 1783 for England and arrived at Gravesend, London, five weeks later.[6]

Bingham took with him letters of introduction from Robert Morris with a view to establishing or re-establishing mercantile contacts—America had now lost its "favored colonies" status and many British merchants had lost shipping and cargoes and were owed pre-war debts. He had a number of other objectives: James Wilson (as ever) wanted Bingham to raise more loans to satisfy his property speculations; father-in-law Thomas was having trouble with an inheritance in England that needed unraveling; John Dickinson wanted books, money, equipment — anything in fact — for his new college in Carlisle, Pennsylvania; and he had to visit Robert Gilmor in Amsterdam. There was much to do, but perhaps most importantly he wanted to see and be seen by all the right people in all the right places. His great wealth and his beautiful wife were going to be his passports.[7]

Bingham rented a house for his family (Anne was now pregnant with their second child, Maria Matilda) in Bloomsbury Square and set about his list of tasks and exploring their new environment. His political rise may have been halted in Philadelphia, but by good management or serendipity he was to find himself in the right place at the right time to meet the right people.[8]

The Binghams' tour started with the Penn family, who still owned property in England, in Richmond, just south of the River Thames. John Penn was the grandson of Pennsylvania's founder William and he made the Binghams particularly welcome (Quaker John Budd was Bingham's great great grandfather, and the Binghams and the Penns also had adjacent homes in Philadelphia). They visited on several occasions over the summer, then the family stayed with the Penn family while Bingham travelled alone to Amsterdam to consult with Robert Gilmor over the progress of the Bingham, Inglis and Gilmor partnership. His attempts to find a loan for James Wilson in Holland were fruitless, however, and he returned to London, where the family moved to a new residence with a more desirable address at 30 Harley Street, Cavendish Square.[9]

Number 30 Harley Street was eminently suitable for entertaining and accommodating guests, the first of which was to be John Jay, recently arrived from the successful peace negotiations in Paris, where Sarah Jay remained. Bingham and John Jay had last seen each other as the *Aurore* left St. Pierre for France four years earlier. Jay stayed with the Binghams at Cavendish Square, his presence attracting yet more visitors, including John Adams, who was making his first trip to London. Silas Deane, now disgraced and exiled, also called to see Jay. Jay had defended Deane against the claims of dishonesty made against him by Arthur Lee, but felt that his loyalty had been compromised by his closeness to Benedict Arnold. Jay refused to see Deane, who was, by now, distressed and bitter.

John Jay had been ill on his arrival in London, and his condition was made worse by an attack of dysentery. He recovered sufficiently for Bingham to take him to the Royal Society and to be introduced to Richard Price, with whom Bingham claimed extravagantly that he was on close and personal terms.[10]

With the excitement of the Jay and Adams visits over Bingham resumed his consideration of mercantile affairs, and in particular trade with Britain. The Treaty of Paris had been a political success for Franklin, Adams and Jay, but of the negotiating commissioners only one had a mercantile background, Henry Laurens, and he had been incarcerated in the Tower of London for almost the entire process. What the peace commission failed to address was the trading arrangements that would prevail after the peace that recognized the United States as a sovereign nation.[11]

While the Earl of Shelburne remained prime minister it would be reasonable to expect his liberal views, particularly on trade, to prevail and become policy. Unfortunately, when William Pitt's conservative administration came to power, British public opinion now drifted away from trade concessions with the United States and the government turned its attentions to financial reconstruction and the establishment of a new British Empire.

Indeed, a pamphlet by Lord Sheffield (possibly written by Silas Deane) in July 1783 argued that the United States now needed trade with Britain more than Britain did with the former colonies and that the ineffectiveness of the Articles of Confederation rendered unified action on import controls on Britain unlikely. He had a point.

On the other hand almost all manufactured goods imported into America were made in Britain and should another non-importation agreement be put in place, employment in Britain would suffer. William Bingham (among others) seized the opportunity, and wrote a response to Lord Sheffield in a pamphlet he wrote and had published entitled "Letter from an American Now Resident in London to a Member of Parliament on the Subject of the Restraining Proclamation, and Containing Strictures on Lord Sheffield's Pamphlet on the Commerce of the United States."[12]

Despite these exchanges of views no change in policy from the British government seemed imminent. Bingham's pamphlet was well received (it was also published in America) on the whole and he decided that he should convince Congress to appoint a commission to hammer out a commercial treaty with Britain. After due consideration he came to believe that he should be the commissioner, and wrote to this effect to his friend Thomas Fitzsimmons to test support in Congress.[13]

William Bingham had already made his fortune; just three miles away in the city of London Francis Baring was intent on making his. While prime minister, Lord Shelburne had already written to his friend Francis Baring that he "needed to have recourse from time to time to Mercantile advice," thus putting their relationship on a more official basis. Baring was already providing information on a number of issues, in particular that of trade with America. Baring continued to advise William Pitt in the new government but also remained a very close confidante of Lord Lansdowne (as Shelburne had now become on leaving office).

It was at this time that the orbits of William Bingham and Francis Baring finally intersected. By his friendship with Richard Price, Bingham was now involved with the circle that Benjamin Franklin had espoused some years earlier in the pre-war years, including Benjamin Vaughan, an "honest Whig" and printer friend of Franklin, Richard Price, Joseph Priestley and Jeremy Bentham. Vaughan had been sent by Shelburne as an unofficial envoy to Paris to sound out the terms of a peace treaty, where he also met John Jay. The exact mechanism is obscure but Benjamin Vaughan later introduced William Bingham to Lord Shelburne, possibly because Bingham's pamphlet on American trade coincided so closely with his own views. It is hard to say whether Bingham engineered all this, but the evidence does suggest some kind of strategic approach.

The Binghams were adopted immediately by Shelburne, who entertained them at Shelburne House (later called Lansdowne House) in Berkeley Square and then at Bowood in Wiltshire, the country seat and hothouse of intellectuals, scholars, scientists and politicians. At Bowood Bingham finally met Francis Baring, who was by now a regular at Shelburne's country gatherings.[14]

On December 9, 1783, Anne Bingham gave birth, and after a three month break the Bingham party moved on to Bath, at the time the out-of-town center of fashionable English society, where Bingham re-acquainted himself with his friend and mutual supporter, the Marquis de Bouille, also in residence there at the time. From Bath the party moved on to Bristol before returning to London, visiting some of England's grandest houses, including Blenheim, Woodstock and Stowe.

Since no word had come from Congress about his (probably fanciful) diplomatic appointment, the Binghams decided it was time to continue their tour into Europe. They made the crossing across the North Sea from Harwich to the port of Hellevoetsluis, then to Rotterdam, and finally to The Hague, the seat of the Dutch government, where they met John Adams once again.

Adams had broken his stay in London on the news that bills had arrived from Robert Morris, drawn on John and Francis Baring & Co. in London, for which there were insufficient funds in Europe to cover. Adams and his son John Quincy returned to Amsterdam to negotiate another loan, raising two million guilders at 6 percent, repayable in 1807. Morris was already a correspondent of Francis Baring. Perhaps Bingham set up the line of credit with Francis Baring?[15] (John Adams was desperate to be appointed to be American minister to the court of St. James. It was also the only job that Benjamin Franklin was prepared to stay on in Europe for. Congress did indeed appoint John Adams and he returned to London the following year, 1785.)

Anne and William Bingham attended a dinner at court with John Adams given in part so that the beautiful Mrs. Bingham could be inspected. After ten days the Binghams left Adams in The Hague and travelled on to Amsterdam, where they were entertained by Henry Hope (of bankers Hope & Co.), following an introduction by their new friend Francis Baring.

While in Amsterdam, Bingham had received the bad news that his partner Samuel Inglis had died quite suddenly at the end of 1783 and that for some reason Willing, Morris & Co. had withdrawn support from the remaining partners. Bingham met Robert Gilmor immediately to establish a new partnership between them, Robert Gilmor and Co. This new partnership was to be based in Baltimore, where Gilmor returned in due course.[16]

After this the Binghams continued their journey to Paris, where they took rooms in the Hotel Muscovy. Word of the famous Binghams had travelled ahead of them, perhaps courtesy of the Marquis de Chastellux's travel revelations. French society was as keen to see them (or at least Mrs. Bingham) as they were to join French society.[17]

Bingham called first on Benjamin Franklin in Passy. Their last meeting had been eight years earlier, when Franklin had given him instructions for his activities in Martinique; this time Bingham was carrying a letter from John Adams. The Binghams then settled in for an extended stay in Paris. Without doubt it was the place to be and to be seen, both for William and Anne.

They called on the Marquis de Chastellux, who was working on a revised version of his *Travels in North America*.

William Bingham called to see Jefferson, who just arrived from America as minister to France. Bingham and Jefferson had already corresponded over mercantile issues and Jefferson had taken a dislike to Bingham, perhaps because of his close association with Robert Morris and Franklin, his Federalist tendencies, his pro–British stance, and his wealth, but more irksome was that he was younger by eight years and had a disarmingly beautiful wife.[18]

Whatever the reasons, he had no time for Bingham, but a great deal of time and affection for Anne; they corresponded in a close, almost intimate way for the rest of her life.[19]

Meanwhile the Adams family, John, Abigail, John Quincy and daughter Abigail (Nabby) moved into a mansion at Auteuil near the Bois de Boulogne. Abigail and Nabby had travelled from Massachusetts to be with John, leaving the younger sons back at the farm.

The Binghams were invited to dine with the Adams on September 25, together with a number of other guests, mainly American. We have a rich source of candid information on these social events in Paris from the letters of Abigail Adams and the diaries of her daughter, Nabby, giving us the perspective of a 19-year-old from New England in Europe for the first time.

Mrs. Abigail Adams writes of the Binghams: "He is said to be rich and to have an income of four thousand a year ... 'tis said he wishes for an appointment here as foreign minister; he lives at a much greater expense than any American Minister can afford to do. Mrs Bingham is a fine figure and a beautiful person; her manners are easy and affable, but she was too young to come abroad without a pilot, gives too much into the follies of this country, has money enough and knows how to lavish it with an unsparing hand. Less money and more years may make her wiser, but she is so handsome she must be pardoned."

Nabby, to whom her new life must have been such a change from Braintree, wrote: "Mr B. is possessed of a large fortune — both very young. Mrs B. is only 20; she was married at 16; she is pretty, a good figure, but rather still. She has not been long enough in this country to have gained the ease of air and manner which is peculiar to the women here; and when it does not exceed the bounds of delicacy, is very pleasing. Mrs B. has been in Europe two years. I admire her that she is not the smallest degree tinctured by indelicacy. She has, from the little acquaintance I have had with her, genuine principles; she is very sprightly and pleasing."[20]

On September 30 the Binghams were dining in style again, this time with Thomas Jefferson and the Adams family. Nabby again enjoyed the company of Anne Bingham, with whom she was becoming quite friendly. On October 19 William Bingham joined John Adams to be presented to the King: "Mr. Bingham came flourishing out in the morning to accompany Pappa to Versailles to be presented to his most Christian majesty, the King of France, with his four horses and three servants, in all the pomp of an American merchant. About twelve they returned, as there was no Court."

A few days later: "We all dined with Mr. And Mrs Bingham at their hotel.... There was much company; Mrs B. gains my love and admiration, more and more every time I see her; she is possessed of more ease and politeness in her behaviour, than any person I have seen. She joins in every conversation in company; and when engaged herself in conversing with you, she will, by joining directly in another chit chat with another party, convince you, that she was all attention to every one. She has a taste for show, but not above her circumstances. Mr B. is an agreeable man, but seems to feel the superiority of fortune more than Mrs B."

John Adams presented Bingham to the French court on the second attempt on October 30, Nabby noting: "Papa went to Versailles by himself last Tuesday: he introduced Mr. J, and Mr. T., and Mr B., the first gentlemen in private characters that have been introduced at this court. Mr B.'s ambition promoted it; what it will promote him to I know not; if to what he wishes, it is easily determined."[21]

Mr. J. was, in fact, Major William Jackson, John Laurens' erstwhile secretary and assistant, now returned to France. Mr. T. is unknown. Nabby was referring, of course, to Bingham's diplomatic ambitions.

Major Jackson was apparently out to make his fortune (a common trait with General Washington's former aides-de-camp, it seems), having failed on his disastrous mission with Laurens and his slightly ignominious return. This time he arrived to see Bingham with letters of recommendation from Robert Morris and proposals for a line of business among the three of them that "promises success equal to the most sanguine wishes."

Major Jackson was now drawn, or drew himself, into Bingham's circle of acquaintances. Jackson had already made an impression on Nabby's father (John Adams): "My papa calls him the Sir Charles Grandison of this age. I was never acquainted with him until I came to France; I consider it an acquisition."

At a party a few days later she described him as "my favorite" but she felt she was losing out to Anne Bingham's charms: "I sat next to Mr. Jackson at table, and next to him was seated Madame [sic] Bingham who by an exuberance of sprightliness and wit slips from the path of being perfectly agreeable; a little judgement would amend whatever defects may appear."[22]

Major Jackson was there to rope in Mr. (and if necessary Mrs.) Bingham, not get entangled with Miss Adams.

In December of 1784 the Binghams moved yet again, this time to the Palais Royal. The season of entertainment continued, with further dinners at Dr. Franklin's, the Marquis de La Fayette's and the Adams' again, this time with the Chevalier de La Luzerne.

Word of Bingham's diplomatic appointments never came and in April 1785 the family returned to London, where they were joined a month later by the Adams, Abigail, Nabby, and John Quincy, who was on his way back to America and Harvard. Congress had finally settled the issue of the American minister to Great Britain in favor of John Adams.[23]

William and Anne Bingham maintained a continuous correspondence with the long-suffering Thomas Willing, widowed of three years, but the letters were a poor substitute for such a long absence from his daughter and granddaughters. He last saw Ann Louisa at just 16 months old and had yet to see Maria Matilda at all. Much of the Bingham/Willing correspondence remains, but Anne's letters have been lost.[24]

Thomas Willing was stoic when Bingham announced that they would stay in Europe for another year: "It was very natural for Nancy [Anne] to wish to gratify her curiosity fully, by staying another year. She had crossed the Ocean already, and had an indulgent friend in you, ready and able to gratify her.... I am contented; and the more so as my state of health is good and I've as fair a chance as ever of living to see her, should your return be delayed till next year."[25]

And later in the year: "Your account of my dearest Nancy and the little ones affords me great joy. I thank her much for her frequent letters to me.

They are sprightly and judicious and would have entertained even a stranger; to me they were as a feast, on which paternal pride and affection had ample room to be gratified. God bless her, you, and those endearing pledges of affection which are with you.... I long to embrace you all."

Having failed in his attempts at diplomatic advance in Holland and France, using all the devices that his money could buy, Bingham now turned his attention to Britain. Back in London he called on American portrait painter Gilbert Stuart. Stuart had trained under another American, Benjamin West, and had recently set up his own studio. His *Portrait of a Gentleman Skating* had been exhibited at the Royal Academy with great success, elevating him to the level of Reynolds and Gainsborough.

Bingham commissioned Stuart to paint a family portrait, which would be a gift to Anne and was intended to make English society take notice of William and Anne Bingham. Stuart accepted the commission with some reluctance and made a start on a romantic scene typical of the style much loved by English aristocracy.[26] Bingham was set in a pastoral scene, dressed in hunting pink, his powdered hair drawn with a bow. Anne was in the center dressed in flowing white, attending the children. But the picture was never finished; perhaps it didn't need to be. Whatever the reasons, however, Bingham and Stuart remained on good terms, the account presumably settled, because Bingham was to commission Stuart a few years later for a portrait that did see the light of day. The painting was not lost, however; it returned to America and was recycled by Henry Clymer (Anne's brother-in-law) into three separate portraits.[27]

Maybe Bingham had no time to sit for Stuart because he took the family off again in the spring visiting the great houses of England, preparing himself, perhaps, for the next attack on English aristocracy to which he felt so attracted. On their return they saw the Adams family again. They learned of Nabby's attachment to another Washington aide-de-camp, this time Colonel Smith, who, like Major Jackson before him, had other, more sinister reasons to become attached to the daughter of an eminent politician.

At the end of July 1785 Bingham was on the move again, this time to The Hague, from where he continued to antagonize Thomas Jefferson, now sole minister to France. While asking Jefferson for an introduction to the French minister, Bingham relayed comments from John Jay that federal (Federalist) ideas were gaining support in Congress. (John Jay was now minister for foreign affairs, having taken over from Robert Livingston, and was considered by the French as favoring Britain over France. His was not a popular appointment in France, either with the French court or with Thomas Jefferson, who was increasingly opposed to a strong federal government.)

Having failed in his mission to The Hague, Bingham returned to Paris, where he met Jefferson again before returning to The Hague once more.

Bingham's shuttle diplomacy continued when he travelled back to Paris and another meeting with Jefferson, but this time Bingham collected his old friend the Marquis de Bouillé to tour Switzerland and Italy, where he may have retraced the steps of his earlier (1773–1774) European travels for the benefit of Anne.

In December 1785 they were back in Paris and announced to the probably relieved Jefferson that they were to return to London and then travel on to America.[28]

Jefferson was pleased to see the back of Bingham but Anne was quite different, and someone for whom he had great affection. He was suspicious of Bingham's motives in the same way that he was to fall out with Adams, Hamilton, Washington, John Marshall and anyone else whose political views did not coincide with his.[29]

Jefferson made his views of Bingham clear some time later in a letter to James Madison from Paris dated January 30, 1787: "Tho' Bingham is not in diplomatic office, yet as he wishes to be so, I will mention such circumstances of him, as you might otherwise be deceived in. He will make you believe he was on the most intimate footing with the first characters in Europe, & versed in the secrets of every cabinet. Not a word of this is true.... He had a rage for being presented to great men, & had no modesty in the methods by which he could if he attained acquaintance. Afterwards it was with such as who were susceptible from the beauty of his wife."

The Binghams arrived back in London in January of 1786. William Bingham's social climb in England was not quite over yet! Anne Bingham had now become something of a celebrity—her picture had been engraved and was on sale, leading Abigail Adams to comment in a letter to her son John on February 16, 1786: "Mr. And Mrs. Bingham arrived here about three weeks ago with a full determination to go out to America in March, but having as usual spared no pains to get introduced to the families of Lord Lansdowne and my Lady Lucans, they are so supremely blest that poor America looks like a bugbear to them.... 'O! I know Mrs. Bingham, you won't go out this spring. Give me but ten years and take all the rest of my life' Who can understand (such) flattery and admiration? What female mind, young, beautiful, rich — must she not be more than woman if vanity was not the predominant passion?"[30]

Nabby endorsed her mother's comments in a letter to her brother:

> Mrs. Bingham called upon us early to request Mamma to present her at Court on Thursday where I suppose she will make a fine figure....
> Mr. Barthelemy and Mr. and Mrs. Bingham called in the evening. They had dined with Lord Lansdowne, and called to let us know it, I suppose....
> Mrs. B is coming quite into fashion here and she is very much admired. The hairdresser, who dresses upon Court days inquired of Mamma whether she knew the lady so much talked of from America — Mrs. Bingham. He had

heard of her from a lady who saw her at Lord Lucan's, where she was much admired. At last, speaking of Miss (Ann) Hamilton, he said, with a twirl of his comb, "Well it does not signify but the American ladies do beat the English all to nothing.

William Bingham had done it. He had finally been presented to the court of St. James as well as to the courts of Holland and France!

The presentation to George III was followed in the evening by a grand ball to celebrate the occasion of Queen Charlotte's birthday, and brought the Binghams' Grand European Tour to a remarkable end.

Ten days later the Binghams called once more on the Adams family to announce their departure for America, and on the following day, March 11, 1786, they set sail for Philadelphia together with eight servants, two carriages and a hold full of new possessions and clothes for Anne.[31]

13. New Country, New Constitution

William and Anne Bingham were not just taking in the sights in their European tour—they were also buying the fittings, furnishing, fabrics and artwork for a new mansion. They weren't leaving the grandeur of the European aristocratic lifestyle behind; they were bringing it with them.

At some stage during the Grand Tour William and Anne Bingham had decided that on their return to America they would build themselves a mansion in Society Hill, Philadelphia, on the block bounded by Third and Fourth Streets, Willings Alley and Spruce Street. Bingham had already acquired the land and sent rough plans to enable a start to be made before their arrival back in Philadelphia in May of 1786.[1]

Work continued apace after their return and they rented a town house on Second Street between Chestnut and Walnut until they could move, in late 1786 or early 1787. Bingham's intention was quite simply to build the best private residence in the new United States, and by general consensus at the time, he succeeded. William and Anne saw no incongruity in copying the luxury and excesses of the Great Britain from which he had helped America to become independent.[2]

The Binghams had decided, apparently without irony, that they would become aristocrats; what in Europe was determined by birth William Bingham decided he could buy with his wealth. He engaged a staff of servants so that he could adopt the style and flamboyance of the royal courts which he and Anne had so successfully infiltrated. Despite the fact that all this was quite contrary to the style of Quaker Philadelphia, apparently no one turned down an invitation to dine at the Mansion House!

Dinners at the Mansion House were conducted in the European style and guests were announced on arrival by a footman. This distinctly un–American activity continued until Senator James Monroe, responding to his name being announced, shouted back:

The Mansion House, Third Street, Philadelphia, residence of William and Anne Bingham. "A View in Third Street from Spruce Street," William Russell Birch, 1800 (I.N. Phelps Stokes Collection, Miriam and Ira D. Wallach Division of Art, Prints and Photographs, New York Public Library, Astor, Lenox and Tilden Foundations).

"Coming!" and on hearing it again called back, "Coming as soon as I can get my greatcoat off!"

With the Mansion House now complete, Bingham launched a spectacular campaign to raise his profile and political credentials, helped to a degree by the timely arrival in Philadelphia of Benjamin Franklin.

Franklin had returned from Paris towards the end of 1785, and once the clamor had died down turned his attention to various unfinished works. He had established the American Philosophical Society in 1743, but in his absence it lacked the funds to prosper. Franklin personally gifted £100 and urged others to do the same. Bingham was one of a number to make a donation, and was subsequently elected to the society. (The society had been given land adjacent to the State House and Philosophical Hall was erected on the site, completed in 1789.)[3] Franklin addressed three successive meetings of the society with papers he had written while on his return journey, any one of which would have been impressive by any scientist at any time. During the course of his journey he had designed a flue for stoves (which was immediately and

Manchester House, London, circa 1800, now Hertford House, home of the Wallace Collection, from Papworth's *Select Views of London* (City of Westminster Archives Centre).

universally adopted), he had observed the course and investigated the science of the Gulf Stream, and he had prepared radical designs for improvements to the rigging of sailing vessels.

Bingham now joined another of Franklin's creations, the Hand-in-Hand Company (actually the Philadelphia Contributionship for the Insurance of Houses from Loss by Fire).[4] He assisted in the advancement of seats of learning; he joined the Board of Trustees of the College of Philadelphia and became its treasurer; and he contributed to Dr. Rush's latest venture, the German College and Charity School in Lancaster, Pennsylvania (later the Franklin and Marshall College).

Bingham's profile, though impressive already in many ways, lacked the military service or the congressional appointments of his contemporaries, and he set about plugging the gaps in his curriculum vitae.

His military standing improved when he was made an honorary member of the Pennsylvania Society of the Cincinnati, the fraternal association formed by officers of the Continental Army, with General Washington as life president. He set up a second troop of militia, the Second Troop of Philadelphia Light Horse. His second in command in this venture was none other than Major William Jackson (now studying law back in America after his mercantile activities in Holland appear to have come to nothing). Perhaps wishing to ingratiate himself with Bingham (again) he transferred his allegiance from the first troop to Bingham's self-styled "gentleman's militia."[5]

It was clear by now, even to William Bingham, that his longed-for diplomatic appointment was not likely to happen, at least in the short term, and he decided that his political future lay in Congress, from where he could develop his Federalist ideas. He did not to have to wait long; he was elected to the Continental Congress as a representative for Pennsylvania at the end of 1786, and in November he travelled with Anne to New York (where Congress had been held, in the New York City Hall on Wall Street, since December 1784).[6]

There was no great exhilaration for Bingham in his new appointment, after the efforts of creating the new independent states and winning a war with Britain, Congress was now a spent force. The Continental Congress of the United States had, under the Articles of Confederation, no formal executive, no judiciary system, no armed forces, no money and a mountain of debt. It did have a federal bank, though, the Bank of North America, but by now that had no money either. The autonomy of the states was preventing Congress from exercising its treaty powers or discharging its obligations. Individual states were organizing their own foreign and Indian policies; the financial system was chaotic; the national debts, or those incurred by Congress, were to foreign lenders, and its inability to repay put the whole question of overseas trade into question; foreign nations were showing contempt for the United States—few had sent ministers, Britain continued to refuse trading agreements, the relationship with France was cooling rapidly, and the relationship with Spain had always been difficult; the Continental Army had been disbanded in 1784, apart from a few garrison forts in the Ohio country and the small unit in West Point, New York; the Continental Navy, such as it was, was sold off; Congress was unable to stop Indian raids; the Spanish controlled the southwest and threatened to close the Mississippi to American trade; the British were still active in the northwest; Congress could do little to reassure settlers on the margins; Washington wrote "the West was on a pivot, ready at the touch of a feather" to turn to the country that offered them some security for the future. Perhaps the greatest problem, though, was the state of the economy (as always): the post-war depression led to inflation; with widespread indebtedness and the lack of gold and silver, states were resorting to printing more and more paper money, adding to the inflationary spiral, and suiting debtors in favor of creditors; and farmers were suffering from low prices and high taxes and property payments.[7]

The increasing discontent would eventually lead to Shay's rebellion, and a very real concern about the direction the nation was heading.[8]

This then, was the sorry state of affairs in 1785 when John Hancock was elected president of Congress. He never turned up. The vote of nine states out of thirteen was required to pass substantive legislation. Real power was in the hands of the state legislatures, where the big hitters from ten years before had returned.

Bingham could have been excused for joining the Pennsylvania State Legislature (where Benjamin Franklin had been appointed life president), but whether it was hubris or a genuine attempt to get something done we do not know. Having made such efforts at the royal courts of Europe, it would be uncharacteristic of him to aim for anything but the top of his country's government.

He wrote to Richard Price in London:

> I must confess that I did not find the United States in as flourishing a situation as I had reason to expect. The specie of the country, which after the war constituted its only circulating medium, has been almost wholly exported; and many of the states have had recourse to the dangerous expedient of paper money, which by not being in general well funded, has in many instances greatly depreciated.... The Confederation is likewise an evil of an alarming nature. It does not possess sufficient power. The Individual states, from the sufferings they are exposed to from the weakness and inefficiency of the Confederacy, seem disposed to vest Congress with such authorities as are necessary to pursue and preserve the general interests of the Union. This will make their administration respectable abroad, and vigorous at home.[9]

Bingham appears to have summed up the situation as well as anyone. Others, of course, had come to the same conclusion. Representatives of five states had already met at Mount Vernon in March 1785 and Annapolis in September 1786 to "review, and if necessary make recommendations for improvements to domestic and foreign trade." James Madison and Alexander Hamilton proposed that discussions should extend beyond this limited remit to include the adequacy of and changes to the Articles of Confederation, at a convention to be held in Philadelphia in May of 1787.[10]

Back in New York Congress limped on; a quorum existed for just one day in January 1787, then lapsed until February when it tried to elect a president, which it failed to do until Arthur St. Clair from Pennsylvania emerged as a compromise candidate. The Treaty of Paris with Britain was discussed, even though two years had elapsed since its ratification. In particular the question of frontier forts that had not been given up by the British was debated. The treaty required the United States to pay the pre-war debts (a substantial debt to British merchants had built up prior to the war, and was never paid off, including to the unfortunate Frenchman Beaumarchais). Since Congress had no money or legislative power to recover it from the states, the debate left the issue unresolved.

Closer to home a copy of Madison and Hamilton's Annapolis resolution to review the Articles of Confederation was debated. Shay's rebellion had been a wake-up call to many delegates and the need for an effective central government was the most pressing issue to be resolved.

Congress passed a resolution endorsing Hamilton's proposal that a convention of delegates assemble at Philadelphia in May "for the sole and express purpose of revising the Articles of Confederation."

Bingham wrote to Lord Lansdowne, with whom he was now a regular correspondent:

> The defects of the confederated systems are so glaring and the necessity of a speedy and effectual revision and amendment so generally acknowledged, that Congress have recommended to the states to appoint, and many of the states have accordingly (and all will) come to the resolution of appointing delegates to a general convention for the purpose of forming and making a report to Congress of such federal constitution as may be suited to the exigencies of the Union....
>
> Having the honor of a seat in Congress, as a representative of the state of Pennsylvania, I was very active in promoting this measure.[11]

A total of 55 delegates formed the Constitutional Convention, which finally convened on May 25, 1787, 11 days late. George Washington arrived on time on May 13, intent on staying at Mrs. House's boarding house, but was persuaded by Robert Morris to stay with him at the Market Street residence. Other, less fortunate delegates boarded at the City Tavern or the Indian Queen Tavern. The delegates were unpaid for their services, though some may have had expenses reimbursed, so it is unsurprising that they were by and large prosperous and well established.[12]

Robert Morris nominated George Washington as presiding officer, and he was elected unanimously. Benjamin Franklin had hoped that his forever-overlooked grandson William Temple Franklin would be chosen as the secretary, but the ubiquitous Major William Jackson was appointed instead, having been nominated by Alexander Hamilton.

The delegates deliberated from May to September 17, when the final document was signed. They had worked six days a week through the heat of the summer; too noisy with the windows open, too stifling with them shut.

Bingham had returned to Philadelphia in March, where there was great deal of entertaining to do, but was encouraged by secretary Charles Thomson to return to New York, to debate the Great Northwest Ordinance which would enable the land north of the Ohio River to become part of the Union. By the time Bingham arrived the ordinance had been passed. Only eight states were present, of which one was against. He was appointed to the now discredited Finance Committee but all minds were now concentrated on events in Philadelphia, and Bingham returned to Philadelphia in August.

Major Jackson left Philadelphia for New York on September 18, arriving the following day and transmitting an engrossed copy of the Constitution to secretary Thompson. On September 26 the Continental Congress, including 12 delegates to the convention, began their consideration of the document.[13]

In December 1787 and January 1788 five states ratified the Constitution. By June 1788, New Hampshire's ratification brought the number to nine, and the Constitution effectively became law. In September Congress named New York as the temporary capital.

For his efforts in getting the Constitution through Congress and the Pennsylvania State Assembly, William Bingham might be forgiven for the belief that a position in the new Congress or the State Assembly or even appointment as the first governor of Pennsylvania under the new Constitution was a just reward.

Despite the approval and ratification of the new Constitution, the last Continental Congress ran its course. Bingham spent much of the year in New York while Anne and the children stayed with the tireless Thomas Willing and returned in the autumn, his time in government over, at least for the time being.

The first president of the United States travelled by coach from Mount Vernon to Philadelphia on his triumphant journey to be sworn in in New York. He was met by Bingham's Second Troop of gentleman soldiers and escorted into the city, where he was provided with a white horse to make the splendid entrance to which he was by now accustomed. The following morning he was escorted to the New Jersey state line. He was taken across the Hudson River in a barge rowed by 13 ship's captains in white dress uniforms. John Jay and General Henry Knox made the crossing in another barge.

George Washington took the oath of office on April 30, 1789. John Adams was elected vice president, John Jay became chief justice of the Supreme Court, with James Wilson one of five associate judges. Thomas Jefferson (although not yet returned from Paris) took the office of secretary of state, Alexander Hamilton became secretary of the treasury, and Edmund Randolph was appointed attorney general. General Henry Knox retained his office from the Continental Congress as secretary of war. Robert Morris was elected to the Senate for Pennsylvania, together with George Clymer and Thomas Fitzsimmons. William Bingham had decided not to stand for election to the new Congress, but he could not have been closer to those who were in high office.

As secretary of the treasury, Alexander Hamilton had by far the most difficult task ahead of him. Foreign debt was over $12 million, in loans and unpaid interest to the French treasury and Dutch banks; domestic debt, in the form of interest-bearing treasury notes, issued to pay war supply contractors, and veterans certificates issued as pay to the Continental Army amounted to over $40 million, much of which was unpaid interest on the notes. Confidence in the notes, especially in the southern states, had collapsed, and they were trading as low as twenty cents on the dollar.[14]

Bingham had known Alexander Hamilton since from his return from Martinique; they had corresponded over that time and had a shared respect for their mentor Robert Morris, and they had almost identical Federalist and economic philosophies. In October 1789 Hamilton wrote to Bingham to request help in formulating his policy by asking a number of specific questions:

> For which purpose I have enclosed a number of queries, to which I shall be obliged by as full particular and accurate answers as possible....
> May I also take the liberty (to request of) you that you will from time to time favor me with communications with regard to ... any thoughts that may occur to you concerning the financing and debts of the United States.[15]

We know that William Bingham was acutely aware of the need to re-establish trade. He had seen firsthand the huge changes that the Industrial Revolution was making to the British economy and the wealth that it was creating. The financial center of Europe was switching from the Netherlands to London. Britain's new and very young prime minister William Pitt had put behind him the loss of one empire; he was busy building a new one.

After the posturing of the Constitutional Convention and the new government, the United States needed someone that could restore the economy and credit, both internally and externally, and create a national or federal central bank and currency that was stable and universal across the states. Because all this was Federalist by its nature, the solutions were likely to be divisive, and they were. President Washington believed that Hamilton was the man for the job; William Bingham felt that he was uniquely qualified to provide Hamilton with a structure that would work.

In response to Hamilton's request for assistance, Bingham wrote a lengthy memorial outlining his proposals in November 1789.[16] The existence of this document was not known until it emerged in 1931, in the archives of the Connecticut Historical Society, when it was studied by Broadus Mitchell, professor of economics (and Hamilton biographer). He wrote: "Correspondence between the advice offered and what Hamilton urged in his first reports is so close as to justify the presumption of strong specific influence."

John C. Miller, professor of history at Stanford University, in his work *Alexander Hamilton: Portrait in Paradox*, concludes: "All the ingredients of what came to be known as Hamiltonian finance were contained in this letter."[17]

Central to "Hamiltonian economics" was that the public debt be wrapped up, consolidated and re-issued with new notes from the Federal Treasury, bearing interest at 6 percent.

The national debt, he argued, should be repaid by a taxation system set up specifically for the purpose, in such a way that foreign nations might have belief in the ability of the United States to honor its existing commitments, and so lend and invest further sums.

Four proposals were submitted by Hamilton to Congress, from January 1790. Hamilton proposed that the United States government would pay off the internal national debt, at par to the current holders of treasury and veteran's certificates; it would assume and repay individual states' war debts; it would set up federal taxes and duties specifically to fund these repayments; it would create a Bank of the United States.

These proposals were hotly contested by the anti-federalist lobby, notably Jefferson and James Madison, but the Funding Act, as it became known, and the legislation to create a National Bank were approved by the Senate (easily) and Congress (with difficulty), and signed by George Washington in August 1790.

The opponents of the new legislation pointed to the asymmetry of northern states recovering more than the southern states, and the owners of certificates, possibly speculators, making huge profits. It may have been a compromise, but it is difficult to see what else could have been done. One perhaps unexpected consequence of this bitter dispute was the inevitable move towards a party political system, something that the founding fathers had tried to avoid. Two groups had now emerged — Hamilton's Federalists and Jefferson's Democratic Republicans.

William Bingham had a vested interest in "Hamiltonian economics" — he had been buying up devalued certificates as early as 1778, while still in Martinique. How much he held is not recorded; in 1789 alone he borrowed £60,000 from Dutch bankers to buy treasury certificates. It is likely that he was holding several hundred thousand dollars worth. On August 4, 1790, William Bingham (and many others, at least 60 million dollars of certificates were in circulation) doubled his money.[18]

Before this time Bingham was considered to be a very rich man; he was now being described as the richest man in America.

While Congress was agonizing over Hamilton's economic package, Benjamin Franklin, who had attended the entire Constitutional Convention, finally succumbed to his long illnesses and died on April 17. Half of the population of Philadelphia turned out to witness the funeral procession from the State House to Christ Church and to the burial ground on Fifth and Arch Streets. The six coffin bearers were General Thomas Mifflin (now state president), Thomas McKean (chief justice), Thomas Willing, Samuel Powel (mayor of Philadelphia), professor David Rittenhouse (College of Philadelphia) and William Bingham. The eulogy was written and delivered by Major William Jackson.[19]

William Bingham had always held Benjamin Franklin in great respect (he was one of the first products of his college, and Franklin gave him the opportunity in Martinique). He had suggested to Franklin (just before his death) and to the Library Company that he would like to commission the Italian sculptor Francois Lazzarini to produce a statue of the great man. Franklin clearly liked the idea, and chose to be sculpted wearing a patrician Roman Toga (surely Franklin was joking?). The finished work failed to arrive before Franklin's death. The directors of the Library Company were pleased with the gift; an alcove was created on the new building for its permanent display. (Unfortunately the soft marble chosen by Bingham suffered from erosion in Philadelphia's climate. It now can be found in the Library Company at 1314 Locust Street, safely inside but sadly having lost its hands to the ravages of time and weather. The one on display today is a replica.)

Later in the year Bingham returned to Philadelphia from New York and was elected to the Pennsylvania State Assembly, of which he became Speaker. In December Congress was back in Philadelphia, the center of society, fashion and government. William and Anne Bingham and the Mansion House were at the very center of this society and what became known as the "Republican Court."[20]

The new government gradually found its feet; Mrs. Washington joined the president; Abigail Adams finally left Massachusetts, reluctantly leaving Nabby (now Mrs. William Smith) behind. Nabby was now expecting their second child, and Colonel Smith was often mysteriously absent in New York.

Foreign diplomats now started to appear, finding Philadelphia a more agreeable and sophisticated posting than New York, and they all migrated to the Mansion House to be entertained by Anne and William Bingham.[21]

Bingham continued to flout his wealth with the furnishings and clothes needed to match the finest houses he had seen in England. Fashions in Europe were changing rapidly, and the Binghams naturally had to be at the vanguard of their introduction to the United States.

Bingham's attempts to lead an aristocracy in America were not going unnoticed, however. Jean-Pierre Brissot, a French republican leader and author under the pseudonym Brissot de Warville, had written in his *New Travels in the United States of America*, published in 1792: "A very ingenious woman in this town is reproached with having contributed more than all others to introduce this taste for luxury. I really regret to see her husband, who appears to be well informed, and of an amiable character, affect, in his buildings and furniture, a pomp which ought for ever to have been a stranger to Philadelphia."[22]

This was written in 1788, well before Bingham's increasing pomp in the 1790s.

Bingham might well have considered how he was being perceived, but apparently chose not to. He was a Federalist among like-thinking friends and political colleagues, particularly Washington, Hamilton, Adams, and Jay. In their absence his future might have been less certain, and he was making an enemy of Thomas Jefferson, who had never had any time for him in any event, despite his feelings for Anne. While attacking his other nemesis, John Adams, Jefferson supported the comments made by James T. Callender, categorizing them together with withering sarcasm: "In the same estimation, do I hold Mr Bingham, the breeches-makers son, at Philadelphia. The trade, I hope, will not take offence at my classing him amongst them."[23]

Bingham appears to have shrugged off these attacks. He was after all dedicating himself to public life, even if many people resented the manner in which the wealth that was allowing him to fund his public life was created.

Hamilton's Bank of the United States duly opened its subscription for shares on Independence Day 1791 by placing 25,000 shares at $400 on sale, which were oversubscribed within two hours. Thomas Willing changed his position as president of the Bank of North America for the role of president of the Bank of the United States. Such was the impact of Hamilton's new economy, competition for one of the seats on the board of the new bank was intense. Coolly Bingham said that such an appointment was a matter of indifference to him — he was elected unanimously and ultimately became one of its most significant directors.[24]

The bank opened its doors in Carpenters Hall on December 12, 1791.

14. Property Fever

Up until the War of Independence the size of Britain's colonies in America was restricted by its ability to defend its borders from French and Indian encroachment, which had prohibited westwards expansion beyond the Allegheny River. But in 1782 the United States was a sovereign nation, and with that constraint effectively gone, expansion was now the art of the possible, at least in theory.

With the post-war slump and the collapse of the economy, there was plenty of land but little money to acquire it. States needed to raise money to clear the debts from the war years and new settlers were needed. Large tracts of state-owned land were put up for auction, starting a wave of speculation by investors who sensed a quick return.

Robert Morris was an early land speculator, as were James Wilson and many others. William Bingham had left James Wilson in charge of the Canaan Company and the negotiations to buy extensive tracts in New York State at the end of 1782. They had started with 30,000 acres straddling the Susquehanna River (part of which became Binghamton). Bingham completed this deal on his return from Europe in 1786 — 32,620 acres at 12.25 cents per acre.[1]

The passing of the Great Northwest Ordinance (in July 1787) opened up new possibilities for expansion and speculation by bringing lands north of the Ohio River into the Union. The Northwest Territory would eventually become the states of Illinois, Indiana, Michigan, Ohio and Wisconsin. (Thomas Jefferson had proposed to split the area into ten states whimsically named Sylvania, Michigania, Chersonesus, Assenisipia, Metropotamia, Illinoia, Saratoga, Polypotamia, Pelispia and Washington.)[2]

Once the Great Northwest Ordinance was signed into law a company was created to exploit the opportunity — the Ohio Company of Associates — which devised a plan to persuade Congress to exchange land for veterans' certificates, then more or less worthless. The company employed secretary of the Treasury Board Colonel William Duer to lobby his fellow congressmen to approve the plan. Congress approved the plan and released five million acres to the Ohio Company.[3]

Property Fever 113

Lansdown House, Philadelphia, built by John Penn in 1773, circa 1800. Acquired by William Bingham in 1797, from an engraving by William Russell Birch.

Bingham passed up the opportunity to invest in the Ohio Company, but the name of Duer would come back to haunt him later. He continued to buy land unobtrusively as the opportunities presented themselves. He acquired large tracts in northern Pennsylvania and acquired shares in (and later became president of) the Lancaster Turnpike Company.[4]

Not content with the Mansion House in Philadelphia, Bingham now extended his family property portfolio and his social ambition by acquiring two large estates. He leased Lansdown House, on the west bank of the Schuylkill River, from his friend John Penn in 1789, and in 1791 he preempted the fashion for summer cottages for the wealthy by 50 years or more when he bought a farmhouse and 200 acres of land at Black Point at the mouth of the Shrewsbury River in New Jersey (now the small town of Rumson).[5]

Bingham had retained his merchant interests since his return to America from Europe, in Robert Gilmor & Co. and also with Mordecai Lewis, and, like Robert Morris, was investing heavily in the "China" trade (a market now available to American merchants following the Treaty of Paris). The returns could be good, but the risks were high, and he seriously considered retiring from these activities to concentrate on speculations closer to home. However this plan was delayed when a series of his "adventures" had successful and profitable conclusions. The *Harmony*, co-owned with Gilmor and Lewis, returned from China and India with cargoes that would net them £17,000, and the *Louisa* was the first tobacco consignment to reach Marseille in the fall of 1791, making a high price, as did the return cargo of vinegar, olives, olive oil and brandy. The round trip made another $20,000.[6]

Bingham's partnerships were not the only ones making money, and this success led to a number of share speculations, especially in the new state banks, whose stocks had been rising on the wave of optimism following Hamilton's economic successes. One man in particular to get himself in deep trouble was Colonel William Duer, Bingham's colleague on the last Continental Congress and supporter of the Ohio Land Company, in which he had invested heavily. Duer now found himself unable to meet his obligations, which included $250,000 to the United States government. Refusing his creditors, he fled to debtors' prison, triggering a run that saw bank shares collapse, taking other stocks with them. The panic selling that resulted created bargain opportunities at distressed prices for those with ready money. The profit from Bingham's successful recent adventures would now find a new home![7]

The Duer Panic, as it became known, did not last long, but it was long enough to have many more recent property speculators desperate to liquidate their investments, presenting yet more opportunities for those with ready funds. Bingham had already acquired substantial property around Philadelphia, in addition to the estate at Bellevue, and he acquired more in New York State and Baltimore. He was offered but declined to purchase tracts of land in the proposed new federal city of Washington on the Potomac.

With the Duer Panic now subsiding, the state of Pennsylvania put four million acres of land on sale, unsurveyed but with no Indian rights attaching. Bingham took warrants on 340,000 acres (at one shilling sterling per acre), and eventually increased this to over one million acres, at a cost of $250,000 (1s was equivalent to about 25c). No land taxes were payable for ten years, and the land could be sold directly to foreign nationals, making it much easier to sell on to European investors. Bingham engaged John Adlum to survey the land, and by early 1793 he had surveyed 430,000 acres of the land, with a further 230,000 to follow. Bingham was not alone in snapping up the warrants for land, and such was the confidence in their value that these warrants were traded readily. There appeared to be no risk, and the potential for enormous profits.[8]

In the Commonwealth of Massachusetts the Land Committee was also attempting to sell vast tracts of land, and two men (Duer and General Henry Knox), by now well known to Bingham, could not miss the opportunity for great and risk-free wealth, and between them acquired just over two million acres at ten cents per acre in July of 1791, and in early 1792 they acquired a further million acres at twenty cents per acre. The down payment for this land in North Massachusetts (now Maine) was $10,000 and the total consideration over $400,000.[9]

The first capital payment fell due while Duer was in difficulty over his Ohio Company debts to the government, and since he was now in debtors' prison he had little alternative but to attempt to liquidate his latest surefire Maine investment.

General Knox, bookstore owner, war hero and secretary for war, had put together military strategy for Washington from the limited manuals that were at hand in his shop. Of modest background and resources, he and his wife Lucy had expensive tastes. They had hoped to build a grand mansion at Thomaston on the St. George River (Montpelier) on land that Lucy had inherited. Henry and Lucy Knox were frequent visitors at the Mansion House, and spurred on by Anne Bingham had planned to match the Philadelphia grandeur in Maine. However Henry Knox lacked Bingham's capital; as the dream started to evaporate with Duer's failure, he approached his old friend Bingham to acquire the Duer share. While Bingham had had no time for Duer, he and Anne had been personal friends of the Knox family since his return from Martinique, and he agreed to talk to Duer.

The Maine tracts were nothing like New York or Pennsylvania; they were very remote, very rugged and very north; their climate did not suit farming well; the only occupation for the sparse population was fishing and lumbering. Throughout his career to this point, as far as can be judged, Bingham's commercial judgment appears to have been impeccable. He gathered what information he could from Knox and what other limited descriptions and statistics that he could find. The news was not good, the general opinion being that this was a territory best avoided. He had already turned down land on the Potomac as being too distant to be easily managed; in any event, either because he saw the opportunity for yet another easy killing or, perhaps more likely, a sentimental attachment from Anne and William Bingham for Henry and Lucy Knox, he agreed to go into partnership and buy out the Duer share.[10]

Bingham's negotiating position would surely have been compromised by going to New York in person, so he engaged an intermediary to close a deal with Duer. Bingham chose none other than Major William Jackson to undertake this commission.

Jackson appears to have made little mercantile progress in Holland or in the mysterious project that Robert Morris had suggested he engage with William Bingham in Paris (while snubbing Nabby Adams). He returned to Philadelphia to complete his studies in law before being chosen as secretary to the Constitutional Convention, after which President Washington employed him as his secretary and travelling companion (Bingham had proposed him for the position of secretary to the United States Senate, but without success). Washington then offered him the prestigious but poorly paid position of Adjutant-General of the Army of the United States (such as it now was).

However, Jackson declined Washington's offer for two reasons, which were in fact the same reason. William Jackson had for some time been attracted to Anne Bingham's younger sister Elizabeth, an interest which was reciprocated. However, Thomas Willing set the bar very high when it came to his daughters and Jackson's impeccable credentials were not backed up by hard cash. His requests for Elizabeth's hand were received by deaf ears. Jackson by this time was clearly well liked by Anne and William, but despite their support, Jackson's love for Elizabeth seemed likely to be unrequited.

For Major Jackson, success in the Duer negotiation could be the answer to the maiden's prayer, perhaps literally. Jackson agreed to become Bingham's agent in exchange for the proceeds of the sale of 100,000 acres of the land. Since no terms were agreed for other payments, expenses, etc, it would seem to both parties that the acquisition and subsequent sale at a profit would be assured and speedy.[11]

Contracts for the purchase were drawn up immediately and Jackson was dispatched with the documents and bills made out to Knox and endorsed to Duer. Although Duer had, in fact, had another offer, the prospect of immediate payment was very attractive to someone in his position, and he duly signed up, allowing Jackson to return to Philadelphia earlier than expected.

Although Duer's share was now Bingham's, the transfer required the authority of the State of Massachusetts, requiring Bingham and Jackson to travel to Boston. They were well received, entertained by the local dignitaries, and on January 28, 1792, the Maine lands were officially Bingham's (they were actually all in his name, although the agreement reached between him and Knox split the profits one-third to Knox, two-thirds to Bingham). Bingham had committed himself to pay $311,250 for his new investment; furthermore he was required to find 2,500 settlers by 1803, with a penalty of $30 per head should he fail to do so.[12]

If Bingham had any concerns about his huge investment, he did not show it, and set about a marketing plan. He (and presumably Knox) planned to sell half of the land to overseas investors to cover the installment payments, while retaining and developing the other half as a long-term investment. The value of the lands could only rise.

With the help of responses to questions that he addressed to General Benjamin Lincoln, he prepared a pamphlet extolling the positive features of the distant lands. In "A Description of the Situation, Climate, Soil and Productions of Certain Tracts of Land in the District of Maine" the advantages of the healthy air, the productivity of the soil and the ocean were well developed, although the remoteness and the need for capital were not.[13]

The pamphlet was published and printed in Philadelphia; Bingham sent his investment proposals and the pamphlet to the financial houses in Europe (with which he and his partners were acquainted) before dispatching an agent to pursue the sale and settlement of the Maine tracts. Bingham again chose the hapless Major Jackson,[14] this time torn between Elizabeth Willing and the fortune that Bingham was offering for a successful conclusion.

Armed with maps, surveys, a supply of Bingham's pamphlet, letters of introduction and a bill of exchange for £200 for his expenses, Major Jackson left Philadelphia for Europe on June 16, 1792.

15. Sir Francis Baring, Bart.

In the decade from the end of the American War of Independence to the French Revolution British Prime Minister William Pitt set about a program of peace, financial reconstruction and economic growth with a certainty sadly lacking across the Atlantic. The effects of the Industrial Revolution were felt everywhere, as Britain became the workshop of the world. A new empire including Canada and India was being built on the ruins of the old one in the Americas and the West Indies.

Pitt had inherited a very capable advisor from Lord Lansdowne in the form of Francis Baring. Pitt and Baring may not have seen eye to eye politically but there was a mutual respect nevertheless.

The business in public loans for the government that Francis Baring had got to grips with dried up during this period of peace, but the growth of business elsewhere more than compensated for the loss. John and Francis Baring & Co. was now becoming a dominant force in the city of London, but despite that the basic structure of the business remained more or less unchanged after partners Charles Wall and James Mesturas were appointed in 1781.

Like Henry Hope in Amsterdam, Francis Baring was starting to consider the succession within the business and the part his own children might play. By 1790, eldest son Thomas was 18 years old, Alexander 16, Henry 14, William 11 and George just 9. Francis Baring was still deeply involved with the East India Company and decided that Thomas and Henry should serve apprenticeships in its service. Thomas was sent to Bengal and Henry to Canton. For Alexander, the middle of the sons, and with the most aptitude for a career in the bank, he had different plans; he would be sent to Amsterdam to learn the business with Henry Hope.[1]

Thirty years of single-minded endeavor was now paying off; in 1792 Francis Baring became chairman of the East India Company, and in 1793 Pitt awarded him the honor of Baronet in recognition of his services (in particular to the East India Company). Lansdowne wrote to him, "I don't congratulate you on your title, because I think in these times you do it more honour that it does you...."[2]

There seems little doubt that Baring had done, or certainly would in time have done enough to be awarded a peerage. But at that time there was still a gulf between trade and aristocracy. That gulf was narrowing, Disraeli claiming (much later) that Pitt had "created a plebeian aristocracy and blended it with the patrician oligarchy.... He caught them in the alleys of Lombard Street and clutched them from the counting-houses of Cornhill."[3]

In fact the only peerage bestowed by Pitt to someone with a mercantile background was Robert Smith, Lord Carrington, whose career had extended well beyond banking. The bankers' time would come, but not for another generation.

Succession in the Hope & Co. business remained a problem for Henry Hope too. John Hope's son Thomas was thought to be a possibility, but in a pattern that was to repeat itself he showed more interest in collecting art than banking, and after a period of travel he settled in Duchess Street, off Portland Place, in London to care for his collection of works of art. To be fair to Thomas Hope, Henry Hope was also attracted to the finer things of life and had long since assumed aristocratic status for himself and his family, as indeed had most of his ancestors. He had purchased a farm and estate named Welgelegen in 1769 and in 1784 had the buildings demolished and a new mansion of vast proportions built in its place, finally completed in 1788. Welgelegen was, and still is, magnificent by any standards, and partly built to house Henry Hopes' own collection of paintings and sculptures.[4] In 1793, by contrast, Francis Baring moved his offices and his home from Mincing Lane to Devonshire Square. He was biding his time.

Henry Hope's search for strong management in the business came to an end, at least for a while, when Peter Cesar Labouchere joined the business initially as a clerk in 1790. Within three years he was in control of the day-to-day running of Hope & Co.

Apart from the difficulties in running the business itself, the political developments in Holland in the 1780s and 1790s were bringing problems of their own. Its own short war with England came to an ignominious conclusion, only to be replaced by internal conflict. The "Patriots" had reduced the power of the Orange Prince William V to the extent that he and his family were obliged to leave the country, to gather support abroad.

On May 30, 1787, a battle erupted between the pro-Orange shipwrights and the Patriotic militia, which ended in a defeat for the Orange faction. On September 16, 1787, Prussian troops occupied Utrecht; the states of Holland surrendered but consented to the restoration of the Prince. This turmoil was not good for the merchant part of the business, but Hope & Co. went from strength to strength in the issue of foreign loans, particularly to Russia.[5]

Henry Hope wrote to his friend Francis Baring in London: "This mis-

Chapter 15

Devonshire Square, London, circa 1800, home of John and Francis Baring & Co. and of Francis Baring (1793–1806) (Baring Archive Ltd., reference #PR060).

erable country, having been devastated and practically ruined during the past ten years by an ambitious faction, is about to take a little rest, but twenty years of economy and industry will not succeed in making good the ruinous losses."[6]

Clearly Henry Hope was starting to despair of the political turmoil in Holland; he was quite right to and it was just about to get very much worse. One chapter in the history of Hope & Co. was closing; another was about to open.

Despite these local difficulties in the Netherlands Hope & Co. was keeping an eye on events in America but resisted getting involved in its catastrophic national financial affairs in the immediate post-war years. It continued to be involved, however, in mercantile arrangements with a number of trusted houses, in particular with Robert Gilmor & Co., successors to Bingham, Inglis and Gilmor. Bingham himself had been entertained by Henry Hope during his Grand Tour, a connection made through their now mutual friend Francis Baring, and he was now in the loop of Hope and Baring and Lansdowne correspondents.

Gouverneur Morris, on business on his own account but also acting for President Washington, visited Henry Hope around the end of 1792 with a view that Hope & Co. might become involved in investment in the financing of the government of the United States (and privately by buying lands owned by him and Robert Morris). Gouverneur Morris left empty handed, but Hope & Co. was becoming increasingly aware of the potential. Indeed one of its own entrepreneurs, Peter Stadniski, was already working on a portfolio of investment opportunities in the United States.[7]

In early 1793 Henry Hope received correspondence from William Bingham describing an opportunity for investment in substantial tracts of land in North Massachusetts. Bingham's approach was noted, but the political situation in Holland was still brittle and Hope took no further action, or at least so it seemed.

To add to the burden of internal political difficulties, the revolution in France was about to impact Holland heavily, and Hope & Co. in particular. In August 1792, the mob arrested 4,000 "suspects," many aristocrats, priests, or those that had fallen foul of the Paris Commune. Fifteen hundred of these were murdered after mock trials; Louis XVI was beheaded in January of 1793; by February France had declared war on Britain and invaded the Southern Netherlands, targeting bankers, speculators and aristocrats, whose property was confiscated in the Reign of Terror.[8] Fearing for their lives, Henry Hope and his family fled to England, but returned briefly in December of 1793.

In July of 1793 Major William Jackson had arrived in London, armed with his letters of introduction, his surveys and his pamphlets. He started his campaign by calling on the American minister, now Thomas Pinckney. He introduced himself to Lord Lansdowne, who entertained him at Bowood; he dined with Benjamin Vaughan and arranged a letter of introduction to William Bingham for Dr. Priestley's son (who was travelling to America to make arrangements for his father's imminent move to Philadelphia).

He introduced himself to Francis Baring, who he found amiable, attentive and apparently disposed to assisting him in the disposal of the Maine lands. He also met Alexander Baring, who was described as "the principal assistant in Mr Hope's counting house." We do not know for sure, but he may well have been introduced to Henry Hope, who was in London at the time.[9]

Jackson's reception in England was impeccable but the results were negligible. He left for France in December 1793, with a special passport from Thomas Pinckney, and letters of introduction from Thomas Jefferson and President George Washington. He was most unfortunate to be imprisoned on his arrival in France and blamed the new American minister to France, Gouverneur Morris, (since 1792) for the delay in releasing him from jail in Boulogne. Jackson spent four months in revolutionary France, and apart from upsetting Gouverneur Morris appears to have achieved nothing.[10]

Jackson returned via Amsterdam, calling on the offices of Hope & Co. without success, and arrived in London in the early summer of 1794 to resume his assault on Francis Baring and Alexander Baring.

By the summer of 1794 the French Army had reached the River Maas, and the Patriots, who had never given up, took up arms against the Regents in Amsterdam. For Henry Hope, now back in Holland, this was the end of the line; on October 17, he and John Williams Hope left from Hellevoetsluis for England (escorted by a British frigate to secure their cargo of gold, silver and works of art), where they joined John's wife and family, who had returned in August. Thomas, Henry Philip and Adrian Elias took their chances in Germany, leaving Peter Labouchere and the "principle assistant," 21-year-old Alexander Baring, at their desks until the last moment.

The last moment came on January 17, 1795, as the first French troops were entering Amsterdam. The weather had been so cold that the estuaries were blocked with packed ice, but the temperature had risen that day sufficiently to free the ice and they were able to make their escape from Den Helder for England.[11]

By the time Alexander Baring and Labouchere were back in London, Henry Hope had acquired for himself a house on Harley Street, off Cavendish Square, suitably extended to accommodate his artworks, and a country estate at East Sheen, Richmond, London. The offices in Amsterdam remained open in the hands of Paulus Tay, a "trusted clerk" to wind up any current business, Hope advertising from London that all future payments would be made by the company from London. Hope was by now convinced that there was no future for their Orange-leaning merchant house in Holland and their removal to England would be permanent.

In April 1795, on the eve of an empty-handed return to America, Jackson was invited to dine with the Barings in Devonshire Square. He drew up a last desperate proposal for the sale of one million acres of Maine; he decided to reduce the price (subject to Bingham's approval) to two shillings or 44 cents an acre.[12]

Francis Baring played his trump card; he announced that Robert Morris and his associates had lately drawn bills on European houses for immense amounts for which no funds were available, and that they had been protested. Baring suggested that this was no time for him to be negotiating with American property interests, whoever they were. Major Jackson was in despair; he would now be returning to a very uncertain future. But on the very eve of his departure, Francis Baring gave him a letter addressed to William Bingham in which he expressed an interest in Jackson's last offer.

The partners of Hope & Co. were now well established in London, and with the "French Terror" coming to an end, business in Amsterdam could now be maintained, albeit with difficulty. However, the bulk of their capital was now in London and uninvested. Alexander Baring was now back in London with Peter Labouchere.

After two years in Europe, Major Jackson sailed from Bristol, empty handed, but with a glimmer of hope, on May 8, 1795. He arrived in Philadelphia a few weeks later to a most unexpected reception. Anne and William (now Senator) Bingham gave him the warmest of welcomes; he should stay with them at the Mansion House until he was settled; the deal he had offered to Baring at the lower price was now quite acceptable: "I think so well of the connection, that I would make great sacrifices to gain it."[13]

And to Jackson's surprise, Judge Thomas Willing now found him a most suitable husband for Elizabeth. They were married at the Willing Mansion on November 11, 1795. It was the Philadelphia society event of the year. Everyone was there, including President and Mrs. Washington. The president offered Jackson the post of surveyor of the customs at the Port of Philadelphia. Major Jackson's rehabilitation was now complete.

Bingham's lands remained, however, firmly unsold, his initial enthusiasm at receiving Baring's letter via Jackson perhaps premature. He revised his strategy and appointed General David Cobb, (another) former aide-de-camp to General Washington, to be his agent to market the Maine lands, this time in smaller parcels for settler groups or American investors, if these were to be found.[14]

Bingham found himself in trouble making the stage installment payment on the Maine land at the end of 1795, telling Henry Knox: "It is quite a novel thing to me to be thrown into such difficulties, and I do not bear the situation with much equanimity."

He was also fearful that the effect of the Jay Treaty, putting the western outposts into American control, would be to encourage settlement westwards rather than northwards. He proposed that either Cobb or Knox return to London to make another attempt at a European sale. He wrote to Francis Baring again repeating Jackson's offer (one million acres at two shillings per acre), for the lands that were appreciating all the time.

Bingham summed up their predicament to Henry Knox, claiming that he was making this proposal "as well to relieve my present difficulties, as from a conviction that such a connection would most essentially benefit the future arrangements of this property," and that should Baring not accept the deal "I shall be in a most cruel and embarrassed position."

Conversely, a successful sale would "set us at our ease and lay the foundation of a lasting fortune, and thereby recompense us fully for our trouble and time."

By this time General Knox was as "embarrassed" as he could be and was in Bingham's hands completely.

Despite the encouraging news in the letter carried by Major Jackson,

Alexander Baring (1774–1848), later Lord Ashburton, by Sir Thomas Lawrence (1769–1830) (Baring Archive Ltd., reference #PT015).

Bingham had heard no more from London, and was beginning to despair when another communication arrived, in which Francis Baring confirmed that he decided to pursue the possibility of a substantial investment in American lands, and that he would send his son Alexander to negotiate a deal. All was not lost.[15]

16. Bingham and Baring Strike a Deal

It may not have been obvious to William Bingham or Major Jackson, but both Francis Baring and Henry Hope were becoming increasingly well disposed towards America during 1795.

Baring was interested in expanding trade with the United States and exploring the possibility of an involvement in government financing, and had already been asked to liquidate $800,000 of U.S. Treasury stock to send to the American minister in Lisbon, David Humphreys.[1] Baring discharged this commission successfully, and indeed was able to put up a further $800,000. Rufus King,[2] now American minister in London, wrote to congratulate him: "I have written to the Secretary of the Treasury on this Subject and shall communicate to him the assurance that I have given you of my conviction that the United States will entertain a proper sense of your Services in this Business."[3]

Henry Hope was more interested in investing the funds that had been liquidated ahead of the French invasion of Holland. Either way it suited both men to have Alexander in the United States for a while. For Alexander it would be a very useful contribution to his career development.

Through his friendship with Rufus King, Bingham now knew enough of Francis Baring to appreciate how important a closer relationship with him could be, not only for the disposal of the Maine lands but for his mercantile prospects in general.

At the same time Francis Baring and Henry Hope had decided that their potential in America would be enhanced by the right connections in commerce, banking and government. Bingham wouldn't know it, but he didn't find them, they found him.

Alexander Baring left England in September of 1795, with letters of introduction from his father and a letter of credit for £100,000, with authority to increase that to £125,000, "if any desirable end may thereby attained." He was instructed specifically not to bring back an American wife: "A wife is best suited to the home in which she is raised, and cannot be formed or trained a second time."[4]

He arrived in Boston on November 29, after a rough and cold Atlantic crossing, where he stayed with merchant John Codman and was then introduced to Boston's finest families.

When Bingham had received the encouraging letter from Francis Baring about a potential sale (to be negotiated by Alexander Baring), he immediately mobilized his team to ensure a successful outcome. Alexander Baring had to be convinced of the value and potential of the Maine real estate, and of an early sale, while not detecting any signs of desperation.

Bingham was probably deluding himself, since he had already asked Baring for a loan against the security of his own stock. Francis Baring had offered a loan for "a sum from five thousand to eight thousand pounds sterling, to be reimbursed from the proposed sale if it shall take place."[5]

General Cobb was sent to Boston to arrange to meet Baring, "by accident," and subtly reinforce the potential of an investment in Maine. Cobb was also instructed to discover, if possible, who else might be talking to him, since Baring's visit was no secret and there were many speculators in Bingham's position, including and especially his old friend Robert Morris.

Cobb did indeed manage to meet up with Alexander Baring, and passed over a letter from Bingham, which he also had with him by accident, perhaps explaining why the lands were not as popular as elsewhere. Baring may well have spotted the subterfuge by now, but was polite enough to Cobb not to cause embarrassment, and suggested that Cobb accompanied his party to New York. On December 31, 1795, Baring and his party of John Codman and David Cobb set off by stage for New York,[6] where Henry Knox had been sent by Bingham to await their arrival.

As soon as the party had reached New York, on January 7, Henry Knox contrived to join them with yet another letter from Bingham. Knox confided to Baring that Bingham was now enthusiastic about a possible deal to make "so respectable connection." He then wrote to Bingham: "In appearance he seems the brother and a strong but large likeness of the young Baring now in Philadelphia — less polish, a countenance rather buttoned up, but without the least particle of disingenuousness or want of candour.... He is intelligent, charmed with the climate and appearance of New England, says ... that the people in Europe have no adequate idea of our happy situation." (The "young Baring" in Philadelphia was Henry, whom Knox had already met.)[7]

Alexander Baring stayed in New York until January 12, attending to business for his father or Henry Hope. Cobb was frustrated by the delay; he and Knox wrote daily to Bingham with progress reports. Knox's financial situation was now so dire that he asked Bingham for a further loan of $5,000 (he already owed $17,500 from an unpaid debt from 1793) and a line of credit from Baring (if that could be arranged): "The sum that would place me completely at my ease would be 50,000 dollar."⁸

Baring and Cobb finally left New York, leaving Knox to his despair, and arrived in Philadelphia on January 15. Cobb escorted Baring to his accommodation before returning to brief Bingham on the current situation. Bingham and Alexander Baring met for the first time on the following morning, which was a Sunday.

It was naive for Bingham to think that Baring would not arrive as well prepared as he was himself. Henry Hope and Francis Baring had already decided on the Maine investment, and that Hope would put up 75 percent of any consideration and Baring the remaining 25 percent. Alexander Baring's job was to strike a deal at the lowest possible price, subject to the investment meeting his approval. Francis Baring was more interested in Alexander making sound commercial arrangements with the best merchant houses in the United States and meeting the right people in Congress. An extended stay in America was beyond these commitments and was not even a consideration. Francis had other plans for Alexander.⁹

Francis Baring was already renowned for the quality of his information and intelligence, and he demonstrated this by arranging for not one but two members of the Baring family to be in Philadelphia ahead of Alexander. Charles Baring, cousin to Alexander (son of Francis' troublesome brother, also Charles), travelled up from Charleston, South Carolina, where he was now settled, and Henry Baring, Alexander's younger brother, was also there en route from his East India Company service in Canton.¹⁰

William Bingham had understood from Francis Baring's letters that the two of them had effectively already reached an understanding about the land sale, and that Alexander might have some discretion on the price, but that was all. He became alarmed when Alexander seemed indifferent to the entire process. Of course Alexander was much better informed than Bingham had guessed, and had decided that he could be as unconcerned about the whole affair as Bingham had contrived to be with him.

Bingham, Cobb and Baring now met daily, and interminably, Baring happy to explore the minutiae of the proposed arrangements. The fact was that Bingham needed this deal much more than Baring. The stark reality for Bingham was that this was the only possible way out, short of liquidating his entire portfolio. He had debts falling due of $213,000 imminently, owing $100,000 to Willinks in Amsterdam, $45,000 to Philadelphia banks, $30,000 to the state of Massachusetts for the installment payment on the Kennebec tract and $38,000 still owing to Duer.¹¹

The bulk of Bingham's fortune, other than his illiquid property investments, was in his successful partnership with Robert Gilmor, as much as $500,000, but accessing that would mean unwinding the fruits of years of work and friendship. He had the offer of the loan from Francis Baring, but accepting that would weaken his negotiating position even further. However, if agreement with Alexander Baring could not be reached there would be no alternative but to unwind his long-established partnership with Gilmor.

Alexander Baring watched Bingham's discomfiture with interest; he was under no pressure from his father or Henry Hope to make a deal at any price. He was essentially spending Henry Hope's money on an investment well away from the problems in Europe. Alexander and Francis Baring were more interested in long-term commercial arrangements in the United States and could take as much time as was needed. Alexander was impressed with Bingham and his connections (although Bingham would never have known), not for the Maine land but for the opportunity, through Bingham, to become the dominant house (with Hope & Co.) in America as well as Europe. Francis Baring had for some time the aspiration to become Europe's first merchant house, with him in London, and in due course Alexander and Hope & Co. in Holland. The opportunity that Bingham had unwittingly offered was a business based on three centers, now to include the United States.[12]

On February 2, 1796, Alexander drew up a lengthy report describing in detail the shortcomings of the lands offered for sale, at the very end of which he made an offer for just one half of the Penobscot lower tract, but at the lower price of two shillings per acre. He found the Kennebec tract unsatisfactory and made no offer on that at all.

Negotiations now stalled; and to make matters worse, Bingham now discovered that Baring had opened discussions with Robert Morris and James Wilson over their land investments.

After another delay of a few days, Bingham and Baring held further discussions at the Mansion House. Baring made a revised offer; he had no interest in the Kennebec tract; of the Penobscot lower tract he would buy half a million acres at two shillings per acre. Of the upper Penobscot tract (on which Bingham had an option, but did not own) he would buy another half million acres, but at the lower price of one shilling and six pence, and only on the condition that the townships in the lower tract (including Gouldsboro) were to be included in the sale.[13]

For Bingham, things were now going from bad to worse. He was as aware as Baring that the Kennebec million was not as attractive a prospect as the coastal lands, and to separate it from the deal could leave it orphaned for ever. To sell half of the upper tract to Baring, he would have first to buy it, stretching his finances even further.

Far from the profit that Bingham, Knox and Cobb had expected, a further $300,000 would have to be found for the upper tract, taking the total obligations to $560,000. He would receive $401,000 from Baring, leaving a cash deficit of $159,400. He would, of course, still own the Kennebec tract and the residue of the upper tract. The attachment of the Baring name should help in the subsequent sale of those, perhaps, but things were not going well.[14]

Bingham spent February 4 discussing the offer with Cobb, and met Baring once again on the fifth. Alexander Baring re-stated his offer, making it clear that there would be no further negotiation, admitting that he had already gone well beyond his original remit, and insisting that he decide within an hour and a half. Bingham, fearful that a deal with Morris might be imminent, duly accepted the terms that he had been offered.

Alexander subsequently wrote to his father and Henry Hope: "When he heard that I conversed with Morris, Wilson, etc., he began to fear he should lose me, and I believe determined to make sure of my offer under the idea that I should not raise it, in which he was mistaken, for I had made up my intention of coming to two shillings for the whole and might perhaps have made some allowance for the additional purchases."[15]

Bingham advised Henry Knox that their profit had, at least for the time being, failed to materialize, and sent him to negotiate the purchase the upper tract with as much credit as the state of Massachusetts would allow. Knox's demand for immediate assistance from Alexander Baring had now risen to $60,000, which he declined, and it was left to Bingham to bail Knox out yet again, for $8,000, followed by a further $17,500, most of which he never saw again.[16]

Alexander Baring's triumphant land purchase was a little slow in completion; Henry Knox had difficulty in extracting all the necessary agreements from the Massachusetts state government and there were other delays in bringing the documentation together for Mr. Wilcocks (Baring's lawyer) to approve. Apparently Wilcocks was hard to please and Bingham's nervousness increased by the day.

In the meantime Alexander was made very welcome at the Mansion House while he and Bingham drew up a development plan for their joint venture to promote Maine as a prime settler destination. Having seen some of the problems with western fringes of the new country Baring felt relieved at the relative security of the northern lands.[17]

Alexander Baring's work was done on the Maine lands, at least for the time being, and with time on his hands turned to his attention to improving his knowledge of American politics. He was well placed to spend time in the public galleries of Congress, and in the mornings in the Senate, which was now open to the public. Alexander was able to observe William Bingham, now a U.S. senator from Pennsylvania, and deeply embroiled in the growing battles between Federalists and Republicans, in particular over the Jay Treaty, which although signed and sealed was still the object of a Republican rebellion. Madison and Gallatin proposed to stop the treaty by voting down the appropriations required, effectively challenging the president's authority. The

Jay Treaty was never popular, considered a sellout to the British by many, but as the Federalists argued, its rejection could lead to war. The Republicans believed that President Washington and the Senate were attempting to override the House.[18]

The constitutional issue lay in the balance; on April 28 Fisher Ames, renowned for his oration, took the floor of the house. In anticipation of what was to come, those that could, including the Senate, which had adjourned for the purpose, packed the gallery. Among the spectators were William Bingham, Alexander Baring and John Adams. Dr. Joseph Priestley, now arrived from England, was also there.

Ames spoke for 90 minutes; Priestley was most impressed with the oratory, placing his performance above that of William Pitt, Edmund Burke and Fox. The house voted 49 for, and 49 against the treaty. Speaker Frederick Muhlenberg, a Republican, cast his vote for the funds to put the treaty into effect, bringing the greatest debate in Congress' short history to an end.

During this time Alexander Baring provided his father and Henry Hope in London with a continuous stream of intelligence, including the Ames speech; the Jay Treaty debate, he believed, showed strength in government that would ensure the security of investing in the new United States and its government.

Despite Alexander Baring's dominance in the Maine land negotiation, he actually got on well with Bingham and respected the depth of his knowledge and experience. He reported to his father that he found him inappropriately aristocratic for his country, but quite acceptable nonetheless. There appears to be an element of hubris about Alexander Baring at this time — he had outfoxed the wily and more experienced man. He may even have felt slightly sorry for Bingham: "I believe I understand pretty well both his disposition and his situation; we are on very good terms and always have been, so much so that I am always confidentially consulted on all important business that regards him and I could I believe lead him to anything within tolerable bounds of reason."[19]

He echoed his thoughts about Bingham again: "He is not generally liked, being rather too high and proud for this country, where very little will do. I agree with him very well and think a good understanding likely to be maintained. He is undoubtedly the richest man in this country and his affairs are not embarrassed or likely to become so by any further speculations. He is a timid and cautious man. His property cannot be short of £4 or 500,000, his expenses annually about £5000. The house he lives in with ground it is estimated worth £50,000."

Young Alexander Baring may have won round one, but "Old" William Bingham was not finished yet.

Despite the scare over the Maine land difficulty, Anne and William Bingham remained at the center of Philadelphia (and at the time, the nation's) high society. William Bingham was reputed to be America's richest man, the Mansion House the grandest in all the country, and William Bingham very well connected. Alexander Baring was still just 21 years old. He could be forgiven for wishing to extend his stay in such exhilarating company a little longer, and was now becoming a permanent feature not only at the Mansion House but now also at the summer residence, Lansdown House on the Schuylkill River. He enjoyed the company of Anne Bingham, herself still only 32 years old, and her daughters Ann Louisa, 15, and Maria Matilda, 13.

We do not know who was really behind the trip to Maine, but Alexander Baring claimed the credit in a letter he wrote home in May of 1796: "I have encouraged Bingham [sic] to take his wife and family as the show will have an effect on the country and the procession make a noise in the New England States from whence the population is expected.... People wonder how such a new country can accommodate such fine ladies in travelling and every Lady's curiosity is raised to the highest. The Ladies company and presence on the lands will be of infinite benefit.... Small causes beget often great effects."[20]

Alexander Baring was going native. He was also free from the control of both his father and Henry Hope. Everyone was now in uncharted territory, and in Alexander's case, quite literally.

William and Anne Bingham now knew the Baring family surprisingly well; they had met Francis and Harriet in London, Henry and cousin Charles in Philadelphia, and, of course, Alexander. The outgoing and affable Henry had made an impact, but he was back in Canton. Of the other brothers Thomas was already in India with the East India Company and William and George were still in their teens. It was clear to the Binghams (probably along with most other observers) that Alexander Baring, although still nominally an employee of Hope & Co., would soon be running the affairs of John and Francis Baring & Co. They had also noticed that Alexander Baring and Ann Louisa Bingham were starting to get on very well, and that the Bingham and Baring families could get a lot closer.

It may have been Baring's idea, but William Bingham soon took control of the Grand Tour to Maine. The party was to consist of Anne and William Bingham, the two girls Ann Louisa (known as Nan in the family) and Maria Matilda, Anne Bingham's youngest sister Abigail (herself only 19), the Vicomte de Noailles, John Richards, Alexander Baring and, of course, an entourage of servants.[21]

The Binghams had become acquainted with the Vicomte de Noailles while in Paris in 1783. Noailles had fought with Washington in 1781. He and his family had suffered badly in the French Revolution; he had managed to leave France, but his wife, her mother and grandmother were all guillotined

Montpelier House, Thomaston, Maine, home of General Henry and Lucy Knox.

in 1794. He had now become, at least for the time being, part of the Bingham household, or as Alexander Baring described him, "a necessary family appendage."[22]

John Richards was an English adventurer whom Alexander Baring had met up with while travelling with General Cobb from Boston to Philadelphia. By chance or otherwise, Richards was carrying letters of introduction to William Bingham written for him by John Jay in London.

The first leg of their pioneering adventure was to New York, by coach, following their departure on June 13, 1796, then after a few days' stay, by boat to Newport, Rhode Island. They had planned to continue by boat to Boston via Providence, but this was abandoned, the ladies in the party having not enjoyed the rough first passage, and they travelled overland by stagecoach.

After an extended stay in Boston of three weeks, during which Baring and Bingham dealt with legal matters, the party moved on to Portland, again by stagecoach, a journey of three days. Portland was the end of the line for travel by stage, and the next part of the trip had to be by boat.

The packet boat *Mercury* was chartered for the next six weeks; the first stop was at General and Lucy Knox's new mansion, Montpelier, at Thomaston a few miles up the St. George River.

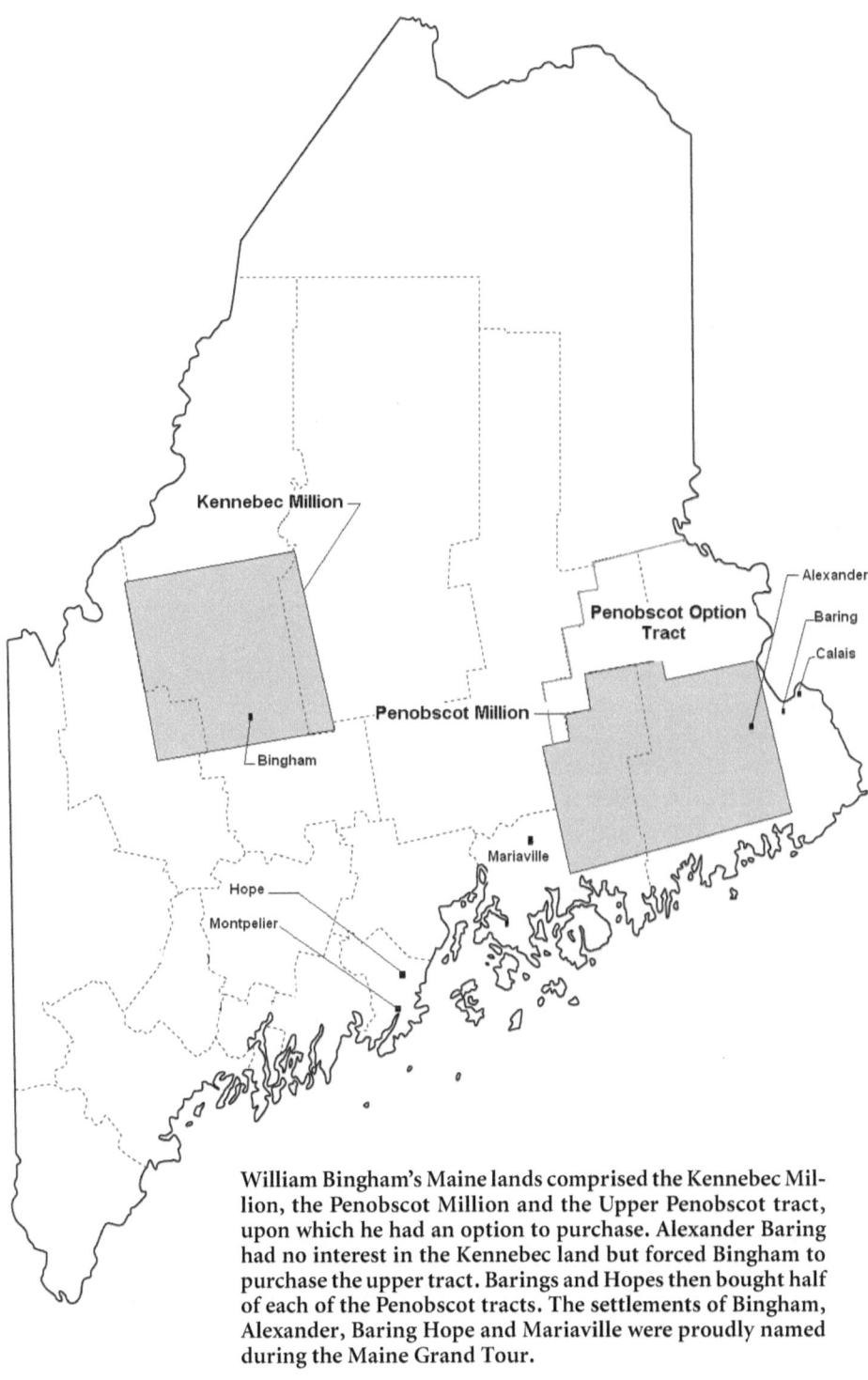

William Bingham's Maine lands comprised the Kennebec Million, the Penobscot Million and the Upper Penobscot tract, upon which he had an option to purchase. Alexander Baring had no interest in the Kennebec land but forced Bingham to purchase the upper tract. Barings and Hopes then bought half of each of the Penobscot tracts. The settlements of Bingham, Alexander, Baring Hope and Mariaville were proudly named during the Maine Grand Tour.

Montpelier and the farm, brickyard, shipyard, sawmills, and gristmills (or the cost of building them) were at the root of Knox's financial woes. Knox was determined to create a viable community, whether he could afford it or not. Alexander Baring dismissed it disparagingly as "an unnecessary expense." Unnecessary or not, it brought many visitors to see it, and Baring might have been more impressed and less churlish if he had seen the lands he had just bought first.[23]

The ladies stayed on at Montpelier while Bingham, Baring, Noailles and now Knox rejoined *Mercury* and sailed up the coast across Penobscot Bay, towards Mount Desert Island (which Knox had bought for £100). At Gouldsboro Bingham and Baring caught sight for the first time of the land that they now owned—flat, barren and remote. They collected General Cobb at Gouldsboro and continued up the coast to the northeastern edge of the Penobscot tract at Passamaquoddy Bay. They sailed up the Schoodic River as far as *Mercury* would take them, St. Stephen, and then by canoe to the falls at Calais. On their return, Knox and Richards sailed in *Mercury* to Gouldsboro, while Bingham, Baring, Noailles and Cobb made the rough 50-mile trip on horseback, encountering a few settlements (Columbia Falls) along the way.[24]

Mercury took the men back to Montpelier, and after a few days the party, still all in one piece (Noailles had nearly drowned apparently), sailed first to Portland and then finally made its way back to Philadelphia on September 22, 1796, after a remarkable trip of 1,500 miles and 100 days.

On his return Baring wrote a lengthy report to Henry Hope, his employer and friend, describing his experiences and their new investment in America, no doubt talking up the value and potential of their purchases.[25]

The purchase of the Maine lands did absolutely nothing for the business of Baring and Hope from the commercial point of view, but without that adventure Alexander Baring's future would have taken a quite different path. It would be the last time Alexander Baring was to buy one million acres of land that he had never seen, but not the last time he would buy a great deal of land.

17. Barings and Bingham — American Consolidation

The intervention of Baring and Hope & Co. in the Maine purchase early in 1796 probably saved Bingham and certainly Knox from financial ruin, but not everyone was as lucky, or in Bingham's case as shrewd. Bingham was right to worry about the need to sign up Baring quickly. The financial panic at the end of 1796 among property speculators soon spread to the business community as a whole, and some of them were very close to Bingham indeed. James Wilson, despite help in the form of a loan from Bingham, was thrown into jail in New Jersey and died the following year overwhelmed by debt and whiskey. The major casualties were, of course, Robert Morris and his property partners James Greenleaf and John Nicholson, but the contagion spread to Alexander Hamilton, John Jay, Thomas Willing and many more. George Harrison, now married into the Francis and Willing families, and not too distant from Bingham, lost his fortune, and with it the $40,000 he owed Bingham.[1]

Robert Morris, a man with such a cool head during the war, was now in difficulty in every quarter; the year before he had started building a mansion on the block bounded by Chestnut, Walnut, Seventh and Eighth streets. The mansion (later described as Morris' Folly) was started with an initial estimate of $60,000, but by mid–1797 when building was finally stopped, the bill had risen to almost one million dollars. Overwhelmed by his debts, Morris was arrested and incarcerated in the debtors' prison on Walnut Street, where he was visited and supported by some of his friends, notably George Washington, who would dine with him in his cell.

Not only did Bingham survive this crisis, but the bankruptcy of James Greenleaf actually provided another investment opportunity. The Lansdown House residence, so popular with Bingham's summer guests, and which he had been renting from the Penn family, had become the property of the unfortunate Greenleaf by marriage. It was sold off by his creditors, and Bingham was able to purchase it at the distressed price of $31,500, acquiring it as a gift for his wife Anne.[2]

Alexander Baring was able to observe this financial panic from the sidelines, but it was already impacting the purchases he had just made. Immigration into America had slowed, at least for the present, and the success of the Jay Treaty was likely to favor the western lands over the northeast. Baring felt that something more had to be done to market the Maine lands, and he became critical of Bingham's failure to put their plans into action. Bingham privately felt that he had already completed his own lengthy and expensive marketing campaign, the result of which had been a timely sale to Hope and Baring, and now was not so keen to invest more time and money.

Just how concerned Alexander Baring was is uncertain, because he still felt happy to embark in early 1797 on another Grand Tour, in this case without Bingham or the ladies, but with the young Henry Philip Hope,[3] who had now arrived from his enforced exile in Germany (via London). Henry Philip had been sent out by Hope & Co. to broaden his horizons and visit their extensive new acquisition in Maine. Whether Francis Baring or Henry Hope already suspected that Alexander was going native is unclear, but they would look forward to Henry Philip's dispatches with interest.

Alexander Baring and Henry Philip travelled south in the spring of 1797, to South Carolina, where they met up with Charles Baring Jr. (who had been in Philadelphia 18 months earlier for his cousin's arrival) in Charleston. Charles Baring's business and its prospects within the overall scheme of things was discussed, before Baring and Hope made their way northwards and into western New York State to look at land developments there (presumably Bingham's investments). From there they journeyed north into Canada and eastwards down the St. Lawrence River to New Brunswick and back into Maine and the Penobscot tract, now the property of Baring and Hope.

Baring returned to Philadelphia in November and unveiled for Bingham's benefit a long and detailed development program for the Maine property. "Every stroke of the axe in your woods should be heard in Massachusetts and Connecticut; every hut should be called a village and every village a town. When you have fixed your Land Office, you should advertise in all the principle New England papers that the tract is ready for settlement, with a short account of the advantages of the country and progress of improvements.... You will find your reputation spread rapidly and visitors to the country will follow."[4]

Why Baring believed that he was in any way experienced or trained enough to pontificate on these matters is not known; maybe Bingham, Knox and Cobb suspected that Baring would soon tire of this activity and return to his mercantile pursuits. To an extent Bingham had made a rod for his own back in extolling the fertility of the soils, because the new Baring plan was predicated on cultivation rather than the ready cash crop of lumber.

By this time John Richards was despairing of ever making progress on the development of the Maine lands, and reported his concerns privately back to Hope & Co. in London. Henry Hope, on reading Richards' report, and knowing the region well (an American himself), was probably right when he suggested that making a success of the Maine lands would require an almost infinite amount of time and money.[5]

With the completion of his unrealistic land proposals, Alexander Baring's duties in America were now more or less complete, and he wrote to his father during his stay in Charleston, in May 1797, saying that he was now prepared to be sent "to any situation or spot on the globe where I thought my duties called me," but then suggested that perhaps he should stay longer to look after the investments in Maine.

Several months later, towards the end of 1797, he told Hope & Co. much the same story, that he would now be happy to be sent "to any part of the world you please," but something had changed, because he was writing to Bingham at the same time suggesting he had reason to curtail his trip with Henry Philip and return urgently to Philadelphia.

The reason was Ann Louisa Bingham, now just turned 16.[6]

Alexander and Ann Louisa had been courting for a while, it seems, and in defiance of his father's express wishes, Alexander proposed in November of 1797. The match was very well received by the Binghams, but grudgingly at first in London — Francis Baring later noted on a letter he had received from Alexander more than a year earlier: "AB proposes to remain in America — his object then must have been a marriage with Miss Bingham."

The wedding date was set for October 1798.[7]

After Alexander Baring had returned from the Maine trip he took the opportunity to observe the politics of the new nation at close quarters. He was, after all, gambling substantial amounts of Hope and Baring money on its future.

By the middle of December 1796 it became clear that John Adams would win the presidency by a very narrow margin from Thomas Jefferson, and that in that case Thomas Jefferson would become vice president, should he be prepared to accept the position. Adams, in the end, won by three electoral votes and Thomas Jefferson accepted the role as his vice president. William Bingham was elected president pro tempore of the Senate.

On Saturday March 4, 1797, William Bingham presided over the Senate, bringing it to order at eleven in the morning. Thomas Jefferson, called to speak by Bingham, gave a short address, emphasizing the importance of the Union, and paying due regard to the qualities of John Adams, his friend of many years, who had preceded him as vice president. Jefferson swore the oath of office administered by Bingham, and took the chair for the first time. Eight new senators were sworn in by Jefferson and the business of the Senate concluded. The Senate then processed to the House, led by Jefferson and Bingham.[8]

Vice President Jefferson took the chair to the side of the Speaker's, in front of the four Supreme Court judges and George Washington, and waited; at noon John Adams entered with his cabinet amid sustained applause and took the Speaker's chair. He rose and delivered a low-key inaugural address. In an effort to avoid further tensions he confirmed that while he had a strong affection for the French nation, having spent several years there, he had no intention of changing the policy of neutrality in the conflict between Britain and France.

Chief Justice Elsworth then administered the oath of office; President John Adams sat in silence for a few moments, rose, and left the House accompanied by his entourage.

The following Monday John Adams and his cabinet met to discuss the pressing issue of worsening relations with France; the eventual approval of the Jay Treaty may have improved matters with Britain, but made war with France a distinct possibility. Adams decided to send an emissary, preferably a Republican, to France for negotiations to improve the state of affairs with France, while at the same time continuing the measures for defense originally proposed to frighten the British.

Adams' envoy became three commissioners, Thomas Pinckney, Elbridge Gerry and John Marshall, after Thomas Jefferson as vice president was ruled out, and James Madison declined the opportunity.

The arch Francophile Thomas Jefferson was now convinced that his new hero Napoleon Bonaparte would overwhelm Britain and bring peace to Europe. Provided he could prevent the Federalists from declaring war on France, a new, more powerful alliance with France was possible: "The best anchor of our hope is an invasion of England. If they republicanise that country, all will be safe with us."[9]

The second session of the Fifth Congress re-convened on November 22, 1797, where President Adams would address both houses on the possibility of descent to war with France. The special envoys Gerry, Marshall and Pinckney had now arrived in Paris (September 1797) but there had been as yet no news from them. Adams advised the joint session that while he hoped for a peaceful settlement, the continuing attacks on American shipping were not acceptable, and that the country and its shipping should be put on a war footing. To the Federalists these were prudent measures to defend the nation's position; to the Republicans it was a declaration of war with France.

The French attacks on American shipping continued unabated; more than 340 ships (worth $55 million) were taken by French privateers. Bingham himself had "adventures" of his own held in French ports. Tempers were running hot in Congress and the popular press, and were now polarized between Franklin Baches' anti–Federalist *Aurora* and *General Advertiser* and William Cobbett's Federalist *Porcupine Gazette*.[10]

By February 1798 there was still no word from the envoys in Paris, and Adams consulted his cabinet colleagues on the position to be taken should negotiations fail. The consensus from his cabinet (and from Hamilton in New York, though out of government still very much involved in formulating Federalist policy) was that while war should be avoided at all costs, the necessary appropriations should be put in place in the event that the talks collapsed, and to send a signal to the French.

In France the new regime was doing very well indeed. Military commander Napoleon Bonaparte was marching through Europe, unstoppable. Bingham's friend Talleyrand was back in France and back in power, and the man who despised all Americans (apart from Hamilton and probably Bingham) refused even to accept the credentials of the newly arrived American envoys.[11] Negotiating peace with Britain 16 years earlier was child's play compared with what was about to unfold. That warm relationship between Franklin and Vergennes was distant history.

Talleyrand continued to have nothing to do with the American representatives, but eventually they received a visit from a "Monsieur Bellami," who identified himself as an agent working for Talleyrand, together with three other gentlemen named as Bellamy, Hottingeur and Hauteval, who proceeded to outline the terms upon which negotiations would continue. First, an apology for the statements made by John Adams in his inaugural address in May the previous year would be required, secondly America must make a loan of $12.8 million to France, and finally that a payment should be made to Talleyrand personally of $250,000.

While the Americans were reeling from the shock of the "new diplomacy" for which they were totally unprepared, they were joined by none other than Caron De Beaumarchais (himself a miraculous survivor of the French Terror) and now presenting his own claims against the United States which stretched back to the days of Hortalez & Co.

Stunned, the Americans rejected this mercenary diplomacy out of hand. Pinckney's blunt response at the time of "no, no, not a sixpence" was revised in the transmission back to the president to "millions for defense, but not one cent for tribute." Beaumarchais helpfully offered to credit Talleyrand's bribe against his own claims, but assured the Americans, as a friend, that failure to comply with the demands would inevitably result in all-out war.

The French position was sent in dispatches to Philadelphia, where they were assimilated in horror by John Adams and the cabinet. Adams was so shocked that he did not release the detail of the reports from France, blandly advising that since the envoys had failed to reach an agreement acceptable to the requirements of the United States the country would continue to re-arm and that American merchant shipping would now be armed.[12]

The Republicans demanded that the dispatches from France be made public, to Congress at least, and the Republican-controlled House passed a motion to that effect. On April 3, 1798, the contents of the dispatches were revealed to the House, the French agents being described simply as X, Y and Z; the fiercely pro–French Republicans had walked into a trap of their own making and voted to keep the information from the general public, a decision that was then overturned by the Federalist Senate, and the text was printed in the newspapers and released as a pamphlet (and became the first publicly printed official United States government document).

John Adams' robust approach now made him the hero of the moment, while Thomas Jefferson sensibly decided to lie low, and when special envoy John Marshall finally returned to Philadelphia via Boston he had the kind of reception seen before only for George Washington himself.

In Congress, William Bingham was at the height of his political power, now perhaps considered the senior Federalist in the Senate. Federalist Senators would meet at William Bingham's Mansion House to hold a "pre-meeting" or "caucus" on major issues, to enable them to vote in Senate en-bloc. Over the ensuing months Congress voted to establish militia totaling 80,000 men and a standing army of 10,000, and to build 12 additional warships. Bingham and the Senate voted appropriations of $250,000 for coastal defense and $800,000 for military supplies. They voted to suspend all relations with France and permit marque and reprisal with the fervor previously applied to the British.[13]

The French themselves, up until now so popular as visitors, had now become persona non grata and new legislation was rushed in by Adams, by executive decree, to restrict the "enemy within." There was now genuine concern for the future of Europe, for Britain and for the United States, Bingham remarking: "The fate of England will have a great influence on the political situation of this country. I cannot but entertain very serious apprehensions for the result when I see the preponderance that France is daily acquiring on the Continent and no union of force or consort of governments to oppose her ambitious projects.... She has impressed a terror which operates like a stroke of a torpedo, and has benumbed all the faculties of the European powers. If she continues a little longer in her career, she will have Europe at her feet."

And in the words of Senator George Cabot: "If England will persevere, she will save Europe and save us; if she yields, all will be lost.... She is now the only barrier between us and the deathly embraces of universal irreligion, immorality and plunder."[14]

While the Republicans remained mesmerized by the French, the Federalists, especially Bingham, were convinced that Bonaparte planned to defeat the British and then re-establish a French empire in North America by assuming control of Florida, Louisiana and Canada.

Rufus King wrote to William Bingham towards the end of 1798: "We deceive ourselves if we believe that the Directory believe us; they and their agents perfectly understand their business, and by our divisions are encouraged to persevere in their fixed purpose to over-throw our government and break up our Union."[15]

Talleyrand's bluff in this quasi-war had been spectacularly successful; French objectives were nowhere near as well formulated as the Americans suspected; Talleyrand was playing for time while he and Napoleon were establishing their own positions. Talleyrand certainly hoped to remain by Bonaparte's side, but if not the increase of his own personal wealth was another major consideration. He realized that he may have gone too far when the United States Navy (as it now was) began engaging French shipping in the Caribbean. France could no more afford a full-scale war with America than America could afford one with France, but Talleyrand kept his nerve.

Amid mounting public pressure John Adams prepared to make a declaration of war, but then fell short of doing so. In an attack on the executive powers of the president, a group of senior Federalists from both houses met at the Bingham Mansion House intent on forcing a vote for war with France. The motion was defeated, William Bingham, who was opposed to a war, voting against.

It was agreed by Adam's cabinet and Alexander Hamilton (though not by Adams himself) to bring George Washington back from his retirement to head (in name at least) the new United States Army. Washington accepted on the understanding that Alexander Hamilton would actually be in command, and that the senior officers met with his approval. Charles Pinckney and Henry Knox were named as third and fourth in line; Henry Knox, as Washington's senior general and secretary of war to two administrations, took this as a snub and turned down the offer.[16]

John Adams added one name to Washington's list — that of Colonel William Stephens Smith, the feckless and largely absent husband of Abigail (Nabby), his daughter.[17]

Alexander Baring continued to report these dramatic events in Congress and a stream of mercantile intelligence to Francis Baring and Henry Hope in London. He had other things on his mind as well — his forthcoming marriage to Ann Louisa Bingham.

The marriage of Alexander Baring and Ann Louisa Bingham was set for October 23, 1798; it had been intended to take place at Lansdown, but another outbreak of yellow fever in Philadelphia forced them out of the city and they were married, no doubt in style, at Bellevue, Black Point, the Bingham family summer cottage in Monmouth County, New Jersey.

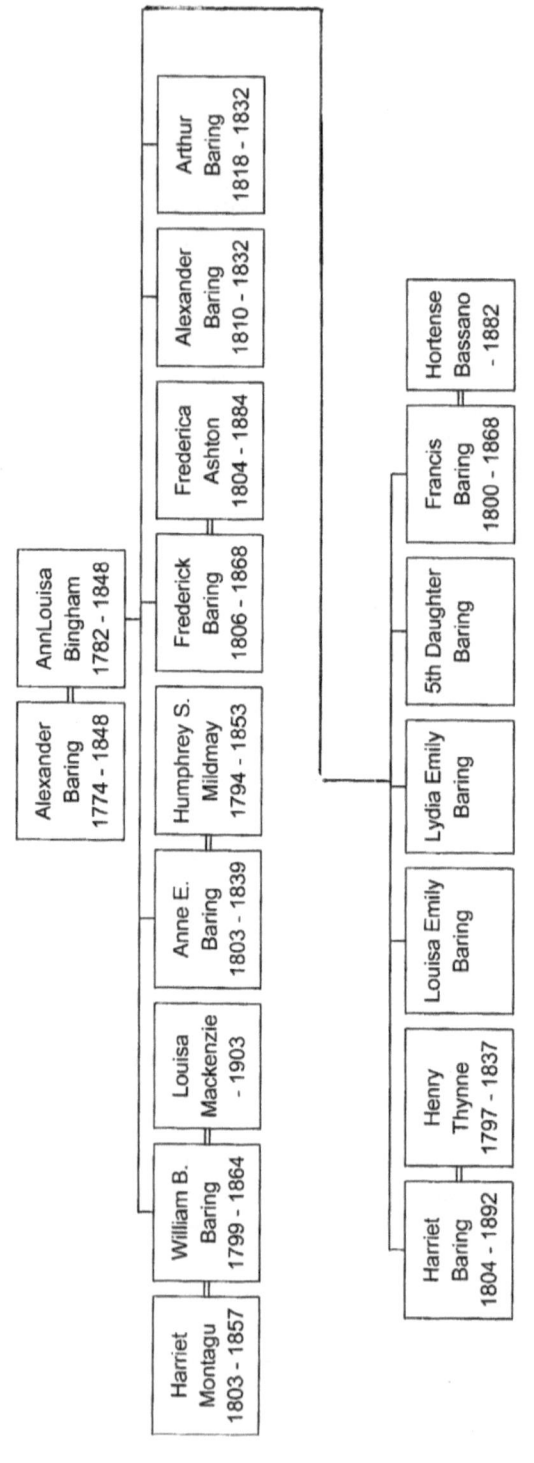

Descendants of Alexander Baring

William and Anne Bingham were as keen to keep Alexander and Ann Louisa in America as Francis and Harriet Baring were to get them back to England — Bingham raised the stakes by acquiring the house on Third Street that had belonged to Ann Bingham's aunt Elizabeth (Powel), the Powel House,[18] and presenting it as a wedding gift (together with an endowment of £500 per year) to the newlyweds.

The Barings, Francis and Alexander, and William Bingham were not only getting closer in business, they were now connected in marriage, and through William and Anne a whole host of other important family and political connections, including Willings, Francis, etc. The business of John and Francis Baring & Co. was also assisting the United States government yet again with weapons procurement; a significant proportion of the arms appropriations that had been approved by Bingham went straight to Barings when Francis was able to source, supply and ship 10,000 muskets and 330 cannon to America. Francis and Alexander Baring, or the "House of Baring," were rapidly becoming a very effective and trusted resource for Congress.[19]

Francis Baring's desire to see his son again was perhaps tempered by the profit now being generated by Alexander's continuing presence in America, but the pressure to return was becoming irresistible.

18. The Death of Anne Bingham and a Turning Point

At the start of the third session of the Fifth Congress in December 1798, the Federalists were demanding a declaration of war on France. John Adams did not declare war on France; instead he sent a coded message to Talleyrand: "to send another minister without more determinate assurances would be an act of humiliation."

Adams did receive assurances from Talleyrand (via Louis Pichon, French minister in The Hague to William Vans Murray, American minister in The Hague) and early in 1799 Adams decided to risk sending another representative to France. Unfortunately, John Adams omitted to advise the Federalists, who were appalled; the Republicans on the other hand, notably Jefferson, were overjoyed. John Adams was now very briefly the darling of the Republicans, while the Federalists, suspicious of his motives, believed that he was currying favor with the Democratic Republicans to secure a second presidential term.

In fact, Adams was actually keeping his head while all around him were losing theirs, as a result of correctly anticipating the turn of events in Europe.

While Congress was wobbling over its approach towards France, Britain was now taking decisive action itself. When the Spanish joined in on the French side and excluded the British fleet from the Mediterranean, William Pitt instructed his inspired choice of Admiral of the Fleet, Horatio Nelson, to recover their position. The subsequent Battle of the Nile, won by Nelson's fleet on August 2, 1798, was a turning point for Britain's naval power, for Britain, and indirectly for the United States.[1]

News of this great victory was late in arriving in London, and later still in Philadelphia, but it did not take long to reach Paris. Talleyrand never wanted to go to war with the United States, certainly not after Britain had asserted itself. He and many others had business interests there to protect, and unknown to America or Britain, he was already having discussions about the future of the Louisiana Territory with Spain, and he needed more time for those.

When Britain regained her naval supremacy, America's Quasi-War with France would soon be at an end, but not as far as Congress was concerned. John Adams continued to be troubled by Federalist senators who were still incensed at his decision to choose William Vans Murray (from his position in The Hague) as envoy to Paris. They were not unhappy about the competence of Murray, necessarily, but they hoped to delay the process indefinitely. To this end it was agreed that Senators Bingham, Jacob Read, James Ross, Sedgwick and Richard Stockton should meet President Adams and express their concerns about a peace mission in general and the choice of envoy in particular. After further discussion amongst themselves it was decided to restrict their objections to the choice of Murray as nominee.

The rebel group of senators requested an audience with Adams, a request that was granted. Adams deeply resented this attempt to diminish his authority and confirmed that he had no intention of changing his mind on the mission or the envoy. The "Bingham caucus" responded by organizing a vote in the Senate to reject Adam's nomination of Murray. Now cornered and fearing a defeat, Adams reluctantly compromised and nominated two new commissioners to join Murray: Oliver Elsworth, chief justice of the Supreme Court, and Patrick Henry. Patrick Henry declined the nomination, and William Richardson Davie, Federalist governor of North Carolina, took his place.[2] Adams' position improved in March 1799, when the American fleet defeated the French Navy in the West Indies, and in May of 1799 when word arrived in Philadelphia that an American peace mission would now be received at the highest level, by Talleyrand himself.

John Adams, having instructed Pickering to dispatch the peace envoys to France in May of 1799, left for the family home in Braintree, but by his return in November they were still firmly in the United States. Adams ordered that they leave immediately, which they did on November 3, splitting the ranks of the Federalists forever. A week later, Napoleon Bonaparte returned to Paris and overthrew the Directory, pronouncing himself absolute ruler of France for a period of ten years.

Concerns about these alarming events in France were overtaken by the news that on December 14, 1799, George Washington had succumbed to complications following an infection in his throat. William Bingham joined a congressional committee to organize a tribute to the great man, which would include the first state funeral, held December 26, 1799. It took one and a quarter hours for the draped (empty) coffin and the procession to make its way through the city of Philadelphia. Similar demonstrations of mourning and respect were held throughout the 13 states, and indeed in Europe, where the British Fleet lowered its flags to half mast, and the French Army was in official mourning for ten days. Six weeks later a "eulogium" was held for George Washington at the German Reformed Church on Race Street; present among the congregation were the President and Mrs. Adams, vice president Thomas Jefferson and British minister Robert Liston, Thomas Willing and William Bingham.

The eulogy was written and delivered by Major William Jackson, former aide and friend.

As the last decade of the eighteenth century drew to a close, William Bingham could reflect on his achievements. He had survived the financial panics that had brought most of his contemporaries down. He had not, though, so far reached the diplomatic positions for which he had strived; nor had he been appointed governor of Pennsylvania. He was, however, a real power broker in government, and had been at the heart of the creation of the bank of Pennsylvania, the Bank of North America and the Bank of the United States. His son-in-law, Alexander Baring, was now established and comfortable in his new home, new country and new family, and there was much satisfaction and joy when that union was blessed in June of 1799 by the birth of a child, named William Bingham Baring.

It had been an interesting and very successful decade for Francis Baring as well, but at its end he was 60 years old and continuing to grapple with the problem of succession in the house of John and Francis Baring & Co. Charles Wall (who had married Francis Baring's daughter Harriet Baring in 1790) was now the senior manager of the business day to day, and although John Baring remained a nominal partner until 1800, new blood would be needed sooner rather than later.[3]

At the end of 1799 Francis Baring took stock of his own children and their likely influence on the future of the business that he was continuing to build on the foundations laid by his father and mother. Of his male offspring Thomas was still serving the East India Company in Bengal, but showed little interest in running the bank on his return, already indicating a wish to follow in uncle John's footsteps in the role of country gentleman.

Alexander appeared increasingly to be a fixture in America, where his success was generating profits and great prestige. Francis had probably not anticipated how well Alexander would do, his ambition for Alexander before his departure to America had been, and still was, to expand with Hope & Co. into a powerful Anglo-Dutch consortium. That plan was clearly on hold, and that left Henry, still in Canton with the East India Company, but something of a loose cannon with a flair for a lifestyle not entirely appropriate to banking. The youngsters William and George had already been sent eastwards with the East India Company as well, but it was far too early to know what might become of them.

With no obvious succession plan available, Francis Baring decided to let matters rest, at least for the time being; there was much to be done, in Europe and America. In Britain interest in American stocks was rising, not least because of the activities of Alexander. Where the house of Barings went, others were now following. Acting with Cazenove and Co., the Barings were now engaged to pay out dividends on all American stock in Britain on behalf of the Bank of the United States. In 1799 Barings bought out the shareholding of the U.S. government in the Bank of the United States for £267,516, and Alexander assisted in raising a $5 million loan for the United States Treasury.[4]

Alexander noted scathingly at the time in a letter to his father: "Our financiers of America as well as our Politicians are quite Novices; they know nothing of what Mr Burke called the small ware of either Diplomaticks or finance."[5]

Although there was now a very strong link between Barings and Bingham through Alexander, it was Francis Baring's relationship with Thomas Willing, started way back in 1774, that was the key connection, and that was now paying off. The houses of Baring and Willing & Morris had been close as merchants and now trading as Willing & Francis remained that way. But it was as president of the Bank of North America and in particular of the Bank of the United States that Thomas Willing drew the business of Barings and the United States closer and closer, assisted by the strong support of Rufus King as American minister in London. Thomas Willing and Francis Baring were now also related through the marriage of Francis' son to Thomas' granddaughter Ann Louisa, the first of a number of significant relationships between the families of Willing, Bingham, Baring (and others) that were already shaping the future of the United States.

Despite Alexander's undoubted success in America, Francis Baring continued to fret about his (and his family's) return to London. In desperation, in November of 1800, he wrote to Alexander's new father-in-law, William Bingham:

"I have been so often disappointed about Alex's return, his presence is so indispensable to a Man of my age, infirmities, and numerous family, that I must request of you to bind him hand and foot, and put him on board some Ship bound for England."[6]

Francis Baring would have to wait a little while longer to see Alexander. After mourning the loss of George Washington, political minds turned to the presidential election to be held at the end of 1800, the first to be held with candidates having party affiliations, just 12 years after the founding fathers believed that government would be possible without such division.[7]

The Federalists believed that they should stay in power for a further four-year term; they had dealt with critical problems with Britain and were attempting to do so with France; Hamiltonian economics and tax-collecting machinery were working well and they had established an efficient executive administration; they had a navy and an army; and although slow to engage with the Industrial Revolution while it freed itself from Britain, America was catching up fast. The United States had just entered the industrial age, and within three generations would be the powerhouse of the world. But as so often happens in these circumstances, many electors were not so impressed and favored a change. Aaron Burr's Republicans took the state of New York, humbling Alexander Hamilton, for whom this was a personal defeat. Aaron Burr was nominated to run as Thomas Jefferson's vice presidential candidate.

Federalist leaders, perhaps reluctantly, proposed that John Adams should be their candidate for president, and Charles Pinckney for vice president. Sensing the opportunity to rid himself of what he saw as the "Hamilton faction," Adams promptly fired Timothy Pickering and James McHenry. John Marshall was appointed to Pickering's position of secretary of state, and Samuel Dexter to McHenry's position as secretary of war. He did not fire Oliver Woolcott.

This was more than Alexander Hamilton could take — in a last-ditch effort to snatch control of the Federalists he wrote, and had printed, a vicious attack on John Adams for distribution to Federalist leaders. Unfortunately for Hamilton, copies fell into the hands of Republicans, and extracts were printed in the *Aurore*. The leading Federalists, including William Bingham, were devastated by Hamilton's conduct, and from then on he was effectively written out of the Federalist future, or what was left of it.

George Washington's wish for the seat of government to be at the new Federal City of Washington on the Potomac River finally materialized in the summer of 1800, during the Sixth Congress. Construction had taken ten years since Washington himself laid the first brick. Bingham arranged to attend the first session, but he had already decided not to seek re-election to the new Congress, whatever the circumstances in the presidential campaign. He may have tired of the recent unseemly squabbling in Congress; he was unsure of the future of the Federalist Party to which he had been so committed. There can be no doubt, though, that the real reason that William Bingham abandoned his political career was the unexpected news that Anne Bingham, now 37 years old, was pregnant, and due in December; she had been in poor health for a while, and her confinement was likely to be a trying time.[8] The future of the Binghams and the Barings was about to be set on a new and unpredictable course.

William Bingham Jr. was born at the end of December, and on January 1, 1801, Bingham left as soon as he could for the new capital for the remainder of the term. Washington's dream of a seat of government on the Potomac was now a reality, but only just; it was in the middle of nowhere (it took Bingham nine hard days carriage drive from Philadelphia), and nothing was complete. The Federal City of Washington consisted of the new Capitol Building (or rather one wing of it), a few makeshift boarding houses and taverns, and a small number of shops, including a grocery store and a printer's shop. A mile to the west the residence for the president of the United States was an unfinished shell, connected to the government buildings by a new roadway, also unfinished, named Pennsylvania Avenue.

The second session of the Sixth Congress and John Adams' administration limped on at the start of 1801, awaiting a decision on the future president. After the disaster of New York, Federalist fortunes improved. Adams had received 63 electoral votes, while Jefferson and Burr had won 73 each. The final decision on president and vice president was left to Congress.[9]

Federalist leaders had been agonizing over whether to support Jefferson or Burr in the final election for president. They wanted neither man, but since they still had a small majority in the House and believed they controlled sufficient states to block Jefferson, the possibility of a deal with Burr might enable them to retain a degree of control. Hamilton had decided much earlier that Jefferson, a man he loathed, would be the better of two evils.

On the due date, Congress duly met and formally confirmed the electoral vote (Jefferson 73 votes, Burr 73 votes, Adams 65 votes, Pinckney 64 votes and Jay 1 vote), having already decided that they would stay in session uninterrupted, in Papal fashion, until a decision was reached. The candidate receiving the vote of nine or more states would be the new president. William Bingham and the Senate continued its business. John Adams was not present; he was in New York mourning for his alcoholic son Charles, who had died alone in New York.[10]

Congress deliberated, ballot after ballot, through Wednesday night. The twenty-seventh ballot was cast early on Thursday morning. At noon the House adjourned until Saturday morning, when three more ballots were taken, and in the absence of a decision adjourned again until Monday, again without success. On Tuesday, after the thirty-sixth vote, Speaker Sedgwick, exhausted, gave the final result; ten states for Jefferson, four for Burr, two abstaining. Jefferson had won, and immediately announced his new cabinet: James Madison, secretary of state, Levi Lincoln, attorney general, Samuel Smith, secretary of the Navy, Henry Dearborn, secretary of war, Albert Gallatin, secretary of the Treasury.

Thomas Jefferson was inaugurated on March 4, 1801, with Aaron Burr as vice president. John Adams had already left.

Alexander Baring reported the events in Washington dutifully back to his father in London: "The [reports of the] accession of Mr Jefferson may have excited apprehension, but you may depend on it that they are unfounded. The personal dispositions of the man are strongly in favour of France, but the party that brought him in is too feeble to admit of his risking a measure that would ruin him.... He is watched with a very jealous eye and I am convinced myself, that he has too much knowledge of the ground he stands on to risk any bold measure."[11]

Unfortunately neither William Bingham nor Alexander Baring was in Washington to hear Jefferson's inaugural speech; they had been overtaken by events.

Bingham had stayed on until the end of February, but left suddenly on the receipt of troubling news of the health of his wife. Anne Bingham had caught cold after a sleighing party (in vogue at the time) and her health declined quickly with "galloping consumption." Alexander Baring, in Philadelphia, now found himself sharing his time between with his wife, Ann Louisa, who was pregnant again, and his mother-in-law, now desperately ill. In a letter of March 29 he wrote to his father: "Though her situation is by no means desperate, it is highly critical. So much so as to leave the hopes and fears of those about her who understand her complaint nearly balanced."

Unfortunately Anne Bingham's situation was indeed desperate, "galloping consumption"—tuberculosis—was generally fatal in those days. A warmer climate was considered her only hope, and Bingham made arrangements for one of his ships, the *America*, to take her and as many family and servants as could be accommodated across the Atlantic to the island of Madeira.

Anne Bingham was carried to the *America* on April 13, 1801, among many onlookers, the news having spread of her plight. Following on foot were her daughter, Maria Matilda Bingham, her younger sister Abigail Willing and William Bingham.[12]

Alexander Baring confided to his father on May 12 (sadly she had already died when Alexander wrote this): "Her case is considered perfectly hopeless here, and indeed she lost so much in the last few days before she was carried on a litter on board ship that our hopes were very faint of her recovering anywhere.... The accounts we have received by the pilot who took the ship out have revived our expectations as she was considerably benefited by the motion and the air of the sea, and we are now in the most anxious impatience to hear from her."

On board *America*, Anne Bingham's condition deteriorated fast and Bingham and Captain Wills changed their immediate destination to Bermuda, which was reached on May 7. She died four days later and was buried at St. Peters churchyard, St. Georges, Bermuda.

Anne Bingham's father, Thomas Willing, wrote in his journal of May 26: "This day Mr. Bingham return'd from Bermuda where my dear daughter died on the 11th May 1801."[13]

Well before the tragic events of early 1801, Alexander Baring had actually been wrapping up his business affairs since his marriage to Ann Louisa in 1798. He wrote to his father in January 1799, indicating that Robert Gilmor could be trusted to act as their agent: "Mr Bingham has separated from Gilmor's House, that his two sons may be admitted into it. You may place implicit confidence in this establishment. Robert Gilmor is worth at least £100,000 sterling."[14]

Alexander was in no rush and the birth of William Bingham Baring in June of 1799 gave him the opportunity to stay on and run what was now the American house of John and Francis Baring & Co. It was clear, though, he would have to decide, once and for all, where his future lay. If lifestyle was the only consideration he would have made his life in America; Philadelphia was very conveniently the center of government and commerce, but that would change when Congress moved to the new Federal City of Washington.

There was also the position of long-suffering employer Hope & Co. to consider. While Hope & Co. was still in London with Labouchere in effective control, Alexander would not have the freedom that he was enjoying in America, but by the end of 1799 Holland was safe enough and its new government very happy to have them back in Amsterdam. An offer of a partnership in Hope & Co. had been made to Alexander as a further encouragement.

Alexander and Francis considered the options available within the family to manage American affairs. Cousin Charles Baring was making a success of his businesses in Charleston (unlike his father) and apparently had no intention of returning to England. Indeed Alexander had talked with his father about sending out help from the Exeter partnership John and Charles Baring & Co. to Charleston: "I have heard nothing of the project of sending Cole of Exeter out to Charles Baring."[15]

Of the other brothers, Thomas Baring had decided to return from Bengal; Henry Baring was still in Canton and despite rumors of his poor health showed no immediate signs of returning to London. William, now also in Canton, was doing well, but like Henry the position did not suit his health. George, on the other hand, became the black sheep of the family, and went his own way in the opium business.

But by the end of 1800 Alexander and Francis had come to an agreement: "I see nothing to prevent our departure now," he wrote in January 1801.[16]

In March, when concerns about Anne Bingham's health first surfaced, he wrote again that "the Binghams propose not to accompany us but to go south to Madeira or Lisbon."

It would seem from this that William and Anne Bingham were also planning to join them in England after the birth of William Bingham Jr., but now intended to travel via Madeira for Anne Bingham's health. On May 12, 1801, Alexander wrote to his father again of Anne Bingham's rapidly declining health, and confirmed that that they would leave "after Mrs Baring's confinement"; Ann Louisa had become pregnant with their second child, Francis, towards the end of 1800 and was due shortly, and they made arrangements to sail for England in August of 1801. By the time Francis Baring received this letter, Anne Bingham had already been buried on the island of Bermuda.

Alexander Baring immediately set about making the arrangements for the continuing control of the Baring's American interests, "that I might never be obliged by my affairs to return."[17]

Thomas Willing Francis (Tench Francis' son and Anne Bingham's cousin) proposed that he join Alexander in partnership. Baring also considered Thomas Willings' son Thomas Mayne, but thought him "a very good young man but idle." Thomas Willing himself was still engaged in the Bank of the United States, but was in any case looking towards his eventual retirement. It was Alexander's firm recommendation that Robert Gilmor Sr., who he described as "by far the best merchant in the United States and the family looks set to last," be appointed to look after the Barings' interests in America.

William Bingham was completely devastated by the death of his wife Anne, a loss from which he never recovered. They had all planned to travel to England together but now he faced losing Ann Louisa, her husband Alexander and his two grandchildren to England, leaving him in Philadelphia in the Mansion House with his teenaged daughter Maria Matilda and his infant son William Jr. He decided that he would travel to London with the Barings and Maria on an extended and indeterminate stay. He left young William in the care of his grandfather Thomas Willing; he left his business affairs as far as he could with Willing & Francis[18] and, like Alexander, left the control of his remaining investments with his old friend and partner of many years, Robert Gilmor Sr. He appointed Charles Willing Hare (Anne's nephew) as his attorney and agent.

In August, as planned, Alexander and Ann Louisa Bingham, their two infants, William Bingham and his daughter Maria Matilda sailed for England.

19. The Louisiana Purchase

Unlike Henry Hope or William Bingham, who both relished the trappings of their financial success, Francis Baring had avoided the signs of ostentation associated with his growing wealth until quite late in life when he was absolutely sure of his circumstances. The premises at Devonshire Square, acquired in 1793, were still the family home right through the final decade of the eighteenth century, and he continued to plough the profits back into John and Francis Baring & Co. until finally in 1796 he acquired a reversionary interest in the Manor House at Lee, near Lewisham, then in the countryside just a few miles south of the River Thames. The lady in residence had a life interest in the property, and Baring had little expectation of taking benefit of the property for many years to come, but she died rather suddenly and Francis Baring found himself the owner in 1800. By this time he was also negotiating to purchase the estate at Stratton Park in Hampshire from the Duke of Bedford, which he acquired in 1801.[1]

He bought several hundred more acres of land around his new estate at Lee and moved in to the house there, while George Dance (the younger) was engaged to remodel the house and gardens at Stratton Park in the neo-classical fashion popular at the time. The work was not completed for two years and Baring busied himself buying adjacent property and land whenever it could be had, and like Henry Hope he started to acquire paintings for his houses, but only the very best, mainly the Dutch artists, Rembrandt, Rubens or Van Dyke.

Francis Baring extended his property portfolio in 1802 when he acquired 33 Hill Street, off Berkeley Square in London's West End. Francis Baring was now almost the complete English aristocrat, but not quite. That final transformation would follow a little later.

Alexander and Ann Louisa Baring and their children, William Bingham and his other daughter Maria Matilda arrived in London from Philadelphia in September 1801, when Francis Baring was reunited with William Bingham for the first time since 1786. They had been correspondents and business associates for most of the intervening period and shared many well-placed friends

The Manor House, Lee, Lewisham, London, circa 1830. Home of Francis Baring, 1800–1810 (Baring Archive Ltd., reference #DEP108).

and acquaintances. Francis and Harriet Baring had not seen Alexander since 1795 and they greeted their grandchildren William and Francis for the first time. William Bingham and Maria Matilda remained the guests of Francis and Harriet Baring in London and at the country estates before taking up rented accommodation in Bath, close to his old friend Lord Lansdowne at Bowood.

Alexander Baring had been back in Britain for just a few months when he wrote to his father, mysteriously, that he might need to return to America on "family business," delaying the opportunity of a partnership in Hope & Co., at least for the time being.[2]

After a few months in Bath, William Bingham returned to London as the guest of Francis and Harriet Baring, and renewed friendships made many years before, in particular with Rufus King (now American minister in London) and Lord Lansdowne, now out of public office but influential nonetheless. This return to London may also have been influenced by Maria Matilda, now 18 years old. Somehow she and Henry Baring, who had met in Philadelphia, had maintained an affectionate long distance relationship, before and after her dalliance with the Comte de Tilly.[3] She and Ann Louisa had entertained Alexander and Henry in happier times at the Mansion House and at Lansdown. Henry Baring, his health apparently now restored, had left his younger brother William behind in Canton and was now back in London,

Stratton Park, Hampshire, country estate of Sir Francis Baring, drawn by J. P. Neale, engraved by J. C. Varrall (Hampshire Record Office TOP/101/2/2).

footloose and fancy free. Following the financial rewards of the Alexander Baring and Anne Bingham match, the attachment of Henry and Maria Matilda seemed almost inevitable, but whatever the actual reasons the match was happily accepted by all, and they were married discretely in London on April 10, 1802.[4] Alexander Baring, now back in Philadelphia, commented to Robert Gilmor that the marriage was "an event which though it did not much surprise me was unexpected."

Bingham's spirits lifted a little after Maria's marriage and he was finally able to face the unfinished business he had left behind in Philadelphia with the help of Alexander, Robert Gilmor, Thomas Willing and General Cobb. The news from Hope and Baring's agent John Richards in Maine was not good, in particular the worrying but not unpredictable lack of settlers: "The advance of this country is slow and gradual.... It is more than ever my fix'd opinion that this will ultimately prove an advantageous speculation, but that the period of winding it up will not arrive for a great many years."

He was right. The failure to find the required 2,500 settlers presented a liability of $62,250, which if unpaid would eventually attach to lands themselves.

But the greatest burden that Bingham was carrying was the unresolved *Pilgrim* affair, which had been weighing on him now for more than 20 years.

He left America with a judgment of $40,000 against him, but had always believed that Congress would underwrite his actions in Martinique as an agent of the government and settle the claims. But now his Federalist support had been swept away and he feared the effects of a Republican backlash.[5]

Having done what he could, and with affairs in America in the capable hands of Gilmor and Baring, William Bingham decided that another Grand Tour was required and set off for Europe with Ann, after she had given birth to her fourth child.

The sequence of events that led Alexander Baring to America and the Maine Trail is remarkable enough, but is more than matched by what transpired over the next 12 months, when Alexander Baring, Francis Baring, Henry Hope and William Bingham found themselves, by chance or otherwise, in the right place at the right time to influence the course of history.

The Quasi-War with France had fizzled out with the toothless Treaty of Mortefontaine which John Adams' envoys had "negotiated" at the end of 1799, and which Congress had debated for weeks the following year. But while Congress returned to internal retrospection and the bitterness of the first political party presidential campaign, Talleyrand and Bonaparte were quietly working on a strategy for world domination, or something pretty close. Talleyrand's plan was to permanently seal off American growth at the Mississippi, and from there build a French North American empire, in which the United States would become a subservient satellite on the fringe.

Louis Andre Pichon had been secretary to the French delegation at Mortefontaine, and had been dispatched to Washington as charge d'affaires, to sound out evidence of President Jefferson's pro–French credentials. He asked Jefferson for the United States position on the island of Santo Domingo, split as it was, into French and Spanish dependencies divided by a mountain range. The French Revolution had triggered a civil war in the French part which had resulted in the emergence of a black leader, Toussaint L'Ouverture, who was attempting to assert independence from France. The island and its sugar plantations had been a rich source of income for France and Talleyrand and Napoleon wanted it back.[6]

Pichon, aware that John Adams had sent Edward Stevens, a friend of Alexander Hamilton, to Cap Francois to urge Toussaint to declare independence, asked what the American response would be if France attempted to regain control of the island. In a complete reversal of American policy, Jefferson replied that "nothing would be easier than to supply everything for your army and navy and starve out Toussaint."

Pichon was delighted and reported this green light from Jefferson back to Talleyrand in Paris. Thomas Jefferson and James Madison had just initiated the second step in Talleyrand's master plan, well before they knew about the first.

The American delegation which agreed to the treaty with the French at Mortefontaine (named after Napoleon's elder brother's chateau where the treaty was signed) would not have been aware, but a second treaty was signed the following day at San Ildefonso in Spain by Lucien Bonaparte (Napoleon's younger brother), and the Spanish King. In this second treaty, Spain would return the territory of Louisiana to France (Louis XV had ceded the territory to Spain to compensate for losses in the Seven Years War with Britain). In return Napoleon agreed to place the son-in-law of the Spanish King on the throne of the Duchy of Tuscany. Napoleon further agreed never to cede Louisiana to any other power. Both parties agreed to the secrecy of this Treaty.[7]

To complete the next stage of the master plan, Napoleon needed to possess Florida and part of what is now Louisiana on the east of the Mississippi, and Talleyrand started negotiations with the Spanish King to acquire these territories. Meanwhile, by October of 1801, the French had agreed to terms for peace with Britain, the Treaty of Amiens, which included British approval for a French expedition to regain Santa Domingo. Talleyrand's stage was set.

Of all this Jefferson and Madison knew nothing. They were concerned, however, about the security of New Orleans, which controlled American trade from the Mississippi. By Pinckney's Treaty of 1795, Americans had the right to store and ship goods, and to navigate the entire river. The Spanish revoked this in 1798, but restored it in 1801, by which time it was actually under clandestine French control.

During 1801 the secret Treaty of San Ildefonso became increasingly less secret in Europe, with rumors of the retrocession of Louisiana to France swirling around.

The rumor had reached William Bingham, and he wrote to Rufus King:

> A rumor prevails that Spain has ceded Louisiana to France.... I most sincerely deprecate the consequences as affecting the United States, by creating separate interests betwixt the eastern and western divisions of the Union, by affording an opportunity of exercising an influence over the inhabitants of our western country, who will be dependent on France for an outlet to their produce.
>
> This country [Britain] is not aware of the advantages this possession will give France as a maritime nation, by the employment of such a quantity of commercial tonnage in transporting the bulky produce of the Mississippi.
>
> General Victor's troops [assembled in Holland] are certainly destined for Louisiana.[8]

Even at this time Bingham, and presumably Jefferson and Madison, were thinking of this as a commercial impediment and had not yet appreciated the real risk that lay in France's intentions.

William Bingham, with Ann Louisa, arrived in Paris during 1802 and remade some of his acquaintances of nearly 20 years earlier. He visited Robert Livingston, now American minister to France (since October 1801), and they discussed the rumors of French aspirations in America. The fears had mobilized opinion in Congress, where there had been calls to take New Orleans by force. Livingston helpfully passed these concerns to Talleyrand, where they were duly noted.

While the reality of Bonaparte's intentions was dawning on Jefferson and Madison, General Leclerc's invasion fleet had left Brest for Santa Domingo, in January 1802. By the time it arrived, the American position, and in particular that of Secretary of State Madison, had reverted to the Adams' embrace of the black ruler Toussaint. Pichon protested to Madison and then to Jefferson, requesting that the Americans make good their pledge of support. Madison had by this time received reports of the size of Leclerc's invasion army and that its ultimate destination might be Louisiana, a question he put to Pichon, who could not confirm or deny this story—he did not know. Meanwhile, Leclerc and his army had arrived in Santa Domingo and were struggling to overcome Toussaint, and at the point that they were about to succeed, the French forces were decimated by a yellow fever epidemic that swept through the ranks. Perhaps surprisingly Toussaint then surrendered and sued for acceptable peace terms, but Leclerc's army had come to the end of the road and Talleyrand's Louisiana dreams with it.[9]

Unaware of the French collapse in Santa Domingo, Jefferson believed that the United States was in real danger from a French invasion, or at the very least that an armed uprising in New Orleans was a real possibility. With little room to maneuver, Jefferson instructed Robert Livingston in Paris to attempt to negotiate the purchase of the Island of New Orleans and the Floridas, which he also now believed to be French possessions. Livingston was authorized to pay up to $10 million for New Orleans and the Floridas or $7.5 million for New Orleans alone. Livingston was no match for Talleyrand, and in March 1803 Jefferson sent James Monroe as minister plenipotentiary to assist Livingston in the purchase, authorizing him to make any advance payments as he thought necessary. He was also instructed to threaten Bonaparte that French occupation of New Orleans or any attempt to close the port to shipping would lead to a strategic alliance between the United States and Britain.

But Jefferson and Monroe were already being overtaken by events. Before Monroe had even set foot in France, William Bingham was apparently meeting his old acquaintance Charles-Maurice Prince de Talleyrand and through a loop probably involving Rufus King suggested that rather than just New Orleans itself, France should sell the entire Louisiana Territory, warning that failing to do so would give Britain the opportunity to take it for themselves. Talleyrand was not prepared to accept the collapse of his plan and was opposed to such a sale, but Napoleon had already decided their American dream was over and instructed Talleyrand to negotiate a deal. Bonaparte had plans to re-open the war with Britain and he needed cash, and lots of it, to re-arm his army and rebuild his shattered navy.

James Monroe and his party finally arrived and were astonished to discover that on April 13, 1803, French treasury minister Francois Barbe-Marbois had already opened discussions on the sale of the Louisiana Territory, which was not even part of his remit, and for which he was not prepared. But in Paris there was one man who was prepared and knew something about buying American real estate; Alexander Baring had completed his business in America and travelled back to Europe, and was now engaged as the financial advisor to the United States government in the negotiations with Barbe-Marbois. He also happened to be acting for John and Francis Baring & Co., Hope & Co. and, of course, William Bingham.[10]

Maybe Alexander Baring knew something that James Monroe did not; in February Alexander Baring had been offered and had accepted the agency of the United States government in London — and had effectively become banker to the United States.

The talks between Monroe and Barbe-Marbois continued satisfactorily and an agreement was reached on April 30, 1803; a treaty was signed, comprising two conventions which outlined how the agreed sum of $15 million

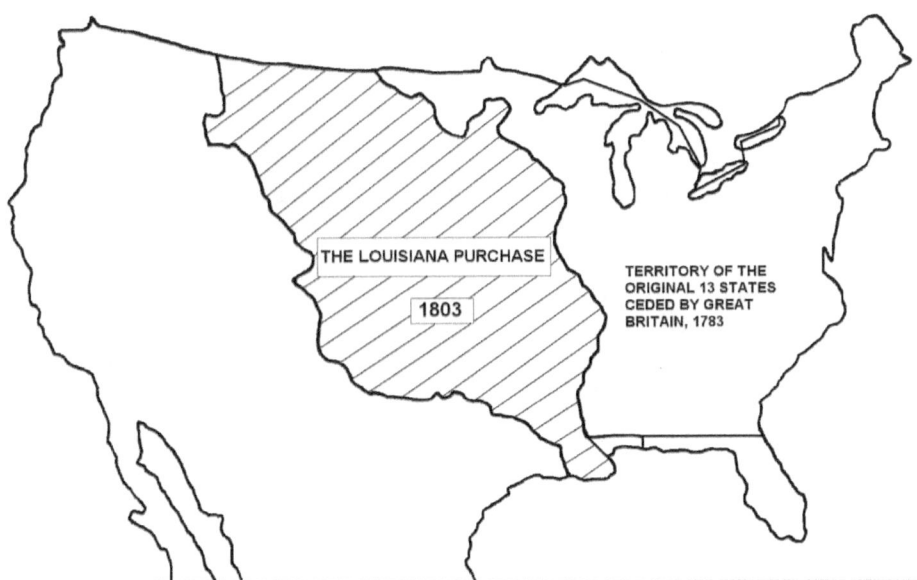

The Louisiana Purchase, 1803.

would be paid for the Louisiana Territory. The sheer size of the deal being undertaken by his son, both in the territory involved and the sums at risk, were almost too much for Francis Baring, with his retirement within sight.[11]

The first convention, signed by Livingston, Monroe and Barbe-Marbois, covered the issue of $11,250,000 of 6 percent United States Treasury stock redeemable in 15 years. The second convention agreed the claims of American citizens against the French navy for seizure of property and goods from American ships, the figure being set at $3,750,000 of stock bearing 6 percent, which the American government would assume and pay in cash, as agreed by Albert Gallatin.[12]

To finance the deal, Barings and Hopes would acquire the $11,250,000 of 6 percent U.S. bonds and pay 52 million francs (in specie) to the French treasury. Barings and Hopes, with help from William Bingham, had just bought Louisiana from France and sold it back to the United States.

Thomas Jefferson had just acquired for the United States 800,000 square miles, or 512 million acres, for $15 million at the price of 30 cents per acre, more than doubling the size of the nation. Only Francis and Alexander Baring, Henry Hope and William Bingham had the connections to pull it off.

Almost as an afterthought Francis Baring told British prime minister Henry Addington of the deal they had just financed. On balance the British government's view was that it was better for Britain for Napoleon to have 11 million dollars than for him to retain Louisiana, and gave Baring the (retrospective) go-ahead. By the time Hopes and Baring started making payments France and Britain were already at war again.[13]

While Francis Baring was attempting to pacify the British government, Alexander Baring sailed for Washington in July 1803 to await congressional ratification for Jefferson's Louisiana Purchase and approval to create the required Treasury stock. During this time he established a strong and lasting relationship with Treasury secretary Albert Gallatin.

Jefferson was troubled about whether the Constitution authorized him to make such a vast purchase of land and considered a Constitutional amendment, but in the end it was put to Congress to agree or not. By this time Barings and Hopes had advanced two million dollars but were awaiting Congress and the bond before paying out any more. Napoleon became increasingly impatient and threatened to pull out of the deal, which was finally ratified by the Senate on October 20, 1803.

Alexander Baring returned to England in February 1804 with one-third of the bonds. The other two-thirds were sent to Livingston in Paris, and from there to Hope & Co. in Amsterdam, where they were discounted to accelerate the transfer of specie for Napoleon's armies.

In all France received just short of nine million dollars in cash. Of the total consideration of $11,250,000, $5 million was payable in Amsterdam and

$6.25 million in London. Hope's portion formed, in turn, the basis of a new loan of 12,500,000 guilders, "share in a joint property of the original American Stocks," of 1,000 guilders each at 5½ percent, thereby generating a margin of half a percent over the U.S. Louisiana bonds, which was used to create a reserve fund. The loan was redeemed in 1819, 1820 and 1821. The reserve fund, when distributed, produced a final bonus of 55.75 guilders per share. The subscription for these was handled by Hope, De Smeth and Willinks. They were quickly placed, even at a premium, and were a great success, and the U.S. never defaulted on the interest payments, even at the height of its subsequent war with France in 1811.[14]

Of the $6.25 million payable in London, Alexander Baring was able to place $500,000 in America, the Barings took $1 million for themselves, $1.7 million went to Henry Hope in London, and $300,000 was transferred to Hope & Co. in Amsterdam. The remaining $2,750,000 was taken up by subscriptions in Britain.

Despite his previous assurances to Francis Baring, British Prime Minister Addington was now under pressure, not surprisingly, to prevent further remittances of cash (from British investors!) to pay for Napoleon's war with Britain, and requested that these transfers be halted. Baring forwarded this request to Hope & Co. in Amsterdam, who chose to ignore it.[15]

Albert Gallatin estimated subsequently that Barings and Hopes had made $3 million profit on the Louisiana Purchase.

William Bingham had no doubt in his mind that it was his intervention that had changed the course of America's history. We will probably never know. His intention to continue his European tour with Ann Louisa was curtailed as the war with Britain flared up again, and he returned to England as Alexander Baring left for the United States.

The Louisiana Purchase had been a political coup for the United States and had made a great deal of money for William Bingham's extended family, but it did not do the chances of disposing of the Maine lands any good at all, in fact the reverse was true. He wrote to General Cobb in Gouldsboro: "In the scale of national policy and individual advantage, the District of Maine presents very superior advantages for settlement. The Atlantic states have now a distinct and separate system to pursue, and every effort should be made to render their population more compact and to prevent their inhabitants from being scattered over that immense western wilderness, thereby weakening the aggregate strength of the country, from their labour turning to so little account."

William Bingham must have had very mixed feelings about his situation; both his daughters were now in London married to two sons of Francis Baring, who had made him most welcome and part of the family. He had left his infant son in Philadelphia with the boy's grandfather Judge Thomas

Descendants of Henry Baring

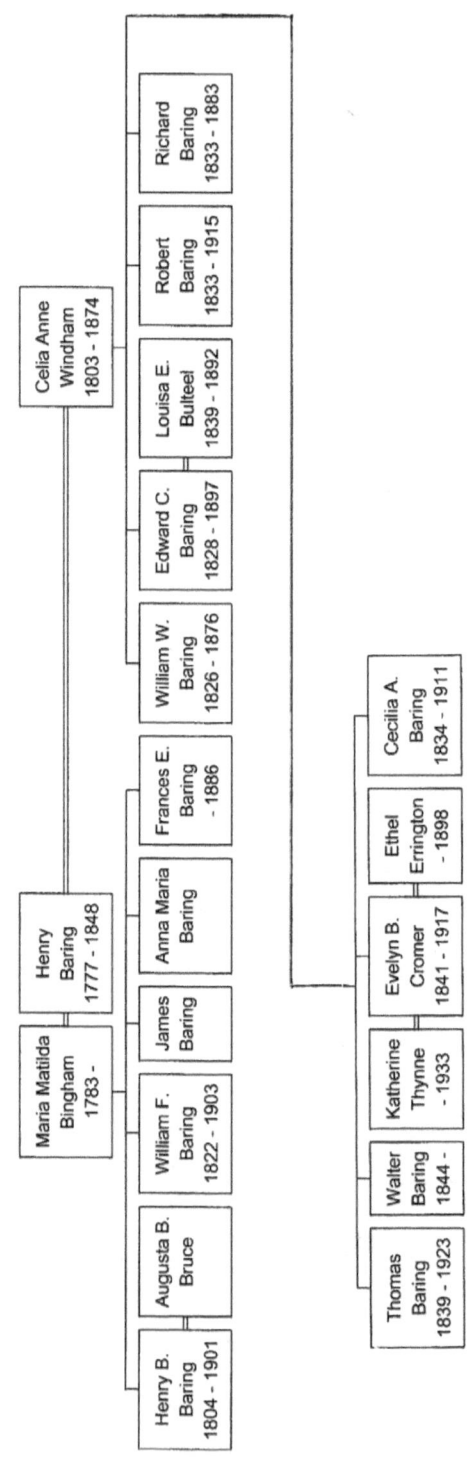

Willing, and had not seen him for more than three years. As a staunch Federalist his political career was probably at an end. In different times and without Jefferson in the White House his country might have recognized his contribution and offered the diplomatic position that he surely deserved and was certainly well qualified to undertake.

He wrote again to General Cobb on October 15, 1803: "The time which I limited for my excursion to Europe being nearly expired.... I contemplate returning next season, except some unforeseen circumstances should occasion a further detention. I shall then be able to fulfil your views. On many points, which cannot be so well effected while we are such a distance. Indeed my affairs essentially require my presence."[16]

Maybe his intention was to return to America to liquidate his affairs before making his home in Britain with young William; certainly the ghosts of the past in the Mansion House would be too hard to bear without Anne by his side.

We will never know what he was planning; William Bingham returned to his lodgings in Bath, but was soon back in London, where he consulted his friend and physician Sir Charles Blagden about his health and the symptoms he was experiencing. His condition declined rapidly and he returned to Bath to put his affairs into order and to complete a will, which he did on January 30, 1804: "being of sound mind but low in health...."[17]

William Bingham died on February 6, 1804, at the age of 52. By his side were his daughters Ann Louisa and Maria Matilda, their children, and Henry Baring. Alexander Baring was on his way back from Washington with the U.S. bonds from the Louisiana Purchase. Francis Baring and Lord Lansdowne were summoned. The funeral was held in Bath Abbey, where he was buried.

Francis Baring wrote to their mutual friend Rufus King (now back in America) on March 1, 1804, advising him of Bingham's death, and the terms of his will.[18]

William Bingham's close friend Benjamin Rush wrote: "Died at Bath, Wm Bingham of this city. He left an estate valued at three million dollars, half a million of which was in stock of different kinds. He was pleasant in his manners, amiable in his temper, liberal but said not to be charitable. He acquired his immense estate by his own ingenuity. In all his money speculations he was fortunate."[19]

The year 1804 closed one chapter in this continuing story, but another was opening.

20. Finale, a Concluding Commentary

William Bingham signed his will on January 30, 1804, just six days before his death. In it he appointed five executors, his sons-in-law Alexander Baring and Henry Baring, his faithful associate and partner Robert Gilmor, his brother-in-law Thomas Mayne Willing and Ann Louisa Bingham Baring's nephew Charles Willing Hare. The terms of the will also created a trust, with the same individuals as trustees, and with the power to create new trustees in perpetuity.

He left £10,000 to his daughter Maria Matilda Baring, and £2,000 to each of the executors and his wife's sister Abigail Willing. To her brother Richard Willing and her niece Maria Clymer he left £1,000 each. The trustees were instructed to divide the residual estate into five equal parts, two parts in trust for the infant son William and three parts shared between Ann Louisa and Maria Matilda. Benjamin Rush estimated Bingham's estate at three million dollars.[1]

Whether it was intended is not clear, but William Bingham's will and the associated trust would make legal history, as an example of what is now known as a federal contract trust. The trust itself lasted for almost 50 years until the death of the last child, and the "Bingham Estate" that it then became lasted for the best part of another hundred years, continuing to pay income to the increasing number of descendents (over 300 at its termination) of Ann Louisa, Maria Matilda and William Bingham Jr. before finally being wound up in 1964.[2]

Alexander and Henry Baring benefited from the substantial income from their wives' legacy, but not from the capital, as was the custom at the time in Britain and America. Francis Baring refers to this, perhaps a little tartly, in his letter to Rufus King of March 1, 1804: "and though my sons do not enjoy some advantages which the customs of America and England sanction, yet I can say most sincerely that they as well as myself are perfectly satisfied and that we shall ever hold his memory in the highest respect and reverence."[3]

Some of the real estate, however, notably Lansdown House in Philadelphia, became Baring property, and was used by the family on occasion for a while and then remained empty until it was burnt down on July 4,1854. The estate was eventually bought by a group of Philadelphia businessmen who donated it to the city of Philadelphia, and it now forms part of Fairmont Park. The Powel House already belonged to Ann Louisa and Alexander Baring, and is now open to the public.[4]

The Binghams' famous and opulent Mansion House and all its contents became the subject of a vast auction sale at the end of 1805. Plans for it to become a gentleman's club fell through and it became the Mansion House Hotel, and also burnt down, in 1847. The plot was bought by the great-great-grandfather of Jackie Bouvier, the wife of John Kennedy, the thirty-fifth president of the United States. Bouvier built a row of houses, some of which still exist.

The trustees of the Bingham estate were burdened by the penalties imposed by the state of Massachusetts for the failure to bring in settlers, but were able to cancel the debt by effectively gifting substantial tracts to leading members of the state Congress in exchange for resolutions that abrogated the settler fees and ensured clear title to the rest. The trustees made no progress in developing the lands for farming, although the unloved Kennebec tract eventually attracted a number of townships. The Penobscot tracts, apart from lumbering, remain mostly wilderness to this day.

Bingham's remaining land in Pennsylvania fared rather better, eventually, when oil was discovered in 1878. Oil rights provided a new source of wealth for the Trust until it was finally wound up in 1964.[5]

Of William Bingham's children, William probably fared worst from the loss of his father and the impact of great wealth. Under the terms of his father's will he stayed in the care of his grandfather Thomas Willing until he was sent to England to be cared for by his sisters. In reality he was bought up in style by Ann Louisa and Alexander Baring as one of their own children, but he did not turn out that way. He did not do well at school and he was undone by the burden of his great fortune. He left England for Canada and married the aristocratic Marie Charlotte Louise de Lotbeniere. They moved to Paris, where they lived in the lavish style reminiscent of his parents back in Philadelphia. He lacked his father's business acumen and lapsed into drunkenness while Charlotte took a stream of lovers into her old age, producing offspring of indeterminate paternity.[6]

Maria Matilda, having run away with the Comte de Tilly, and having been "rescued" by William Bingham and Alexander Baring, married Alexander's brother in 1802. The income from her legacy probably suited Henry and his somewhat dissolute lifestyle well. Henry became a partner in the bank, technically at least, in 1804. He was a renowned gambler, and was removed from the partners' room in 1823 after a scandalous and very public divorce from Maria Matilda, after he had finally (apparently) been able to separate her from most of her money. This marriage produced three sons and four daughters.

Maria Matilda moved to Paris and married a French nobleman, the Marquis de Blaizel, another gambler bent on spending what was left of her fortune.

Ann Louisa, through her marriage to Alexander Baring, had by far the greatest impact on the history of Britain and the Baring family. Anne and Alexander had ten children whose progeny have percolated through English aristocracy for the last 200 years. Appendix D has more detail.

For Sir Francis Baring, 1804 was an eventful year. His son-in-law William Bingham's death in March was followed by the passing of his wife, Harriet Baring. Francis Baring now had his three older sons back in Britain, and they were now as ready to take on the challenge as he was to retire from it. Thomas, Alexander and Henry joined Charles Wall as the new partners of Baring Brothers & Co. (as it would be known from 1807). In 1806 the firm moved from Devonshire Square to number 8 Bishopsgate, which remained its offices until the 1970s.[7]

Francis Baring died in 1810, leaving an "official" estate of £625,000, although his real worth was considered to be closer to two million pounds. The eldest son Thomas assumed his father's baronetcy on his death and retired, at the same time as Charles Wall, leaving Alexander to run the business with new partners Thomas Nixson and Swinton Holland, with Henry Baring a rare visitor to the partners' room.

Lord Lansdowne had previously described Francis Baring "a prince of merchants"; Lord Erskine went one further, writing after his death: "he was unquestionably the first merchant in Europe; first in knowledge and talents, and first in character and opulence."[8]

Henry Baring married Cecilia Anne Windham after divorcing Maria Matilda. Henry and Cecilia had eight children. It is said that he won his London house, 11 Berkeley Square, in a game of cards. He served as MP for Winchester from 1806. Henry Baring is probably best known for the success of some of his children — see Appendix E.

The bonds between Hopes and Barings continued to strengthen towards the end of the 1790s, helped no doubt by the marriage of Peter Cesar Labouchere to Francis Baring's daughter Dorothy.

Although Henry Hope & Co. were well established in London, they had always intended to return to Holland when the opportunity arose, and the Treaty of Amiens which ended hostilities between France and England in March of 1802 (temporarily) gave them the opportunity. Hopes of London took a five million guilder share in the Amsterdam house, with Labouchere as the senior partner in the new business. Plans to admit Alexander Baring as a partner were shelved; Francis Baring was, in fact, considering opening his own house in Antwerp or merging Barings and Hopes, but was overtaken by the events surrounding the Louisiana Purchase, which gave both houses a great deal to digest.[9]

The re-established Hope & Co. continued to prosper from foreign government loans, until 1810 when the business started to unravel. Henry Hope Jr. resigned in 1810, and Peter Labouchere decided to relinquish day-to-day management when Holland was annexed by France. Henry Hope died in February 1811, much like William Bingham, "attacked by a disorder which baffled all medical skill."[10]

After Henry Hope's death the other partners fell out with Labouchere when they proposed that the business be liquidated; John Hope died in February 1813, and his wife remarried and demanded that her share of the assets be realized by liquidation. Thomas and Henry Philip resolved this immediate problem by buying her out for £183,509 sterling, but this triggered the final disintegration of the former partnership, and Thomas and Henry Philip transferred the assets of Hope & Co. and Henry Hope & Co. (in London) for £250,521.[11]

Francis Baring's plan of an Anglo-Dutch banking empire was finally realized, but he had not lived to see it. Hope & Co. reformed in 1815 with Alexander Baring's brother-in-law Labouchere at the helm. Amsterdam's position as the financial center of Europe had now passed to London, but Hope & Co. continued as a leader in foreign loans, in particular in the United States and Russia.[12]

In the latter part of the twentieth century Hope & Co. became Bank Mees and Hope NV, and then ABN AMRO, before being acquired with disastrous consequences by the Royal Bank of Scotland in 2006. Whether anyone spotted at the time that Hopes had returned to its place of birth is uncertain.

As we have seen, Henry Philip Hope continued a flamboyant lifestyle, including the acquisition of the Hope Diamond, until his death in 1839.[13]

After the death of Francis Baring, Alexander Baring took a firm grip on Baring Brothers & Co., and made enormous sums from financing the Napoleonic wars from every side. This was the time when the Duc de Richelieu made his famous but probably apocryphal statement that "There are six great powers in Europe, England, France, Prussia, Austria, Russia and Baring Brothers."[14]

Britain's war with the United States in 1812 caused some embarrassment, but Alexander Baring was able to exploit the strong relationship he had with America's peace emissary, Albert Gallatin, and was actually employed by the British government to act as an intermediary.

In 1817 Alexander Baring acquired the estate of Grange Park in Hampshire, adjacent to Stratton Park (which was by then the property of his elder

Grange Park, Hampshire, country estate of Alexander Baring (1174–1848), later Lord Ashburton, drawn by J. P. Neale, engraved by W. Watkins (Hampshire Record Office 15M84/P3/464).

brother Thomas) from fellow banker Henry Drummond. From then until his death he continued to acquire property; by 1850 various Barings owned between them a very significant proportion of the county of Hampshire.[15]

Alexander Baring was elected an MP first for Taunton, and remained in the House of Commons until 1835, when he was raised to the peerage as Lord Ashburton. In 1832 he had been offered the post of chancellor of the exchequer in the Duke of Wellington's putative ministry in 1832, but thought better of it and withdrew. He died in 1848 while visiting his daughter Harriet (now married to the Marquess of Bath) at the family seat of Longleat at the age of 73.[16] He was described by Benjamin Disraeli as "the greatest merchant banker England perhaps ever had."[17]

Back in Philadelphia, Thomas Willing continued to look after his grandson William Bingham Jr. until the boy left to join his sisters in England in 1810. Thomas resigned as president of the Bank of the United States in 1807, after a stroke. He died in 1821 at the age of ninety, leaving an estate of over $1 million, including the 122,000 acres of Pennsylvania he had purchased with William Bingham. He was a modest man with roots in the west of England whose descendents through his daughter and William Bingham have played a major role in British history, as of course have his American descendents in American history.[18]

In terms of sheer ability, Alexander Baring may have been the high-water mark for Baring family members running the business, but the business continued to grow through the nineteenth century, bringing in new blood from outside when needed. The first prominent outsider was Joshua Bates, who was taken on in 1828 and dominated the partner's room for 30 years. Baring Brothers Bank had a head start on the Rothschilds, whose European integration (from their arrival on the scene in 1804) propelled them to become formidable opponents. They would eventually overtake Baring as the foremost merchant bank, but that would take decades to achieve.

By the 1860s the old order was changing and control of the business reverted to descendents of Alexander and Henry Baring, cousins in fact, Edward Charles Baring and Henry Bingham Mildmay, when the Bingham name reappears.

By the late 1880s the bank and its new partners was about to face the greatest challenge in its history.

21. Epilogue

I have to admit that I rather stumbled on this story while researching the events of a century later, but decided to try and answer the questions that stemmed from the later research — what factors catapulted John and Francis Baring & Co. to preeminence in the world of banking; who was the senator from Philadelphia and how did his family and that of the Hopes of Scotland and Holland intertwine to produce such formidable results that changed the history of the times? I have presented the facts as accurately as my research resources have allowed and I will leave it to the reader to judge whether I have answered the questions satisfactorily. There are still many loose ends that should be followed up at some stage.

At the same time I have also tried to write two stories superimposed on each other, the evolution of the merchant and banking operations on the one hand and the human story of the people and families that were caught up in the events from the American War of Independence to the Louisiana Purchase on the other.

The answer to the first question, with hindsight, is fairly straightforward. Before the Seven Years War and the American Revolution government finance was all about current income and current expenditure and the taxation (or overseas plundering) to pay for the hostile activities that were so popular at the time. The Dutch banks, in particular Hope & Co., as a result of republican political stability through most of the eighteenth century, and a population interested in and prepared to invest in joint stock enterprises, made the first big leap towards government loans funded by individual investors.

What Francis Baring did above all was recognize this potential and add this activity to the financing of trade rather than trade itself, which was his first big idea. It was not as simple as it sounds and he had some very helpful and influential associates along the way, which led him to the second big idea — the combination of trade and politics.

One of those useful associates was, of course, William Bingham, and we now know who he was. Also key to Francis Baring's success were Henry Hope and his political patrons on both sides of the Atlantic, in particular the Earl of Shelburne and Rufus King in America.

On the assumption that all these assertions are correct, why do we know so little of the individuals concerned? Why is there no Bingham monument in Philadelphia or memorials to Francis and Alexander Baring in Trafalgar Square, or a Henry Hope plaza in Amsterdam?

In the case of William Bingham, he was simply overwhelmed by time and the tide of events. He had made a great deal of money, and the manner in which he flaunted it was at odds with the changing times. His main Federalist political allies such as Washington and Hamilton were gone; John Adams never had much time for him and Thomas Jefferson despised him. He had missed out on the great offices of state and the diplomatic posts, even the governorship of Pennsylvania, at any of which he would probably have excelled; there seems to be no doubt of his political and intellectual ability and his communication skills were faultless.

The death of his wife Anne was the real turning point, though. He left America in haste to be with Alexander Baring and Ann Louisa and his grandchildren, leaving his infant son, William, behind, but he clearly intended to return at some stage, if only to tidy up his business affairs.

Although he left much of his wealth behind in America, it was largely in real estate and the "richest man in America" tag faded over the years. His children were now in England or France, where they became part of British or French history, not that of the United States. Some of his close allies, such as James Wilson and Robert Morris, were also under something of a cloud; Thomas Willing's influence was waning, and Thomas Jefferson and James Madison had no time for him or for the First Bank of the United States that he did so much to create. Philadelphia's social elite, the "Republican Court," was now history, and its queen and the brief Federalist society that went with it was gone.

By the middle of the nineteenth century William and Anne Bingham had become footnotes to the history of the Federal era of the early years of the United States. But without Bingham (and his connections)[1] Alexander Baring would not have acquired the agency of the United States, and without that they may have been overtaken by Rothschild as the world's banker much sooner than they eventually were. In the histories of Barings that have been written so far Bingham is characterized as a "rich senator from Philadelphia" without any real attempt to find out more. The Barings have not been known for acknowledging the influence of non-family members in the success of the enterprise, and as a result William Bingham was effectively assimilated into Baring history.

Francis Baring was already the "first merchant in Europe" when the British government, and in particular William Pitt, recognized his contribution in restructuring the East India Company and in raising money to fight the French, but a Baronetcy was the greatest honor available to a mere merchant in the reign of George III, and you will not see his likeness on a plinth anywhere in London. Control of Baring Brothers Bank effectively passed to Alexander Baring in the early years of the nineteenth century, and he remained the senior partner from 1804 until he retired to his vast estate at the Grange in Hampshire in 1830. He was considered the greatest banker of his generation, and possibly of the nineteenth century. His mastery of the art of government financing and of world trade earned him the peerage in 1835, as Lord Asburton, that his father never acquired. But no statue to Alexander Baring exists either. It was the "political" Barings that emerged from the banking Baring wealth that are captured forever in bronze.

Hope & Co., and in particular Henry Hope, was critical in the emergence of Barings, by introducing them to the opportunity to finance foreign governments as well as world trade. Perhaps in the end they were less cohesive as a family; they had already made a great deal of money, enjoyed the good life, were weakened by the political events in Holland at the end of the eighteenth century, and in the end ran out of family members prepared to carry on. By 1814 the "principle assistant in Mr Hope's counting house," as Alexander Baring was described by Major William Jackson, had swallowed Hope & Co. whole.

But maybe the real reason that history has "lost" these bankers is because politicians tend to write history. Before the War of American Independence, there were merchants, and there were governments with their treasuries. By the time Messrs Baring, Bingham and Hope had financed the Louisiana Purchase there were merchant banks, capable of financing governments. Perhaps the first and certainly the foremost was Baring Brothers Bank, set up in 1762 in London by second-generation German immigrants, and from that day to this the merchant banker, or as we would say today the investment banker, is never far from the center of government.

There seems little doubt that the main characters in this book were clever and resourceful men, and may well have changed the world on their own, but it is fascinating to reflect on the unlikely circumstances that brought them together in such an effective way.

Looking back, the key event for Barings' growth during the nineteenth century was the acquisition of the agency of the new United States. In 1774 very few observers would have tipped John and Francis Baring & Co. to be the foremost merchants and bankers in the world, but in 1774, of course, the United States did not exist.

It would seem that Francis Baring and William Bingham were on some kind of preordained and inevitable collision course; if William Duer, and as result, Henry Knox had not been in financial difficulties during the property fever in America in the 1790s, Bingham would not have had the opportunity to acquire the Maine lands. If Napoleon Bonaparte had not invaded Holland, Hopes and Francis Baring would not have sent Alexander Baring to America to invest the money they were sheltering from the French. If Alexander Baring had not fallen for Ann Louisa Bingham he would have returned to London; without William (now Senator) Bingham he would not have had the introductions to the political heart of the United States government, particularly James Madison and Albert Gallatin, that would lead to the agency of the United States and the Louisiana Purchase. Today it seems quite staggering that Baring, Bingham and Hope could find 11 million dollars in gold (admittedly in staged payments), with absolutely no security other than the trust in Jefferson, Madison and Gallatin that the United States would pay it back.

But then, further back in time, if Thomas Willing and Robert Morris and Henry Hope had not become correspondents of Francis Baring, William Bingham would not have targeted Baring to sell the Maine lands. And without the Revolutionary War Bingham would not have made the fortune in Martinique and elsewhere to be able to speculate so boldly.

And if Benjamin Franklin and Robert Morris had not sent Bingham to Martinique there would have been no fortune to make.

Without the patronage of the Earl of Shelburne, Francis Baring would not have reached the highest echelons of British government, and a whole host of other connections including Rufus King would probably not have been made.

If Shelburne (by then Lansdowne) had not sent Talleyrand (who was escaping to America from the French Terror) with introductions to Bingham in Philadelphia, the two of them would not have been in a position to discuss the wider possibilities of the Louisiana Purchase in 1803.

So how have these events of over 200 years ago changed the course of history, assuming that they have?

Politically, the independence of the United States is the most significant event of the time. The pressure for independence in the American colonies came from merchants concerned about the effect that British measures were having on trade, and lawyers and politicians offended by the infringement of their rights and liberties. The decision to assert independence was made, in the end by politicians, but it was achieved by merchants and soldiers, and the soldiers needed the merchants to finance and supply them.

The loss of the American colonies, disastrous as it seemed at the time for Britain, triggered a new British Empire that would be financed by a new breed of merchant bankers and set in motion the creation of a superpower; and the Louisiana Purchase made sure of it.

As we have seen, in the overall scheme of things, history has not treated our triumvirate of Barings, Bingham and Hope particularly well, but it can be argued that their influence at the time matched the political names that we do remember. They were present and involved, like Forest Gump, in some of the most critical events of the period, but they seem somehow to have been air-brushed away. Perhaps it is because they were merchants and bankers, motivated above all by the creation of wealth, at which they were successful almost without parallel, but as we have seen in very modern times that is not the way to a nation's heart.

Nevertheless, I would suggest that as we look at the shape of the world today we think of those first merchant bankers—let's hear it for Baring, Bingham and Hope!

Appendix A — The Historical Value of Money

The very rough conversions in the year 1800 were:

   £1 = $5 = 25 livres
   $1 = 4 shillings sterling = 5 livres Paris
   £1 = 12.5 fl (Dutch guilders)
   $1 = 2.5 fl

The U.S. dollar was broadly equivalent to the Spanish milled dollar.

The calculation of relative purchasing power is complex. In pure currency inflation terms, to get to a crude comparison with today, dollar values in 1800 can be multiplied by 30, and sterling values by 50 or more.

Sources

The Smithsonian Institution, http://www.smithsonianeducation.org/educators/lesson_plans/revolutionary_money/
The Inflation Calculator, S. Morgan Friedman, http://www.westegg.com/inflation/
Measuring Worth, 2009, http://www.measuringworth.org/exchangeglobal/
Measuring Worth, 2009, the purchasing power of the British pound, http://www.measuringworth.com/ppoweruk/?redirurl=calculators/ppoweruk/
Federal Reserve Bank of Minneapolis, Consumer Price Index Estimate, 1800–2008, http://www.minneapolisfed.org/community_education/teacher/calc/hist1800.cfm

Appendix B — Genealogy

These charts and reports are as accurate as can reasonably established, but there may well be errors that have resulted from transcription over the years. I apologize for these inaccuracies or omissions; the information should be used for general guidance only.

Descendants of John Baring (1697–1748)

Generation No. 1

1. JOHN BARING was born 1697 and died 1748. He married ELIZABETH VOWLER 1729, daughter of JOHN VOWLER and ELIZABETH TOWNSEND. She was born 1702 and died 1766.

    Children of JOHN BARING and ELIZABETH VOWLER:
    i. JOHN BARING, b. 1730; d. 1816.
    ii. THOMAS VOWLER BARING, b. 1733; d. 1758; m. ELIZABETH PARKER, 1758; b. 1731.
    iii. FRANCIS BARING, b. 1740; d. 1810.
    iv. CHARLES BARING, b. 1742; d. 1829.
    v. ELIZABETH BARING, b. 1744; d. 1809.

Generation No. 2

2. JOHN BARING was born 1730 and died 1816. He married ANNE PARKER 1757, daughter of FRANCIS PARKER. She was born 1729 and died 1765.

    Children of JOHN BARING and ANNE PARKER:
    i. JOHN BARING, b. 1760; d. 1837.
    ii. ANNE BARING, b. 1758; d. 1804.
    iii. ELIZABETH BARING, b. 1759; d. 1801.
    iv. FRANCIS BARING, b. 1762; d. 1810.
    v. CHARLOTTE BARING, b. 1763; d. 1833; m. JOHN JEFFERY SHORT, 1786.
    vi. MARGARET BARING, b. 1765; d. 1851.

3. FRANCIS BARING was born 1740 and died 1810. He married HARRIET HERRING 1767, daughter of WILLIAM HERRING and DOROTHY DAWSON. She was born 1750 and died 1804.

    Children of FRANCIS BARING and HARRIET HERRING:
    i. DOROTHY BARING, b. 1771; d. 1839; m. PETER CESAR LABOUCHERE, 1796.
    ii. THOMAS BARING, b. 1772; d. 1848; m. MARY SEALEY, 1794; d. 1846.

iii. ALEXANDER BARING, b. 1774; d. 1848; m. Ann Louisa BINGHAM, 1798; b. 1782; d. 1848.
iv. HENRY BARING, b. 1777; d. 1848; m. (1) MARIA MATILDA BINGHAM, 1802; b. 1783; m. (2) CELIA ANNE WINDHAM, 1825; b. 1803; d. 1874.
v. WILLIAM BARING, b. 1779; d. 1820; m. FRANCES PAULETT THOMPSON, 1810; d. 1877.
vi. GEORGE BARING, b. 1781; d. 1854; m. HARRIET HADLEY D'OXLEY.
vii. HARRIET BARING, d. 1838; m. CHARLES WALL, 1790.
viii. MARIA BARING, m. RICHARD STAINFORTH, 1790.
ix. FRANCES BARING, m. THOMAS READ KEMP, 1808.
x. LYDIA BARING, b. 1787; d. 1843; m. PHILIP LAYCOCK STORY, 1806; d. 1843.

4. CHARLES BARING was born 1742 and died 1829. He married MARGARET GOULD 1767, daughter of WILLIAM GOULD and MARGARET BELFIELD. She was born 1743 and died 1812.

Children of CHARLES BARING and MARGARET GOULD:
i. JACQUETTA BARING, b. 1768; d. 1841; m. SIR STAFFORD HENRY NORTHCOTE, 1791.
ii. FRANCES BARING, b. 1769; d. 1769; m. WILLIAM JACKSON, 1790.
iii. WILLIAM BARING-GOULD, b. 1770; d. 1846; m. DIANA AMELIA SABINE, 1801; d. 1869.
iv. MARY BARING, b. 1772; m. (1) HUGH MAIR; m. (2) J. PELLET.
v. CHARLES BARING, b. 1774; d. 1865; m. (1) SUSAN HEYWOOD (nee COLE), 1797; b. 1763; d. 1845; m. (2) CONSTANCE DENT, 1847; b. 1816; d. 1891.
vi. EMILY BARING, b. 1775; d. 1847; m. SIR SAMUEL YOUNG 1ST BARON FORMOSA.
vii. LUCY BARING, b. 1778; d. 1815; m. THOMAS LOUIS MALLET, 1808.
viii. CAROLINE BARING, b. 1783; d. 1825.

5. BARING was born 1744 and died 1809. She married JOHN DUNNING 1780. He was born 1731 and died 1783.

Child of ELIZABETH BARING and JOHN DUNNING:
i. RICHARD DUNNING, d. 1823.

Descendants of Francis Baring (1740–1810)

Generation No. 1

1. HERRING FRANCIS BARING was born 1740 and died 1810. He married HARRIET 1767, daughter of WILLIAM HERRING and DOROTHY DAWSON. She was born 1750 and died 1804.

Children of FRANCIS BARING and HARRIET HERRING:
i. DOROTHY BARING, b. 1771; d. 1839.
ii. THOMAS BARING, b. 1772; d. 1848.
iii. ALEXANDER BARING, b. 1774; d. 1848.
iv. HENRY BARING, b. 1777; d. 1848.
v. WILLIAM BARING, b. 1779; d. 1820; m. FRANCES PAULETT THOMPSON, 1810; d. 1877.
vi. GEORGE BARING, b. 1781; d. 1854; m. HARRIET HADLEY D'OXLEY.
vii. HARRIET BARING, d. 1838.
viii. MARIA BARING, m. RICHARD STAINFORTH, 1790.
ix. FRANCES BARING, m. THOMAS READ KEMP, 1808.

x. LYDIA BARING, b. 1787; d. 1843; m. PHILIP LAYCOCK STORY, 1806; d. 1843.

Generation No. 2

2. DOROTHY BARING was born 1771 and died 1839. She married PETER CESAR LABOUCHERE 1796.

    Child of DOROTHY BARING and PETER LABOUCHERE:
    i. HENRY LABOUCHERE 1ST BARON TAUNTON, b. 1798; d. 1869.

3. THOMAS BARING was born 1772 and died 1848. He married MARY SEALEY 1794, daughter of CHARLES SEALEY. She died 1846.

    Children of THOMAS BARING and MARY SEALEY:
    i. FRANCIS THORNHILL BARING, b. 1796; d. 1866; m. (1) JANE GREY, 1825; d. 1838; m. (2) ARABELLA HOWARD, 1841; d. 1884.
    ii. THOMAS BARING, b. 1799; d. 1873.
    iii. JOHN BARING, b. 1801; d. 1888; m. AMELIA PORCHER, 1842; d. 1846.
    iv. CHARLES BARING, b. 1807; d. 1879; m. (1) CAROLINE KEMP; d. 1885; m. (2) MARY SEALY, 1830; d. 1840.
    v. CHARLOTTE BARING.
    vi. EMILY BARING.
    vii. FRANCES BARING, b. 1813.
    viii. MARY BARING.
    ix. LYDIA DOROTHY BARING.

4. ALEXANDER BARING was born 1774 and died 1848. He married ANN LOUISA BINGHAM 1798, daughter of WILLIAM BINGHAM and ANNE WILLING. She was born 1782 and died 1848.

    Children of ALEXANDER BARING and ANNE BINGHAM:
    i. WILLIAM BINGHAM BARING, b. 1799; d. 1864; m. (1) HARRIET MONTAGU, 1823; b. 1803; d. 1857; m. (2) LOUISA MACKENZIE, 1858; d. 1903.
    ii. FRANCIS BARING, b. 1800; d. 1868; m. HORTENSE BASSANO, 1832; d. 1882.
    iii. ANNE EUGENIA BARING, b. 1803; d. 1839; m. HUMPHREY ST. JOHN MILDMAY, 1823; b. 1794; d. 1853.
    iv. HARRIET BARING, b. 1804; d. 1892; m. HENRY THYNNE, 1830; b. 1797; d. 1837.
    v. FREDERICK BARING, b. 1806; d. 1868; m. FREDERICA ASHTON, 1831; b. 1804; d. 1884.
    vi. ALEXANDER BARING, b. 1810; d. 1832.
    vii. ARTHUR BARING, b. 1818; d. 1832.
    viii. LOUISA EMILY BARING.
    ix. LYDIA EMILY BARING.
    x. 5TH DAUGHTER BARING.

5. HENRY BARING was born 1777 and died 1848. He married (1) MARIA MATILDA BINGHAM 1802, daughter of WILLIAM BINGHAM and ANNE WILLING. She was born 1783. He married (2) CELIA ANNE WINDHAM 1825. She was born 1803 and died 1874.

    Children of HENRY BARING and MARIA BINGHAM:
    i. HENRY BINGHAM BARING, b. 1804; d. 1901; m. AUGUSTA BRUDENELL BRUCE.
    ii. WILLIAM FREDERICK BARING, b. 1822; d. 1903.
    iii. JAMES BARING.
    iv. ANNA MARIA BARING.

v. FRANCES EMILY BARING, d. 1886.

Children of HENRY BARING and CELIA WINDHAM:
- vi. WILLIAM WINDHAM BARING, b. 1826; d. 1876.
- vii. BULTEEL, 1861; b. 1839; d. 1892.
- viii. ROBERT BARING, b. 1833; d. 1915.
- ix. RICHARD BARING, b. 1833; d. 1883.
- x. CECILIA ANNETTA BARING, b. 1834; d. 1911.
- xi. THOMAS BARING, b. 1839; d. 1923.
- xii. EVELYN BARING 1ST EARL OF CROMER, b. 1841; d. 1917; m. (1) KATHERINE THYNNE; d. 1933; m. (2) ETHEL ERRINGTON; d. 1898.
- xiii. WALTER BARING, b. 1844.

6. HARRIET BARING died 1838. She married CHARLES WALL 1790.

Child of HARRIET BARING and CHARLES WALL:
- i. CHARLES BARING-WALL.

Descendants of Thomas Willing (1731–1821)

Generation No. 1

1. THOMAS WILLING was born 1731 and died 1821. He married ANNE MCCALL 1763.

Children of THOMAS WILLING and ANNE MCCALL:
- i. ANNE WILLING, b. 1764; d. 1801.
- ii. CHARLES WILLING, b. 1766; d. 1799.
- iii. THOMAS MAYNE WILLING, b. 1767; d. 1822.
- iv. ELIZABETH WILLING, b. 1768; d. 1858.
- v. MARY WILLING, b. 1770; m. HENRY CLYMER; b. 1767.
- vi. DOROTHY WILLING, b. 1772.
- vii. GEORGE WILLING, b. 1774.
- viii. RICHARD WILLING, b. 1775; d. 1858; m. ELIZABETH MOORE.
- ix. ABAGAIL WILLING, m. RICHARD PETERS, 1804.
- x. WILLIAM SHIPPEN WILLING, b. 1779.

Generation No. 2

2. ANNE WILLING was born 1764 and died 1801. She married WILLIAM BINGHAM 1780, son of WILLIAM BINGHAM and MARY STAMPER. He was born 1752 and died 1804.

Children of ANNE WILLING and WILLIAM BINGHAM:
- i. ANN LOUISA BINGHAM, b. 1782; d. 1848; m. ALEXANDER BARING, 1798; b. 1774; d. 1848.
- ii. MARIA MATILDA BINGHAM, b. 1783; m. (1) COMTE DE TILLY, 1799; m. (2) HENRY BARING, 1802; b. 1777; d. 1848; m. (3) MARQUIS DE BLAIZEL, 1826.
- iii. WILLIAM BINGHAM, b. 1800; d. 1864; m. MARIE CHARLOTTE DE LOTBENIERE.

3. CHARLES WILLING was born 1766 and died 1799. He married (1) ROSALIND EVANS. He married (2) ANNE HEMPHILL.

Children of CHARLES WILLING and ROSALIND EVANS:
- i. ELIZABETH WILLING.

ii. THOMAS WILLING, d. 1834.
iii. RICHARD WILLING.

Child of CHARLES WILLING and ANNE HEMPHILL:
iv. GEORGE CHARLES WILLING, d. 1834.

4. THOMAS MAYNE WILLING was born 1767 and died 1822. He married JANE NIXON, daughter of JOHN NIXON and ELIZABETH DAVIS.

Children of THOMAS WILLING and JANE NIXON:
i. ELIZABETH WILLING.
ii. CHARLES WILLING.
iii. ANNE WILLING.
iv. EMMA WILLING.

5. ELIZABETH WILLING was born 1768 and died 1858. She married WILLIAM JACKSON 1795 in Christ Church. He was born 1759 and died 1828.

Children of ELIZABETH WILLING and WILLIAM JACKSON:
i. CAROLINE ELIZABETH JACKSON.
ii. WILLIAM JACKSON.
iii. ANNE WILLING JACKSON.
iv. MARY RIGAL JACKSON.

6. GEORGE WILLING was born 1774. He married (1) REBECCA HARRISON BLACKWELL, daughter of ROBERT BLACKWELL and REBECCA HARRISON. She was born 1782. He married (2) MARIA BENEZET 1795, daughter of JOHN BENEZET and HANNAH BINGHAM.

Children of GEORGE WILLING and REBECCA BLACKWELL:
i. MARIA WILLING.
ii. HARRIET WILLING.
iii. REBECCA HARRISON WILLING.
iv. ELIZA MOORE WILLING.
v. DOROTHY FRANCIS WILLING.
vi. CHARLES WILLING.

Descendants of William Bingham (1752–1804)

Generation No. 1

1. WILLIAM BINGHAM was born 1752 and died 1804. He married ANNE WILLING 1780, daughter of THOMAS WILLING and ANNE MCCALL. She was born 1764 and died 1801.

Children of WILLIAM BINGHAM and ANNE WILLING:
i. ANN LOUISA BINGHAM, b. 1782; d. 1848.
ii. MARIA MATILDA BINGHAM, b. 1783.
iii. WILLIAM BINGHAM, b. 1800; d. 1864; m. MARIE CHARLOTTE DE LOTBENIERE.

Generation No. 2

2. ANN LOUISA BINGHAM was born 1782 and died 1848. She married ALEXANDER BARING 1798, son of FRANCIS BARING and HARRIET HERRING. He was born 1774 and died 1848.

Children of ANN BINGHAM and ALEXANDER BARING:

i. WILLIAM BINGHAM BARING, b. 1799; d. 1864; m. (1) HARRIET MONTAGU, 1823; b. 1803; d. 1857; m. (2) LOUISA MACKENZIE, 1858; d. 1903.
ii. FRANCIS BARING, b. 1800; d. 1868; m. HORTENSE BASSANO, 1832; d. 1882.
iii. ANNE EUGENIA BARING, b. 1803; d. 1839; m. HUMPHREY ST. JOHN MILDMAY, 1823; b. 1794; d. 1853.
iv. HARRIET BARING, b. 1804; d. 1892; m. HENRY THYNNE, 1830; b. 1797; d. 1837.
v. FREDERICK BARING, b. 1806; d. 1868; m. FREDERICA ASHTON, 1831; b. 1804; d. 1884.
vi. ALEXANDER BARING, b. 1810; d. 1832.
vii. ARTHUR BARING, b. 1818; d. 1832.
viii. LOUISA EMILY BARING.
ix. LYDIA EMILY BARING.
x. 5TH DAUGHTER BARING.

3. MARIA MATILDA BINGHAM was born 1783. She married (1) COMTE DE TILLY 1799. She married (2) HENRY BARING 1802, son of FRANCIS BARING and HARRIET HERRING. He was born 1777 and died 1848. She married (3) MARQUIS DE BLAIZEL 1826.

Children of MARIA BINGHAM and HENRY BARING:
i. HENRY BINGHAM BARING, b. 1804; d. 1901; m. AUGUSTA BRUDENELL BRUCE.
ii. WILLIAM FREDERICK BARING, b. 1822; d. 1903.
iii. JAMES BARING.
iv. ANNA MARIA BARING.
v. FRANCES EMILY BARING, d. 1886.

Descendants of Alexander Baring (1774—1848)

Generation No. 1

1. ALEXANDER BARING was born 1774 and died 1848. He married ANN LOUISA BINGHAM 1798, daughter of WILLIAM BINGHAM and ANNE WILLING. She was born 1782 and died 1848.

Children of ALEXANDER BARING and ANN BINGHAM:
i. WILLIAM BINGHAM BARING, b. 1799; d. 1864.
ii. FRANCIS BARING, b. 1800; d. 1868.
iii. ANNE EUGENIA BARING, b. 1803; d. 1839.
iv. HARRIET BARING, b. 1804; d. 1892; m. HENRY THYNNE, 1830; b. 1797; d. 1837.
v. FREDERICK BARING, b. 1806; d. 1868; m. FREDERICA ASHTON, 1831; b. 1804; d. 1884.
vi. ALEXANDER BARING, b. 1810; d. 1832.
vii. ARTHUR BARING, b. 1818; d. 1832.
viii. LOUISA EMILY BARING.
ix. LYDIA EMILY BARING.
x. 5TH DAUGHTER BARING.

Generation No. 2

2. WILLIAM BINGHAM BARING was born 1799 and died 1864 He married (1) HARRIET MONTAGU 1823, daughter of GEORGE SANDWICH and LADY LOWRY-

CORRY. She was born 1803 and died 1857. He married (2) LOUISA MACKENZIE 1858. She died 1903.

    Child of WILLIAM BARING and HARRIET MONTAGU:
    i. ALEXANDER BARING, b. 1828; d. 1830.

    Child of WILLIAM BARING and LOUISA MACKENZIE:
    ii. MARY FLORENCE BARING, b. 1860; d. 1902; m. 5TH MARQUESS OF NORTHAMPTON, 1884.

3. FRANCIS BARING was born 1800 and died 1868. He married HORTENSE BASSANO 1832. She died 1882.

    Children of FRANCIS BARING and HORTENSE BASSANO:
    i. ALEXANDER BARING, b. 1835; d. 1889; m. LEONORA DIGBY, 1864; d. 1930.
    ii. DENZIL BARING, b. 1837.
    iii. DAUGHTER BARING.

4. ANNE EUGENIA BARING was born 1803 and died 1839. She married HUMPHREY ST. JOHN MILDMAY 1823, son of HENRY ST. JOHN and JANE MILDMAY. He was born 1794 and died 1853.

    Child of ANNE BARING and HUMPHREY MILDMAY:
    i. HENRY BINGHAM MILDMAY, b. 1828; d. 1905; m. GEORGIANA FRANCES BULTEEL, 1860; b. 1834; d. 1899.

Descendants of Henry Baring (1777–1848)

Generation No. 1

1. HENRY BARING was born 1777 and died 1848. He married (1) MARIA MATILDA BINGHAM 1802, daughter of WILLIAM BINGHAM and ANNE WILLING. She was born 1783. He married (2) CELIA ANNE WINDHAM 1825. She was born 1803 and died 1874.

    Children of HENRY BARING and MARIA BINGHAM:
    i. HENRY BINGHAM BARING, b. 1804; d. 1901; m. AUGUSTA BRUDENELL BRUCE.
    ii. WILLIAM FREDERICK BARING, b. 1822; d. 1903.
    iii. JAMES BARING.
    iv. ANNA MARIA BARING.
    v. FRANCES EMILY BARING, d. 1886.

    Children of HENRY BARING and CELIA WINDHAM:
    vi. WILLIAM WINDHAM BARING, b. 1826; d. 1876.
    vii. EDWARD CHARLES BARING, b. 1828; d. 1897.
    viii. ROBERT BARING, b. 1833; d. 1915.
    ix. RICHARD BARING, b. 1833; d. 1883.
    x. CECILIA ANNETTA BARING, b. 1834; d. 1911.
    xi. THOMAS BARING, b. 1839; d. 1923.
    xii. EVELYN BARING 1ST EARL OF CROMER, b. 1841; d. 1917.
    xiii. WALTER BARING, b. 1844.

Generation No. 2

2. EDWARD CHARLES BARING was born 1828 and died 1897. He married LOUISA EMILY CHARLOTTE BULTEEL 1861, daughter of JOHN BULTEEL and ELIZABETH GREY. She was born 1839 and died 1892.

Appendix B — Genealogy

Children of EDWARD BARING and LOUISA BULTEEL:
- i. ARTHUR BARING, b. 1862.
- ii. JOHN BARING, b. 1863; d. 1929.
- iii. CECIL BARING, b. 1864; d. 1934; m. MAUDE LORRILARD, 1902.
- iv. EVERARD BARING, b. 1865; d. 1932; m. ULRICA DUNCOMBE.
- v. SUSAN BARING, b. 1871; m. JAMES REID.
- vi. MARGARET BARING, b. 1868; d. 1906; m. CHARLES ROBERT SPENCER; b. 1857; d. 1922.
- vii. MAURICE BARING, b. 1874; d. 1945.
- viii. HUGO BARING, b. 1876; d. 1949; m. EVELYN ASHLEY COOPER, 1905; d. 1931.
- ix. RUPERT BARING, b. 1878; d. 1878.
- x. ELIZABETH BARING, m. VALENTINE CHARLES BROWNE (5TH EARL OF KENMERE).

3. EVELYN BARING 1ST EARL OF CROMER was born 1841 and died 1917. He married (1) ETHEL ERRINGTON. She died 1898. He married (2) KATHERINE THYNNE. She died 1933.

Children of EVELYN CROMER and ETHEL ERRINGTON:
- ii. ROWLAND BARING, b. 1877; d. 1953.
- iii. WINDHAM BARING, b. 1880.

Child of EVELYN CROMER and KATHERINE THYNNE:
- i. EVELYN BARING, b. 1903; d. 1973; m. MARY GREY.

Appendix C — Heritage Locations

A remarkable number of the places and buildings that feature in this book still exist in one form or another.

Much of eighteenth-century **Philadelphia** still exists, and in the area around Independence National Park can be seen:

The Powel House, 244 South Third Street, in the Society Hill district, the former home of Anne Willing Bingham's aunt Elizabeth (Powel) and the wedding gift from William Bingham to Alexander and Ann Louisa, is maintained by the Philadelphia Society for the Preservation of Landmarks and is open to the public daily.

The American Philosophical Society is at 104 South Fifth Street, and next door at 105, the Library Hall has Bingham's (replica) statue of Franklin proudly displayed in its alcove, while the original can be seen at the Library Company at 1314 Locust Street. The Historical Society of Pennsylvania is close by at 1300 Locust Street.

The Philadelphia State House, Independence Hall, site of the United States Congress, and Carpenters Hall, briefly the home of the Bank of the United States, are both on Chestnut Street. The site of Gilbert Stuart's house, with a plaque commemorating Anne and William Bingham's commission to Gilbert Stuart for the Lansdowne portrait of George Washington can be found on Fifth Street, close to the statue of Robert Morris which stands slightly forgotten and neglected on its plinth in the park.

The City Tavern (reconstructed but very close to the original) at Second and Walnut, the site of many important meetings, is very much still open for business.

William Bingham's Mansion (at 258-262 South Third Street) is long gone, but much of the area keeps its Georgian ambience.

The Willing Mansion was at Third Street and Willings Alley and was demolished during the nineteenth century, but the Stamper Bingham Blackwell Mansion at 224 Pine Street still exists.

The Penn-built mansion, Lansdown, on the Schuylkill River is gone, but the estate now forms part of Fairmont Park.

In **New York State**, the town of Binghamton marks Bingham's profitable land purchases there.

William Bingham probably started the fashion for summer cottages with the purchase of Bellevue at Blackpoint, Monmouth County, New Jersey. Now called Rumson, the area has remained popular with the rich and famous, including Frank Sinatra and Bruce Springsteen, both of whom have owned property there. Bellevue is gone, but the memory of Anne and William live on in the street names of Bellevue Road, Bingham Avenue, Black Point Road and Bingham Hill.

In the state of **Maine**, the townships of Bingham, Baring, Hope, Mariaville, and Alexander, named on the "Maine Grand Tour," all still exist. General and Lucy Knox's (reconstructed) mansion, Montpelier, at Thomaston is well worth a visit and Gouldsboro is the first sight that Bingham and Baring had of their speculation. It's a shame for Bingham and Baring that tourism would not exist for another hundred years or more, certainly long after the lands were finally disposed of.

The Kennebec tract covers much of today's Somerset County, and Penobscot much of Hancock County. To the north of the Penobscot tract is the border with Canada, the position of which was finally settled by Alexander Baring and Daniel Webster in the Webster-Ashburton Treaty.

In **Martinique** (still very French after a spell under British rule) Fort Royal is now the capital. The volcano of Mont Pelee, so redolent in Bingham's description of his arrival in Martinique on *Reprisal*, is no more — it disappeared and St. Pierre with it when it blew up in 1908.

In **Bermuda**, the grave of Anne Willing Bingham can be visited at St. Peters Church in St. George.

In **Paris**, the seat of French government, in particular the palace of Versailles, can, of course be visited, as can The Hague in Holland. Henry Hope's magnificent mansion Welgelegen has been owned by the Dutch state since 1812 and is now the seat of government of the Province of North Holland.

In **Britain** there is much still to see and visit that provides some of the atmosphere of the period.

In London, Mincing Lane and Cheapside in the City of London are still there of course, but much changed. Devonshire Square, home of Francis Baring, his family and the business from 1793, remains in its Georgian splendor. Number 11 houses the offices of many major businesses today.

Bloomsbury Square, the Binghams' first home in London, remains home to the wealthy. Harley Street is now the preferred address for expensive private medicine, in particular number 30, which today houses many exclusive clinics. Hill Street and Berkeley Square are very desirable addresses indeed.

The house in Manchester Square that captivated the Binghams' imagination (and upon which the Mansion House on Third Street was modelled), now called Hertford House, is the home of the Wallace Collection of Fine Art.

Francis Baring's first "proper" country house, Lee Manor, Old Road, Lewisham, is now a public library.

Francis Baring's pride and joy, Stratton Park in Hampshire, was largely demolished by John Baring, Lord Ashburton in 1960, but the magnificent portico has been retained by its present owners as a vast surreal garden ornament.

Next door is the even grander Grange Estate, acquired by Alexander Baring in his pomp in 1817. His portico is even bigger, an attempt to trump his father-in-law at Lansdown perhaps?

The estate was sold by the Baring family, but re-acquired in 1960s. Lord Ashburton failed to demolish this house after a public outcry and it passed into the protective custody of the Department of the Environment. It still stands but most of its interiors are lost. It is now the home of the "Grange Park Opera."

Further west in Wiltshire Lord Lansdowne's home at Bowood is still very much alive, and although what was called the "Great House" has gone, what remains is pretty impressive. It is still home to the present Lord Lansdowne and is open to the public.

Further west still in Exeter, bits of John Baring's Larkbeare House remain, although it is very much not in the country any more.

And finally in the South Hams of Devon are Flete House, Mothecombe House and the remains of the Membland Estate which feature very strongly in the next phase of the rise of Baring and the ghost of William Bingham. But that is for the next book.

Appendix D — Anne Willing Bingham

There is no doubt that Anne Bingham was a remarkable woman. She grew up in one of Philadelphia's most prominent families, in the mansion built by her grandfather Charles Willing. As a teenager she was a favorite of George Washington as he lodged nearby during the War of Independence.

As we have seen, her marriage to William Bingham came as no great surprise. They were a remarkable pair at a remarkable time.

Their impact on the social life of Philadelphia, America, and indeed of Europe was unmatched at the time, or possibly since. Margaret L. Brown covers their successes in detail in her work, *Mr. & Mrs. William Bingham of Philadelphia, Rulers of the Republican Court.*[1]

But Anne was clearly much more than just Mrs. William Bingham, and the attempts at aristocracy were clearly relished by both of them.

Both Anne and William had solid yeoman roots in England but seemed determined to become aristocrats in a country which was basing itself on a more egalitarian society. They saw no irony in re-creating a mansion in Philadelphia to rival the most opulent in Europe.

But the social microcosm in which they lived was transient, in the end swept away after the short-lived Federal era. What would have become of them in Jefferson's United States we will never know, since Anne died so young and William passed way in England soon afterwards.

There is no doubt that Ann loved to be the center of attention and she seems to have created a sensation wherever she went. Her appearance and style gave the Binghams unrivalled access to the royalty and high society of Europe, which the less charismatic William would not have achieved on his own despite his wealth.

She was completely at ease in the company of her contemporaries, Georgiana Cavendish, Duchess of Devonshire and her namesake Lady Anne Bingham, daughter of Charles Bingham, first Earl of Lucan.

She was well educated and fluent in French, certainly, and it is easy to see why she and the urbane William found life so much easier in Paris than, say, John and Abigail Adams.

Although now largely forgotten, she has left her mark in several ways. It was she that commissioned Gilbert Stuart to paint, and persuaded George Washington to sit for, the famous "teapot" portrait in 1796. This picture was to be a gift for Lord Lansdowne, to whom it was duly sent. The Binghams' had Stuart make a replica for themselves.

Lansdowne was thrilled with the picture and the associated flattery; it did the cause of the Binghams (and indirectly the Barings) a world of good. A plaque in Independence National Park in Philadelphia on the site of Gilbert Stuart's house shows the Lansdowne portrait and a self-portrait of Gilbert Stuart and Washington's words: "Sir, I am under promise to Mrs. Bingham to sit for you tomorrow at 9 o'clock, and wishing to know if it be convenient to you that I should do so, and it shall be at your house."[2]

It is said that Washington was wearing an ill-fitting set of false teeth, and Gilbert Stuart produced the distorted view of his face we see today. Stuart was apparently no great respecter of most of his subjects.

Apart from Bingham's copy of the Lansdowne portrait, Stuart made several more copies, generating a considerable amount of money in the process. One copy hangs in the East Room at the White House, and has been the property of the mansion since 1800. It is the only object known to have remained in the White House since that year apart from a period after 1814 when the British burnt it down. The first lady, Dolley Madison, had refused to abandon the picture as she fled. She wrote to her sister on the day of the fire:

> Our kind friend, Mr. Carrol has come to hasten my departure, and is in a very bad humor with me because I insist on waiting until the large picture of Gen. Washington is secured, and it requires to be unscrewed from the wall. The process was found to be too tedious for those perilous moments; I have ordered the frame to be broken, and the canvas taken out; it is done, — and the precious placed in the hands of two gentlemen of New York, for safe keeping. And now, dear sister, I must leave this house, or the retreating army will make me a prisoner in it, filling up the road I am directed to take.[3]

It was not the first time that Stuart had worked for the Binghams; in 1785 during the Grand Tour, Bingham had sensed that a Stuart portrait of him and his family would be very effective in raising their profile. The painting was never finished, but eventually made its way back to America. Stuart was also engaged to paint family portraits at Lansdown House in 1796.

What happened to Anne Bingham's likeness from the Stuart portrait is

Opposite: The "Lansdowne" portrait of George Washington, by Gilbert Stuart, 1796, commissioned by Anne Bingham as a gift to Lord Lansdowne (**National Portrait Gallery, Smithsonian Institution Art Resource, New York**).

lost in the mists of time, but there is a strong view amongst numismatists that it is her likeness (as Miss Liberty) that made its way onto the first federal coinage of the United States. She was certainly an attractive woman and William Bingham was a key director of the Bank of the United States. These "draped bust" coins were in circulation from 1795, the last coin being minted in 1808, and are now prized by collectors across the world.[4]

Apart from Gilbert Stuart, Anne and William Bingham were patrons to other artists, in particular the engraver and enamellist William Russell Birch. Birch, born in Warwick, England, had become a very successful engraver, working closely with Joshua Reynolds. On the death of Joshua Reynolds, Birch (who had family connections in America — his uncle Thomas Russell (1696–1760) was among the founders of the first iron forge in America, together with George Washington's father and half brother) emigrated to Philadelphia in 1794 to make his fortune.

He introduced himself to the Binghams with a letter from Benjamin West (who painted the Francis Baring portrait in this book). William Bingham took Birch into his employment and he established a workshop to produce enamel portraits, the first of which were of William and Anne. Birch worked with Gilbert Stuart on his return to Philadelphia at the end of 1794, and between them they made substantial sums from reproducing the Lansdowne portrait of George Washington.[5]

Anne Bingham was not just a pretty face and could hold her own in political discussion, and she was a firm believer in the rights of women, like her friend Abigail Adams. The two knew each other well and although Abigail was attracted to Anne's charm initially, in the end that turned to dislike as the Binghams flaunted their wealth.

Also attracted to Anne Bingham from before her marriage to William Bingham to her death in 1801 was Thomas Jefferson. Anne had corresponded with Thomas Jefferson for some time and they had a warm and friendly relationship, particularly after the death of Jefferson's wife in 1782. They saw each other in Paris when Jefferson was American minister. On her departure for England and then America in 1786, Thomas Jefferson urged her to write to him within 12 months. On February 7, 1787, he wrote to her in Philadelphia to remind her of her pledge "to tell me truly and honestly whether you do not find the tranquil pleasures of America preferable to the empty bustle of Paris."[6]

Draped bust dollar of 1795, believed to be the image of Anne Willing Bingham.

Anne duly replied on June 1, 1787. In the only letter written by Anne Bingham known to have survived she suggests that she still prefers the style, glamour and greater emancipation of women in (pre-revolutionary) Paris to America's "tranquil pleasures." She signs off her letter, with a request for "another book of fashions" with a gentle rebuke. "It is time I bid you adieu, but remember this first of June I am constant to my former opinion, nor can I believe that any length of time will change it. I am determined to have some merit in your eyes, if not for taste and judgement, at least for consistency."

Despite Anne's wrong answer in Thomas Jefferson's view, he wrote to her again on March 11, 1788, enclosing some theatrical pieces and fashion books. "A gentleman going to Philadelphia furnishes me the occasion.... You will change your opinion, dear Madam, and come over to mine in the end."[7]

Had more of her letters survived we would know much more about her, perhaps, but she has left her mark in perpetuity through her descendents in English aristocracy and public life. See Appendix E for more detail.

Appendix E — Baring and Bingham's Aristocracy

The impact that the Baring family (and indirectly the Bingham family) have made on the English aristocracy is quite astonishing.

Francis Baring was made a baronet by a grateful William Pitt in 1793. His eldest son, Thomas (1772–1848), became the second baronet on the death of his father. His son Francis Thornhill (1796–1866) went a stage further to become the first Baron Northbrook (he was Britain's viceroy to India). His son Thomas (1826–1904) inherited the title as the first Earl Northbrook. His son Francis George (1850–1929) became the second Earl on the death of his father.

Francis Baring's sister, Elizabeth (1744–1809), married John Dunning in 1780. He was created first Lord Ashburton (of the first creation) shortly before his death in 1783. Their son Richard inherited the title as the second Lord Ashburton. This title became extinct on his death in 1823.

Francis Baring's second son Alexander (1774–1848) became the first Baron Ashburton (of the second creation) for his services to the British government. Alexander Baring and Ann Louisa Bingham's son William Bingham Baring (1799–1865) inherited the title as the second Baron Ashburton and married Harriet Montague, the daughter of the Earl of Sandwich. Their son Alexander died in infancy and the title passed to William Bingham Baring's brother Francis (1800–1868) as the third Baron Ashburton. William Bingham Baring married a second time to Louisa Mackenzie, and their daughter Mary married William Compton, the fifth Marquess of Northampton.

One of Alexander Baring and Ann Louisa Bingham's five daughters, Harriet, married Henry Frederick Thynne (1797–1837), the third Marquis of Bath (of Longleat House) in 1830.

Francis and Harriet Baring's third son Henry Baring (1776–1848) married Ann Louisa Bingham's sister Maria Matilda in 1802. They had three sons and two daughters. Henry Baring divorced Maria in 1823 and married Cecilia Windham in 1825, at which point he styled himself as Henry Baring of

Cromer Hall. Their offspring created no less than three peerages between them. Their second son Edward Charles Baring (1828–1897) later became the first Baron Revelstoke. Their sixth son Evelyn (1841–1917) was one of Britain's most eminent politicians and became the first Earl of Cromer. He married Ethel Errington and their first son Rowland inherited the title as the second Earl of Cromer. Evelyn Baring married a second time, Lady Katherine Thynne (see above!). Their son, also Evelyn, married the eldest daughter of the fifth Earl Grey, Lady Mary Grey (who inherited the estate of Howick in 1963). Evelyn had a distinguished career in the British Colonial Service and became the first Lord Howick of Glendale in 1960.

The titles of Northbrook, Ashburton, Northampton, Bath, Cromer, Revelstoke and Howick continue to this day.

The daughter of Edward Charles Baring (1828–1897) and Louisa Emily Bulteel, Susan, married Charles, the sixth Earl Spencer (1839–1892). Lady Diana Spencer (1961–1997) was their great-great-granddaughter and mother to William and Harry Windsor.

Source

The principal source of information for Appendix E is www.thepeerage.com, an online genealogical survey of the peerage of Britain.

Appendix F — William Bingham and the *Pilgrim* Affair

William Bingham's success at establishing a network of privateers operating from Martinique almost led to his undoing.

In January 1779 the Massachusetts privateer *Pilgrim* brought the ship *Hope* into St. Pierre as a prize, but she was carrying Danish papers and her crew appeared to speak only Danish. She was in the process of being seized by the prize master when Bingham became aware of the situation. As a neutral vessel the seizure was illegal and Bingham returned her to the Danish captain. The cargo was not so lucky, and, being perishable, was sold on General Bouillé's orders. A proportion of the proceeds was returned to the captain, the remainder being held until such time as Congress could determine the legality of the situation.

Unknown to Bingham at the time, the owners of *Pilgrim* filed a lawsuit against him personally for the loss of what they considered to be legitimate prize cargo and obtained a judgment against him which attached to his property in Massachusetts and Pennsylvania.

Congress showed no signs of assisting Bingham, perhaps because his lawyer in Boston, William Tudor, subsequently confirmed that *Hope* was carrying two sets of papers and probably was British, and therefore a legitimate prize. Bingham raised the problem with John Jay in December of 1779, who wrote to president Samuel Huntington, but no further progress was made until his return to Philadelphia in the spring of 1780, when he submitted a report and requested a hearing. Congress upheld Bingham's actions in restoring *Hope* to its owner, and agreed to indemnify him against current and future litigation, and requested the court in Massachusetts to lift the charges on his property.

Bingham could have been forgiven for believing that the matter was over, but he was shocked to discover 12 years later, in 1793, that the case against him was still very much alive, and attempts were being made to make distraints on his property, which after his Maine acquisitions were now very substantial indeed. Again he asked Congress for assistance and President Washington instructed the attorney general to defend the suit. Bingham was asked to put up $30,000 as security at a time when his cash flow was critical. Despite the intervention of the attorney general, Bingham was ordered to pay (conveniently) damages of $30,000 plus costs, but this judgment was again reversed two years later in 1795.

The Cabots, owners of the *Pilgrim*, obtained yet another judgment in their favor three years later, by default (the district attorney in Massachusetts had failed to defend the suit as instructed), this time for $37,000. Bingham engaged Fisher Ames and Harrison Gray Otis to defend this latest claim, but the Cabots now introduced the conclusive evidence of the British ownership of *Hope*, which they had apparently withheld in 1793. Bingham believed that the Cabots were attempting to acquire his Maine land by skulduggery.

The matter was unresolved after Anne Bingham's death. Before leaving for England (with the Barings) and with a judgment of almost $40,000 against him, he put his side of affairs in a pamphlet. His counsel, Fisher Ames, advised that the case was lost; Bingham feared that if he paid up he would have little chance of recovering the debt from a Republican Congress.

Unfortunately, William Bingham took his worries over injustice of the *Pilgrim* Affair to the grave, as it was still unresolved in 1804.

It was left to his wife's nephew and trustee of the Bingham estate, Charles Willing Hare, to settle Cabot's claim of $37,000 in full. There is no record of Congress honoring the resolutions of June 20, 1780, and indemnifying him (or his estate) against the claim for the lost cargo of flour.

Sources

Alberts, Robert C. *The Golden Voyage: The Life and Times of William Bingham, 1752–1804* (Boston; Houghton Mifflin, 1969), p. 520.
Allis, Frederick S. *William Bingham's Maine Lands, 1790–1820* (Boston: Colonial Society of Massachusetts, 1954), pp. 1125, 1127–38, 1174.
Bingham, William. Letter to Congress, February 22, 1779.
Brown, Margaret L. "William Bingham, Agent of the Continental Congress in Martinique." *Pennsylvania Magazine of History and Biography* 61 (January 1937), pp. 83–87.
The full texts of the *Pilgrim* cases, *Bingham v Cabot*, are available online from the U.S. Supreme Court: U.S. Supreme Court Cases, *Bingham v Cabot*, 3 U.S.19, 1795 (http://supreme.justia.com/us/3/19/case.html); U.S. Supreme Court Cases, *Bingham v Cabot*, 3 U.S. 382, 1798 (http://supreme.justia.com/us/3/382/case.html).
See also *Mifflin v Bingham*, 1788.

Chapter Notes

The following source abbreviations are used in the chapter notes that follow; full citations are also found in the Bibliography.

AB Alexander Baring.

AH American history database, *http://www.americanheritage.com/*.

ALLIS Allis, Frederick S. *William Bingham's Maine Lands, 1790–1820.* 2 vols. Boston: Colonial Society of Massachusetts, 1954.

APS American Philosophical Society, Philadelphia, *http://www.amphilsoc.org/*.

AR American Revolution, the Preservation Society for the American Revolution, *http://www.americanrev.org/*.

BBA The Baring Archive, London, *http://www.baringarchive.org.uk*.

BBO Orbell, John. *Baring Brothers & Co, a History to 1939.* London: Baring Brothers, 1985.

BBZ Zeigler, Philip. *The Sixth Great Power, Barings 1762–1929.* London: Collins, 1988.

BDUS Biographical Directory of the United States Congress, *http://bioguide.congress.gov/biosearch/biosearch.asp*.

BFM Morgan, Edmund S. *Benjamin Franklin.* New Haven, CN: Yale University Press, 2002.

CH Colonial Hall.com — Biographies of the United States Founding Fathers, *http://colonialhall.com/index_t1.php*.

CIA Central Intelligence Agency, *https://www.cia.gov/index.html*.

COE Christie, I. R. *Crisis of Empire, Great Britain and the American Colonies, 1754–1783.* New York: W. W. Norton, 1966.

CSC The Committee of Secret Correspondence of the Continental Congress.

DRO Devon Record Office, Exeter and Plymouth, *http://www.devon.gov.uk/record_office.htm*.

EB 1911 Encyclopaedia Britannica, Cambridge University Press, now in the public domain.

ECE Ashton, T. S. *An Economic History of England: The Eighteenth Century.* London: Routledge, 2005.

FA Famous Americans—virtual American biographies, *http://www.famousamericans.net/*.

FB Francis Baring.

FP Young, Eleanor. *Forgotten Patriot: Robert Morris.* New York: Macmillan, 1950.

GV Alberts, Robert C. *The Golden Voyage: The Life and Times of William Bingham, 1752–1804.* Boston: Houghton Mifflin, 1969.

HAPJ Johnson, Paul. *A History of the American People.* London: Weidenfeld & Nicholson, 1997.

HBAT Hidy, R. W. *The House of Baring in American Trade and Finance.* Cambridge, MA: Harvard University Press, 1949.

HSP   Historical Society of Pennsylvania, Philadelphia, *http://www.hsp.org/*.

LCP   The Library Company, Philadelphia, *http://www.librarycompany.org/*.

LCRK   King, Charles R., ed., *The Life and Correspondence of Rufus King*. 6 vols. New York Putnam, 1894–1900.

LLI   The Lilly Library, Indiana University, Bloomington, Indiana, *http://www.indiana.edu/~liblilly/overview/history_in.shtml*.

LOC   Library of Congress, Washington, D.C., *http://www.loc.gov/index.html*.

LODC   Library of Congress, Letters of Delegates to Congress, 1774–1789, Law Library of Congress, *http://memory.loc.gov/ammem/amlaw/lwdg.html*, *http://memory.loc.gov/ammem/amlaw/lwjc.html*, *http://memory.loc.gov/ammem/collections/continental/*, *http://memory.loc.gov/ammem/amlaw/lawhome.html*.

LPF   Fleming, Thomas. *The Louisiana Purchase*. Hoboken, NJ: John Wiley, 2003.

LW   Clark, William Bell. *Lambert Wickes: Sea Raider and Diplomat*. New Haven, CT: Yale University Press, 1932.

MBA   Brown, Margaret L. "William Bingham, Agent of the Continental Congress in Martinique." *Pennsylvania Magazine of History and Biography* 61 (Jan. 1937): pp. 54–87.

MBM   Brown, Margaret L. "William Bingham, Eighteenth Century Magnate." *Pennsylvania Magazine of History and Biography* 61, no. 4 (Oct. 1937): pp. 387–434.

MBP   Brown, Margaret L. "Mr. & Mrs. William Bingham of Philadelphia, Rulers of the Republican Court." *Pennsylvania Magazine of History and Biography* 61, no. 3 (July 1937): pp. 286–324.

MHS   Massachusetts Historical Society, Boston.

ND   Newman Dorman, W. A. "The Second Troop of Philadelphia Cavalry." *Pennsylvania Magazine of History and Biography* 45, July 1921: pp. 257–291, vol. 46, January 1922, pp. 57–77, April 1922, pp. 154–172; vol. 49, January 1925, pp. 75–94.

NP   Northbrook Papers at the Baring Archive, London.

PC   The Peerage.com — genealogical survey of the peerage of Britain, *www.thepeerage.com*.

PG   Pennsylvania Gazette.

PHL   Haymer, Philip May, George C. Rogers, and David R. Chestnut, eds. *The Papers of Henry Laurens*. Columbia: University of South Carolina Press, 1972.

PHLP   Laurens, Henry. *The Papers of Henry Laurens*. Laurens Papers Project, Department of History, Columbia: University of South Carolina.

PHMB   *Pennsylvania Magazine of History and Biography* *http://www.hsp.org/default.aspx?id=68*.

RDC   Wharton, Francis, ed. *The Revolutionary Diplomatic Correspondence of the United States*. 6 vols. Washington, D.C.: Government Printing Office, 1889.

RGM   Gilmor, Robert. *Memoir or sketch of the history of Robert Gilmor as derived from his books and papers in the possession of his eldest son, and from the conversations with his father and mother on the subject at various times*. Baltimore: privately printed, 1840.

RGS   Gilmor, Robert. *Memorandums Made in a Tour of the Eastern United States in 1797*. Boston: Bulletins of the Boston Public Libraries, 1893.

RMPF   Oberholzer, Ellis Paxton. *Robert Morris: Patriot and Financier*. New York: Macmillan, 1903.

RR   From Revolution to Reconstruction — a hypertext on American history from the colonial period until modern times, University of Groningen, *http://www.let.rug.nl/usa/index.htm*.

SC   The Secret Committee of the Continental Congress.

SCON   Ferris, Robert G., and James H. Charleton, *The Signers of the Constitution*. Flagstaff, AZ: Interpretive Publications Inc., 2001.

SH   Howard, James I. *Seth Harding: A Naval Picture of the Revolution*. New Haven, CT: Yale University Press, 1930.

SHE   Trevelyan, G. M. *A Shortened History of England*. London: Penguin Books, 1942.

SNF   Buist, Marten G. *At Spes Non Fracta*. Amsterdam: Bank Mees & Hope, 1974.

SSC   Wright, Robert K., Jr., Morris K. MacGregor, Jr. *Soldier-Statesmen of the Constitution*. Center of Military History, United States Army, Washington, D.C. 1987, http://www.history.army.mil/books/RevWar/ss/ss-fm.htm.

SWA   *Supplying Washington's Army*, United States Army Center of Military History, Washington, D.C., http://www.history.army.mil/books/RevWar/risch/rischfm.htm.

SWI   Auger, Helen. *The Secret War of Independence*. New York: Duell, Sloan and Pearce, 1955.

TAM   Teaching American History — Ashbrook Center for Public Affairs, Ashland University, Ohio, http://teachingamericanhistory.org/.

TNA   Chastellux, Francois Jean. *Travels in North America, 1780, 1781, 1782*. London, 1787.

UDL   University of Delaware Library, Newark, Delaware.

UKNA   UK National Archives, Kew, London, http://www.archives.gov/.

UPENN   University of Pennsylvania Archives, Philadelphia, http://www.archives.upenn.edu/.

USH   U.S. History.org — the Independence Hall Association in Philadelphia, http://www.ushistory.org/index.html.

USNA   U.S. National Archives, Washington, D.C., http://www.archives.gov/research/alic/index.html.

WB   William Bingham.

WBP   Sawtelle, William Otis. *William Bingham of Philadelphia and His Maine Lands*. Philadelphia: Genealogical Society of Pennsylvania, 1926.

WGW   Fitzpatrick, John C., ed. *The Writings of George Washington*. 39 vols. Washington, D.C.: Government Printing Office, 1931–1944.

WHS   Whitehouse Historical Society, Washington.

WIPJ   Jackson, Joseph. "Washington in Philadelphia," a paper read to the Historical Society of Pennsylvania on March 14, 1932, Philadelphia. *Pennsylvania Magazine of History and Biography* 56, 1932.

WL   Winterthur Library, at the Winterthur Museum and Country Estate, Delaware, http://www.winterthur.org/about/library.asp?sub=whats_new.

WSS   Conway, Stephen. *War, State and Society in Mid-Eighteenth Century Britain and Ireland*, New York: Oxford University Press, 2006.

Chapter 1

Chapter 1, "Early Days in England," draws on various sources, including *Baring Brothers & Co., Ltd., a History to 1939* (BBO) by John Orbell, and *The Sixth Greatest Power* (BBZ) by Philip Ziegler.

1. BBO, pp. 1–2, BBZ, pp. 13–14. Just 70 years earlier in Bremen, Germany, Johann Baring was born to Pastor Doctor Franz Baring and Rebecca Vogels. Doctor Franz followed in a long line of Protestant clerics stretching back to the end of the fifteenth century. Franz (1656–1697), the youngest son of Johann (1620–1676) and Anna Hildebrand, became a professor of theology and married Rebecca Vogels, the daughter of one of Bremen's leading wool merchants, and by doing so made the first significant step in the creation of the Baring banking dynasty.

2. In 1717 £500 sterling was a considerable sum of money. Appendix A attempts to convert historic sums into today's equivalents. During the eighteenth century Exeter

was a much more significant port than it is today.

3. John Vowler (1667–1748) was born in Bell Air, Heavitree, Exeter, son of another John Vowler (1620–1697). They are described in Land Transfers in the Devon Record Office as "grocers," and apparently with substantial property. They were business associates of Edmund Cock (the elder and the younger), described as "fullers" (the process of thickening cloth, as in serge). Johann Baring was sent to Exeter to work with Edmund Cock in 1717, and it is likely that his business was incorporated into the Baring enterprise (DRO).

John Vowler married Elizabeth Townsend (1679–1703). Their daughter Elizabeth Vowler (1702–1766) married Johann Baring (1697–1748) about 1729. John Vowler settled a total of £20,000 on Elizabeth (BBZ, p. 15).

4. BBO, p. 2.

5. BBZ, p. 16.

6. Thomas Vowler Baring and John Baring married the daughters of wealthy land owner Francis Parker of Blagdon, Devon, in 1757.

7. Samuel Touchet (d. 1763) is described by Ziegler (BBZ, p. 18) as a leading Manchester and West Indian merchant (of Aldermanbury Square, London). The relatively innocuous term "Manchester and West Indian merchant" actually describes the triangular slave trade of the eighteenth and nineteenth centuries. Slave-grown cotton from the West Indies was woven in Lancashire, England, into "coarse checks" (cloth with a pattern of crossed line) which was traded in Africa for slaves who were shipped back to the West Indian plantations (later American plantations) in the same vessels, thus completing the triangle and contributing immensely to Manchester's prosperity.

Samuel Touchet was from a family which was prospering from this trade. Samuel moved to London, sometime around 1740, representing the family business, and by the mid 1750s was apparently a very successful merchant in the textile trade with the Continent, the West and East Indies, America and West Africa (Senegal and Sierra Leone). He also became a ship-owner, insurance broker, speculator in naval prizes (by Royal Commission), sugar merchant and slave trader.

Francis Baring joined him in 1755, by good fortune, perhaps, and to learn the trade. There can be little doubt that the young Francis Baring learned a lot more than the textile trade in his time in Aldermanbury Square (as with all apprenticeships at the time, Elizabeth Baring would have paid Touchet to train Francis; as a quid pro quo, however, Touchet contributed to the original share capital of John and Francis Baring & Co. (BBO, p. 3).

During the Seven Years War he became increasingly close to the British government, first as a contractor supplying the garrisons of an expanding empire (including the American colonies) and later lending money to the treasury. He became a member of Parliament in 1761.

Touchet was acutely aware of the need to bring down costs in textile production, to maximize profits and fend off competition from the Orient. He became involved in the first "cotton mill" (mechanized cotton spinning) at Edward Cave's mill on the river Nene at Northampton in 1755. The mill used the first roller spinning machinery patented by Lewis Paul in 1738 (*Source: Cotton-spinning in Northampton: Edward Cave's Mill, Northamptonshire Past and Present, 1996*). Lewis' machines appear not to have been profitable, and Touchet terminated his involvement in 1755, at the time of Francis Baring's arrival in London. It is not unreasonable to speculate that this technological failure may have been a factor in Baring's attitude to the risks associated with new technology. (Richard Arkwright perfected and patented his Water Frame in 1769).

Touchet was accused repeatedly of trying to secure monopolies on materials, particularly the import of cotton yarn. Together with partner Joseph Hague he was summoned before a Parliamentary Committee examining the complaints of the northern weavers. Although no action was taken, Touchet's business crashed spectacularly in 1763 shortly after the formation of John and Francis Baring & Co. He escaped the normal penalties of bankruptcies, with further criticism, as a result of Parliamentary privilege.

Despite his considerably straightened circumstances Touchet maintained his influence in high government circles, in particular with Henry Fox and Charles Townshend. In the spring of 1767 Touchet advised Townshend on the specific items that would attract the most revenues in the much-hated "Townshend Duties" that played such a significant part in the revolution of the American colonies.

In 1766 Touchet was granted rights to a plantation in Florida which were never taken up. He was a close associate of merchant and member of Parliament Anthony Bacon.

Touchet's colorful life came to an end in May 1773 when he hanged himself.

Sources: ECE, Samuel Touchet's Florida Plantation, 1771, James C. Frazier.

8. Nathaniel Paice is described by John Orbell (BBO, p. 3) as the Baring family representative in London from as early as 1717, the date that Johann Baring first appeared in Exeter. He may well also therefore have been the agent for the Vogel's family business (BBO, p. 5).

Paice is described in Kent's Directory as a director of the South Sea Company of Cloak Lane, London, in 1740, and in 1763 in The London Directory as "a New York merchant and director of the South Sea Company" of Cloak Lane, College Hill, London. He was a correspondent of the firm of Austin, Laurens & Appleby of Charlestown, South Carolina, in the West Indian trade (*Source:* Laurens, *The Papers of Henry Laurens*). Henry Laurens, later president of the Continental Congress and peace negotiator, was the father of John Laurens, who was sent by Congress to assist Franklin in negotiating French loans in 1781.

On his retirement in 1763 Paice suggested that Francis Baring take over his merchant business to form the basis of John and Francis Baring & Co.

9. BBO, p. 5.
10. BBO, p. 5.
11. BBZ, p. 20, Elizabeth Baring to Francis Baring, March 1766, NP.
12. Fate of Samuel Touchet — he went bust.
13. BBZ, p. 21.

Nevertheless, cumulative profits for the years 1762 to 1765 amounted to just £1,377, and a disastrous "adventure" in 1766 led to a write-off of £3,091, leading to a cumulative deficit that remained on the books until 1770 (BBZ, p. 373, BBO, p. 5).

14. BBZ, p. 27.
15. PC.
16. BBO, p. 7.
17. W. English, *The Textile Industry* (London: Longmans, 1931).
18. BBO, p. 7.

Charles Baring (1742–1829) was born in Exeter in 1742, the youngest son of Johann (John) Baring and Elizabeth Vowler. He was sent to London with his elder brother Francis in 1755 for his education. He was recalled to Exeter in 1758 when Thomas Vowler Baring died suddenly at the age of 25, to help John Baring and their mother, Elizabeth, in the running of the manufactories, leaving Francis Baring in London with Samuel Touchet.

Francis Baring was scathing about his younger brother in Exeter, claiming that Charles "was not calculated for the management of the house, an establishment which depended on steady order and attention, ill suited to his disposition of catching every new project that offered." Charles had travelled in Spain and Portugal, journeys which had proven expensive and unsuccessful. "This is not stated as a reflection on his intention, but solely to impeach the want of commercial knowledge and judgement, which he has manifested through life." Unsuccessful trips to the Continent were one thing, but interfering in London was quite another, having "interfered too much with the house in London, but by degrees he formed partnerships, connexions and speculations, of a wild, strange, incoherent description; and what is particularly unfortunate, not one of them has proved successful" (BBZ, p. 22, NP).

Elder brother John also heaped scorn on Charles, writing later in a family history: "The weakness, the capriciousness, the greediness, the shabbiness of Charles are so abominable it is hoped no occasion will arise again to mention him" (BBZ, p. 22, NP).

The relationship between Charles and John and Francis deteriorated to the extent that the three bothers signed an agreement that if one of them died £2,000 should be deducted from Charles' capital in the business to account for his speculations (BBZ, p. 23, NP).

Francis Baring felt, rightly or wrongly,

that Charles was making demands on family capital that could better be employed in London. "Your unceasing projects, by absorbing so large a part of the family and of the Bank, hung as a dead weight and impeded my progress for years" (BBZ, p. 23, Francis Baring to Charles Baring, NP).

Charles, no wilting violet himself, would have none of this, claiming in effect that the London house would fail and that Francis would have to fall back on Exeter.

While Francis Baring was struggling to establish himself in London, John and Charles Baring also became financiers in their own right by creating the Devonshire Bank in Exeter in 1770.

At this distance in time it is difficult to assign blame in the breakdown of the relationship between Charles and his elder brothers. Certainly Charles might have felt aggrieved at Francis' preferment by the family as far as his education was concerned. Francis also seems very single-minded in his intention to get on. Change, it appears, was inevitable, and the arrival in London of "three low persons, projectors, who had offered a plan for spinning wool by machinery" was the last straw. The partnership between Exeter and London was ended in 1776 (BBO, p. 7).

Francis Baring had seen Samuel Touchet's difficulty with spinning cotton by machinery a few years earlier, which appears to have created a lifelong aversion to the effects of the Industrial Revolution, and a fear that pervaded Barings Bank for generations to come.

Richard Arkwright had patented his water frame in 1769, precipitating an enormous growth of the textile business in the new mills in Lancashire. It is fascinating to reflect on the possibility of Charles and his "low projectors" actually being successful in their bid to spin wool by machines in Devon, which may then have become the woollen textile capital of Britain and its empire. Of course it didn't happen and Exeter continued to hand-make its serges for a market that would dwindle and eventually disappear.

Charles Baring married Margaret Gould, daughter of William Drake Gould and Margaret Belfield, in 1767. On the death of her brother Edward Gould in 1788 Margaret inherited the property and estates of that family. They had eight children, of whom William Baring and Charles Baring have continuing significance. William Baring (on the condition that he adopted the name Gould, becoming William Baring Gould) inherited the Lew Trenchard estates, and his grandson was Sabine Baring-Gould, prolific writer of novels and hymns (notably "Onward Christian Soldiers") and rector of the family parish of Lew Trenchard.

Their second son, Charles Baring (1774–1865), having not inherited the family estate, had to make his own way in life. We will hear more of him later.

Charles Baring's fortunes remained chaotic (the Lew Trenchard estates having jumped a generation to William Baring Gould). He tried for the Parliamentary seat of Tiverton, but was rejected. He continued to indulge in a series of business ventures, including Barings, Short and Cole, formed in 1788. The partnership of John and Charles Baring continued until 1801 when Francis was required to assist in unwinding their affairs. By 1801 Charles' financial affairs had apparently returned to form and Francis had to make him a loan to keep him going.

Charles (less arrogant than 25 years earlier) claimed, "You are exalted with every success, I am of late oppressed with many troubles" (BBZ, p. 24, NP). Francis' withering response was: "You never did understand your own Character and your own situation. We have a very long test of your conduct in the almost monstrous management of the original and chief dependence of the Baring family and you are disposed to impute your want of success to the want of luck.... In this I cannot agree with you as there is not a single instance which has come to my knowledge in which ultimate miscarriage was not to be discovered at the outset."

Margaret Baring died in 1812 and Charles Baring in 1829.

John Baring (1730–1816) was the first child of John Baring and Elizabeth Vowler, born in 1730. As the eldest he took the senior role in running the Baring business after the death of his father in 1748. Thomas, the second son, was also brought into the business while Charles and Francis were sent to London. John spent a period on the Continent developing correspondents and contacts for the business, returning in 1755 (BBO p. 2).

Thomas Vowler Baring died suddenly in 1758, and as a result Charles was recalled from his studies in London to assist John with the running of the business.

John appears to have enjoyed the trappings of the family wealth and was comfortable in the role of country gentleman. He acquired the Mount Radford estate and its fine Georgian house in 1755. From 1758 the day-to-day running of the business was in the hands of Charles and their mother Elizabeth. It seems hardly surprising that the relationship between Charles and his elder brothers became so strained.

John married very well to Anne Parker (daughter of Francis Parker of Blagdon) in 1757, (while Thomas married her sister Elizabeth in 1758). The Parker family owned and still owns substantial property in Devon.

John Baring and Anne Parker had five children, Charlotte, John, Francis, Anne Elizabeth and Margaret. Charlotte Baring married John Short of Bickham (a country estate near Exeter), who had business connections with John and Charles Baring & Co.

John Baring tried for Parliament for Honiton in 1774 but was defeated by fellow Exeter merchant and second-generation émigré John Duntze. Stung by this defeat he contested Exeter in 1776 when Duntze's son-in-law John Cholwich stood on a platform claiming, among other things, that the Baring influence was too great in the city. John Baring won the election at great personal financial cost (£6,000). His re-election in 1790 cost him even more (£10,000). His opponent, Sir Charles Bampfylde, cried foul, raising a petition claiming bribery and corruption. Baring won the day when the House of Commons decided that he had been properly elected. He remained MP for Exeter until 1801 (BBZ, p. 35). He was a magistrate of the Devon Quarter Sessions (DRO).

He remained a partner of John & Francis Baring of London until 1800. Although his involvement had never been substantial, John Baring appears in a triple portrait commissioned from Thomas Lawrence in 1806. This painting featured prominently in the Partners Room of Barings Bank until its demise in 1995.

The partnership with Charles Baring was wound up in 1801. John Baring retired a prosperous man but there was much sadness in his life before he died in 1816. Two of his three daughters died and his second son committed suicide (BBZ, p. 43).

Elizabeth Baring (1744–1809), the youngest of the children of Johann (John) Baring and Elizabeth Vowler, was born in 1744, just four years before the death of her father. We know very little of her early life, her education or her involvement in the family business. As the only daughter of a wealthy family she would have had a good education and would have expected to marry well. She certainly married well, but she married very late by the standards of the time. She was 36 when she married John Dunning in 1780. John Dunning was 13 years her senior, from Ashburton in Devon (close to the Baring family home in Exeter), a lawyer who rose to the top of his profession, making himself a fortune at the bar. Dunning had been appointed Solicitor General in 1767 and elected member of Parliament for Calne (in Wiltshire) in 1768, a seat secured for him by the Earl of Shelburne. He was elevated to the peerage as Lord Ashburton in 1782.

John Dunning was a very important and influential lawyer and politician. His connection to the Baring family through Elizabeth would have a profound effect on the future of John and Francis Baring & Co.

John Dunning and Elizabeth Baring had one son, Richard Barré Dunning, born in 1782. He assumed the title of second Lord Ashburton on the death of his father in 1783. Elizabeth Dunning was therefore married for just three years. She died in 1809. Richard Barré Dunning died in 1823, at which time the title became extinct, to be revived in 1835 by Alexander Baring, Francis Baring's second son.

Chapter 2

Chapter 2, "Early Days in Philadelphia," draws in particular on Robert Alberts' *Golden Voyage* (GV) and Margaret Brown's *William Bingham, 18th Century Magnate* (MBM).

1. Thomas and Charles Willing were the sons of merchant Thomas Willing and Anne Harrison, of Bristol, England. Thomas was sent to Philadelphia and he was joined two years later by his younger brother Charles (1710–1754).

2. Joseph's father Edward, born in Methley, Yorkshire, England, in 1639, immigrated to Boston in 1668, where he set himself up as a merchant. Edward married Quaker Elizabeth Lybrand in 1671. She died in 1688 and Edward moved to Philadelphia around 1693, having subsequently married Rebecca Howard in 1689.

Edward Shippen's wealth and character soon brought influence and position in his newly adopted home of Philadelphia. In 1695 he was elected to the Assembly, and in 1696 to the Provincial Council, where he remained a member until his death. In the same year he was appointed a justice of the peace and in 1697 the presiding judge of the Courts of Common Pleas. In 1701 he became mayor of Philadelphia. He was treasurer of the city from 1705 until his death in 1712. He married his third wife, Esther Wilcox, in 1706, which led to his departure from the Society of Friends. He built a grand house — "Shippen's Great House." Edward Shippen, it was said, was characterized by three things — "the biggest person, the biggest house, the biggest carriage."

Joseph Shippen was born in Boston in 1679, where he completed his education and started a mercantile career. He married Abigail in 1702 and they moved to Philadelphia in 1704. Abigail and Joseph had eight children, including Edward (born 1703) and William (born 1712), whose descendents were to continue the family tradition of great achievement in Pennsylvania over the next century. Anne Shippen, who was later to marry Charles Willing, was born in 1710. Abigail Shippen died in 1716, and Joseph subsequently married Rose Budd in 1721. Joseph was a man of science and philosophy and was invited to join Benjamin Franklin's Junto in 1727.

Sources: UPENN, WL, FA.

3. Samuel Powel (1738–1793) inherited substantial wealth at an early age from his grandfather, his father having predeceased him. The family wealth had been acquired through marriage and shrewd property development. He travelled extensively in Europe after graduating at the College of Philadelphia, and married Elizabeth Willing, daughter of Charles and brother of Thomas Willing, in 1769. He purchased the Georgian house on Third Street, Philadelphia, from Charles Steadman. There Samuel and Elizabeth Powel entertained the city's high society, including George and Martha Washington, John and Abigail Adams, the Marquis de Lafayette and Benjamin Franklin. He was mayor of Philadelphia before and after the American Revolution. He was a trustee of the Academy and College of Philadelphia, subsequently the University of Pennsylvania. The Powel House was subsequently acquired by William Bingham, who gave it as a wedding gift to his daughter, Ann Louisa, and Alexander Baring.

Sources: UPENN, USH.

4. Charles Willing (1710–1754) built up America's foremost merchant house, Charles Willing & Co, later becoming Willing and Morris & Co. Thomas Willing, his son, was one of, if not the wealthiest merchant and businessman of his time. He left a reputed $1 million on his death in 1821. He played a critical role in supplying Washington's Continental Army, together with Robert Morris. He was the president of the Bank of North America, and later of the Bank of the United States. He formed a lifelong relationship with Francis Baring from 1774 to Baring's death in 1810.

Sources: UPENN, BDUS.

5. Robert Morris Sr. (1711–1750) was sent to America as a factor for Foster, Cunliffe & Sons of Liverpool, England, around 1738. His father Andrew Morris (1689–1728) was a sailor, believed to be active in the trade with the Chesapeake Bay, quite possibly Foster, Cunliffe & Sons vessels. His mother was Magdalene Simpson (1689–1729).

Robert Morris married Elizabeth Murphet (born about 1712 in Lancashire, England) and had eight children by her. Margaret was born in 1732 in Liverpool, England, and died in 1799 in Lincoln, North Carolina, and Robert Morris Jr., was born in 1734 in Liverpool, England, and died in 1806 in Philadelphia, Pennsylvania.

Elizabeth Murphet appears to have stayed in Liverpool, where she presumably died.

Robert Morris had another child, Thomas Wise Morris (born 1751 in Maryland, died 1778 in Nantes, France), with Sarah Wise.

All the prominent English merchant firms had representatives in Oxford, Maryland, because of its excellent harbor. For 12 years Robert Morris remained in Oxford in charge of the business of his Liverpool firm and of the various sub-agencies established at Cambridge and Dover on the Choptank River and other points on the Wye and Chester Rivers.

Robert Morris Sr. had accumulated considerable assets, including a library, which was most unusual for someone in his position at the time.

Sources: RMPF, SCON, UPEN, EB, BDUS, CH.

6. English-born Robert Morris Jr. (1734–1806) has been described as "the financier of the American Revolution." He was strongly opposed to British restrictions, in particular the Stamp Act, and together with Thomas Willing joined the first Continental Congress and its Secret Committee in 1775. Robert Morris became the second chairman of the Secret Committee after Thomas Willing. He became a member and vice-president of the Pennsylvania Council of Safety in 1775.

The firm of Willing and Morris, and in particular Robert Morris, became the predominant means by which the Continental Army was financed and armed. They used their own credit to finance purchases and shipping, honor bills of exchange, etc., and were also liable for their own debts. In exchange they were entitled to reclaim commissions from Congress for purchases, financing, storage and sale.

Robert Morris used his wide mercantile contacts to set up a supply chain involving agents in Europe and the West Indies (St. Pierre, Martinique, Cape Francois in Santa Domingo and St. Eustatius). These agents were not only merchants, but also "secret agents" since the trade was clandestine, particularly before the Declaration of Independence. They included Oliver Pollock at New Orleans, Silas Deane in Paris and William Bingham.

Between 1775 and 1777 the Secret Committee disbursed over $2 million (say £100,000,000 in today's terms), much of it directly through Willing, Morris & Co. The controls on the disbursement of funds were limited, and it was quite possible for committee funds to be used for private ventures, and public vessels to be used for private cargoes. Morris took advantage of this situation to divert £80,000 dollars to his own use in 1776. The money had been granted by the Secret Committee to purchase goods for shipment to France. The goods were not exported but the money was not returned. This profiteering was probably inevitable, and Congress was not unhappy that its merchant members should benefit from the supply of the Continental Army, but it would appear that Robert Morris stretched the business code of the time to the breaking point. On the other hand there is no doubt that without his personal credit the incipient revolution would have fallen at the first hurdle.

Following the victory of the Americans at Saratoga in 1777, France entered into an alliance with the United States (as it now was), and supplies could then be shipped by the French navy, effectively bringing the "secret" phase to an end.

Morris' financial assistance did not end there, however, since he was involved with Benjamin Franklin in arranging and subsequently renegotiating substantial French loans.

He retired from Congress in 1778 and was at once sent to the legislature, serving in 1778–1779 and 1780–1781. He became superintendent of finance, a position he held from 1781 to 1784, and continued to use his personal credit to facilitate the needs of the department. He proposed heavy taxation to repay the French loans that he had renegotiated, to which Congress would not agree, and he resigned in 1784.

With Thomas Willing, William Bingham and others, he established in 1781 the Bank of Pennsylvania, later renamed the Bank of North America.

He served as senator to the U.S. Congress in 1789–1795 for Pennsylvania. He was offered and declined the position of secretary of the Treasury, suggesting that the post should go to Alexander Hamilton.

The partnership between Thomas Willing and Robert Morris continued until 1791 but their business activities diverged after the end of the Revolutionary War. He became involved in the "China" trade and engaged extensively in property speculation, owning at one time or another nearly the entire western half of New York state, two million acres in Georgia and about one million each in Pennsylvania, Virginia and South Carolina.

However, the land investments proved slow to liquidate, he was defrauded by a partner, suffered a bank failure in London and finally became overwhelmed by the taxes on the land. His ultimate financial embarrassment ended in bankruptcy and the debtors prison in Philadelphia, in which he was interned from 1798 to 1801. He never recovered from this disastrous sequence of events and died in 1806. He is buried in the family vault of William White in the Churchyard of Christ Church.

He had a son, Thomas, who was a member of the New York State Assembly from 1794 to 1796 and was elected to the Seventh Congress as a Federalist, 1801–1803. He was United States marshal for the southern district of New York from 1816 to 1829, and died in 1849.

Sources: RMPF, FP, UPENN.

7. RMPF.

8. Anne Budd's grandfather was the Rev. Thomas Budd, born in England in 1716 and an early convert to Quakerism. In 1761 he refused to take the Oath of Obedience to the Church of England and was jailed. He died in prison nine years later. His son William left England, settled in Burlington, New Jersey, and married Ann Clapgut.

9. Bingham family history, GV, pp. 10–14, UPENN, MBM.

10. The college (later university) was the vision of Benjamin Franklin to create a seat of learning intended not just to train clergymen (as was the case in New England, Virginia and Europe) but to develop a business and governing class for Philadelphia, then the foremost city in colonial America. His ideas were well received by the merchants of the city, and in 1755 Franklin and his board of founding trustees secured a charter for the College of Philadelphia. The class of 1757 was the first to graduate. Franklin's college would not only go on to produce the business and political leaders of the future, but a network of individuals who, twenty years later, would be able to manage a revolutionary war.

11. GV, p. 11.

Research has not turned up much on John and James Bingham. We do know from the will made by William Bingham's sister Anne in 1779 that John had already died and James was still alive (WL).

12. GV, p. 13.

13. Wharton Family History, UPENN, VIRT.

14. William Bingham's Grand European Tour, MBA, p. 55, GV, p. 13.

Chapter 3

Chapter 3, "Trouble Brewing," draws on the following works: I. R. Christie, *Crisis of Empire 1754–1783*, Foundations of Modern History (New York: W. W. Norton, 1966), (COE); G. M. Trevelyan, *A Shortened History of England* (London: Penguin Books, 1942), (SHE); Niall Ferguson, *Empire* (London: Penguin Books, 2004); the 1911 Encyclopaedia (EB); Paul Johnson, *A History of the American People* (London: Weidenfeld and Nicholson, 1997), (HAPJ); Alistair Cooke, *America* (London: Weidenfeld and Nicholson, 2002).

1. COE, p. 38.
2. COE, p. 45.
3. Described in the 1911 Encyclopaedia Britannica as a "British soldier and politician," Isaac Barré (1726–1802) was born in Dublin, the son of a French refugee. He was educated at Trinity College, Dublin, and entered the British army in 1746.

He fought alongside General James Wolfe during the defeat of the French on the Plains of Abraham in the Battle of Quebec in September 1759. Wolfe was fatally shot during the battle and Barré himself received a severe bullet wound to his right cheek. This wound blinded his right eye and distorted the appearance of his face.

Barré did not get the army promotion that he expected (and deserved), and after years of commendable service, returned to England and entered Parliament under the auspices of Lord Shelburne, apparently as a blunt instrument to attack William Pitt. He sat for Chipping Wycombe from 1761 to 1774 and for Calne from 1774 to 1790. He opened his parliamentary career with a bitter attack on Pitt (and was later rewarded with the rank of Lieutenant Colonel by Lord Bute).

During the North Briton controversy in 1762–1763 Barré supported the rights of John Wilkes in Parliament, for which he was temporarily stripped of his military rank.

The Stamp Act (a sales tax introduced to pay for the protection of the American colonies) was introduced in 1765, and Barré was its most vocal opponent in the House. He predicted rebellion and described the colonists in a famous speech, "Sons of Liberty." His eloquence did not, however prevent the passage of the Stamp Act through Parliament. The expression "sons of liberty" was adopted with passion by the Americans and radical groups were formed to oppose the new act by civil disturbance.

The Stamp Act was repealed in 1766 and a portrait of Barré was hung in Fanueil Hall in Boston in his honour. The picture was destroyed by British troops during the siege of Boston in 1775.

Barré was appointed treasurer of the Navy in 1782 by his long-time patron (and now prime minister), Shelburne. This well-paid sinecure caused much discontent, and in its place he was appointed clerk of the Pells (by William Pitt the Younger), which was not paid for from the public purse.

At other times Barré had held the offices of Adjutant General of the British Army, governor of Stirling Castle and vice-treasurer of Ireland.

As a result of his earlier war wound, he became blind in 1785, but retained his seat in Parliament until 1790.

Colonel Barré died without heir at his home on Stanhope Street, Mayfair, in July 1802 (EB).

English radical, journalist, politician, and member of the Hellfire Club, John Wilkes (1725–1797) was a bitter opponent of Bute. He created his own weekly, *The North Briton* (an ironic reference to Bute's own paper, *The Briton*), to attack the establishment and Bute in particular. These attacks proved sufficiently virulent to unseat Bute. He was a staunch supporter of the rights of the American colonists and opponent in Parliament of the Stamp Act (together with Isaac Barré). He was, therefore, by definition, popular in America, and his erratic career was followed with interest.

4. James Otis, COE, p. 69.

5. Charles Townshend asked his friend Samuel Touchet to advise on taxes that might be appropriate to extract money from the American colonists. Touchet was by this time bankrupt but survived through the privilege of his Parliamentary seat.

Chapter 4

Chapter 4, "City Tavern — The Eve of War," draws from GV, COE, and the Letters of Delegates to Congress (LODC).

1. GV, p. 14.
2. Proceedings of the First Continental Congress, September 1774.
3. GV, p. 3.
4. HAPJ, p. 154.
5. HAPJ, p. 155.
6. GV, p. 16.
7. LODC, WB — Congress June 29, 1779.
8. Thomas Jefferson, Notes of Proceedings in Congress, June 7–28, 1776; July 1–July 4, 1776.
9. The Declaration of Independence, July 1776.

Chapter 5

Chapter 5, "The Secret War — A Parisian in America," draws from various sources, including GV, and E. Morgan, *Benjamin Franklin* (BFM).

1. Franklin to Dumas, December 9, 1775.

Charles W. F. Dumas (1721–1796) was a friend and very useful correspondent of Benjamin Franklin, providing intelligence to the Committee of Secret Correspondence at the start of the Revolutionary War. He devised ciphers used by the committee to communicate with agents such as Deane and Bingham. He acted as John Adams' secretary at The Hague and in Paris. He died in 1794 (CIA).

2. BFM, p. 203.

Arthur Lee (1740–1792) was born in Virginia, and sent to England for his education (Eton College and the University of Edinburgh, Scotland, where he studied medicine). He studied law in London, where he was admitted to the bar and practiced from 1770 to 1776. After acting as agent for Massachusetts and Congress he returned to Virginia in 1780. He was a member of the Continental Congress in 1782–1784. He was the brother of Francis Lightfoot Lee and Richard Henry Lee (BDUS).

3. Pierre Augustin Caron de Beaumarchais (1732–1799) was a French dramatist, courtier, speculator and watchmaker. He was born to a watchmaker in Paris. He insinuated himself into the French court and assumed a patent of nobility by purchasing the office of secretary to the King. He made a fortune in speculation with banker Joseph Duverney. He was engaged by the King of France (Louis XVI) as agent in London, where he acquired an interest in and supported the American colonial cause. He proposed that France take direct steps to support America in its struggle with Britain. With the approval of the French court he organised the Hortalez & Co. arms shipments to America with Arthur Lee and Silas Deane.

He was never reimbursed, however, by the American government for his personal contribution in the supply of arms. The United States government finally made a settlement with his descendents in 1835.

He was also an accomplished playwright, writing two well-known comedies, *the Barber of Seville* and the *Marriage of Figaro*. He was suspected of treason during the French Revolution and imprisoned in 1792, and then exiled. He returned to Paris 1796 and died suddenly May 1799 (EB, pp. 589–590).

4. Committee of Secret Correspondence (CSC) to Deane, March 2, 1776.

Charles Gravie, Comte de Vergennes (1717–1787) was a French statesman and diplomat. He became French foreign minister after the accession of Louis XVI. His foreign policy was characterized by a resentment of British fortunes after the Seven Years War. He took a close interest in the American colonial rebels and made an early strategic decision to support the split with Britain. His financial and then military support to the American rebels greatly damaged the French economy and indirectly led to the French Revolution of 1789.

5. Livre conversion, as a very rough guide, at around 1800:

1 livre Paris was worth about 20 cents, $1 was worth about 5 livres, $5 was worth about £1, and 1 million livres was equivalent to about £50,000 or $200,000. See Appendix A for more detail.

6. Silas Deane (1737–1789) was born in Groton, Connecticut, studied law at Yale and was admitted to the bar in 1761. He became a merchant in Wethersfield and was active in opposition to British taxation. He was appointed to the First Continental Congress as a delegate from Connecticut. He served on Congressional Committees and was sent as agent to France in 1776.

He was successful and effective with his negotiations with Vergennes and Beaumarchais in securing early military supplies for shipment to America, and credited with enlisting the services of Lafayette, among others. However, he was recalled to Congress to answer charges of embezzlement, where he was defended notably by John Jay and John Adams. He returned to France in 1781, but became disillusioned with the American cause and spent several years in England. He died on the ship in Deal harbor that was to take him back to the United States. No evidence of any dishonesty or wrongdoing was found and Congress voted $37,000 to his descendents in 1842 (EB).

7. Deane to Jay, December 3, 1776, RDC.

Chapter 6

Chapter 6, "William Bingham's Martinico Odyssey," draws on GV, *Supplying Washington's Army* (SWA), William Bell Clark's *Lambert Wickes: Sea Raider and Diplomat* (LW), Margaret Brown's *William Bingham: Agent of the Continental Congress* (MBA), and LODC.

1. SWA, chapter 12.
2. GV, p. 20.
3. LODC, Willing, Morris & Co. to William Bingham, June 3, 1776.
4. LODC, Willing, Morris & Co. to William Bingham, June 3, 1776.

5. On the same day the Committee for Secret Correspondence wrote to William Bingham concerning Adrien Le Maitre and Richard Harrison and to Le Maitre and Harrison themselves. The Secret Committee also wrote to Le Maitre and Harrison, who were already in Martinique as agents for Virginia.

6. "The privateer," once suitably licensed, was authorized by the State to treat captures as "prizes" and take them to a compliant port for sale. This process was highly structured and not only the captain and owners of the vessel would share in the proceeds, but also the crew, on an established sliding scale. For the ordinary sailor this was an opportunity to accumulate wealth; the risk of so doing was considered part of the life of a merchant sailor, who was likely to have left an environment where there was little or no chance of acquiring any property at any time. The circle of privateer and prize was completed when the captain and crew were given the opportunity to rejoin the "prize" which was now turned and operating for the (in this case) American cause. The captain of such a vessel may have had qualms about this and would be allowed to go his own — usually difficult — way, but the average sailor would have little choice but to accept his new terms of employment. In any case his potential prize earnings may be greater, and being a long way from home the risks lower. In normal circumstances (if such a thing existed), the private merchant owner of the vessel and cargo would be compensated in due course by the government issuing the letters of marque in the first place.

The line between privateering and piracy from a historical perspective seems very fine. The principle continued to be applied until such time as merchant vessels differed from men-of-war essentially only in what they were carrying.

7. Robert Morris appointed agents in each colony to manage his supply chain, including Oliver Pollock in New Orleans. William Hodge was appointed to travel to Europe after Silas Deane to endeavor to procure arms (10,000 stand of arms, 1,000 barrels of gunpowder, etc.) and two "fast cutters, well armed and manned" from his own merchant contacts (Jean Wanderwoort). His instructions were included in a letter from the Secret Committee dated May 30, 1776. Congress allowed him to take a 2 percent commission on his purchases. Unfortunately the brig *Polly* which was taking him to Europe was captured by the *Orpheus* on July 3, 1776, as Deane was arriving in Paris and William Bingham was en route to Martinique on board *Reprisal* (Secret Committee [SC] to William Hodge, May 30, 1776, LODC).

8. Committee of Secret Correspondence (CSC) to William Bingham, June 3, 1776 (LODC).

9. GV, p. 20.

10. LODC, Marine Committee to Wickes, June 10, 1776.

11. LODC, Wickes to CSC, June 16, 1776. A shallop is small open boat with sails and oars for use in shallow waters.

12. *Reprisal* was the first to bear the illustrious name in what was to become the United States Navy. Formerly the merchantman *Molly*, she was purchased by the Marine Committee on March 28, 1776, refitted and renamed.

After Wickes' triumphant return to Philadelphia, he and *Reprisal* took Benjamin Franklin to France and then was tasked with cruising British waters. On February 5, 1777, she captured the *Lisbon Packet* in the Bay of Biscay.

During April 1777 *Reprisal* was joined by *Lexington* and *Dolphin*, forming a squadron under Wickes' command. Between them they captured a total of 18 prizes, before returning to France to refit.

On September 14, 1777, *Reprisal* and *Dolphin* left France for the United States. *Reprisal* was lost off Newfoundland with the loss of all on board apart from the ship's cook (*Source:* Allen, *Naval History of the American Revolution*).

13. Wickes' naval exploits are covered in detail in William Bell Clark's *Lambert Wickes: Sea Raider* (LW).

14. For details of *Reprisal*'s prizes, see GV, p. 481.

15. HMS *Shark*, 16 guns Royal Navy sloop-of-war, commanded by Captain John Chapman.

16. Lambert Wickes (1735–1777) was originally from Maryland and a former ship's master employed by Willing, Morris

& Co. He died in 1777 when *Reprisal* was lost off Newfoundland.

His astonishing tally of prizes seems to single him out as a latter-day Bluebeard, but there appears no doubt that in his way he was as much a patriot as Adams, Jefferson or Franklin.

Chapter 7

More information on William Bingham's activities in Martinique can be derived from GV and LW.

1. LW, GV, p. 27.
2. LODC, WB to Deane, August 5, 1776.
3. LW, pp. 61–62; GV, pp. 4, 82.
4. LODC, WB to Congress; GV, p. 30.
5. LODC, CSC to WB, June 3, 1776.
6. LODC, WB to CSC, August 4, 15, 26, 1776.
7. GV, p. 482.
8. LODC, WB to Deane, December 24, 1776.
9. LODC, SC to WB, October 21, 1776.
10. LODC, Robert Morris to WB, September 27, 1776.
11. LODC, SC to William Hodge, October 3, 1776.
12. LODC, CSC to WB, October 1, 1776; GV, pp. 41–42.
13. William Hodge was engaged by Congress to get the treaty documents to Paris, at which he succeeded. His overt anti-British sentiments embarrassed the French authorities to such an extent that he was held in the Bastille for a period. (GV, pp. 41–43, SWI). Congress had every reason to be concerned about secrecy and the potential damage that might be caused by the interception of confidential information being transmitted to France via William Bingham. Benjamin Franklin had met Dr. Edward Bancroft (1744–1821) in London while acting as agent for Pennsylvania prior to the Revolutionary War and as fellow scientists they had become good friends. Bancroft became a useful source of information for Franklin, passing intelligence to him on British political activity. When Franklin was sent to Paris as commissioner, Bancroft was recruited by Paul Wentworth (of what would now be called the British Secret Service) as a double agent. Bancroft travelled to Paris and Franklin engaged him as his private secretary. Bancroft then passed any information of interest to the British via a dead-letter drop. He wrote his reports using invisible ink and addressed them to a Mr. Richards, signing as Edward Edwards. He was instructed to seal these dispatches in a bottle and hide them in a hole in a tree on the south terrace of the Jardin des Tuilleries. These bottles were collected after 9.30 P.M. every Tuesday evening and replaced with instructions for Bancroft to retrieve. Franklin never suspected that Bancroft was a British double agent, although Arthur Lee had his suspicions, but not of his own secretary, Holker, who had also been engaged by Wentworth! Bancroft returned to America after Independence and remained a friend of Franklin for the rest of his life.

14. LODC, CSC to WB, September 21, 1776.
15. LODC, Deane to Morris, September 17, 1776.
16. LODC, Morris to WB, October 21, 1776.
17. The day after leaving Martinique, *Seine* was intercepted by HMS *Seaford*. She was tried and condemned in Dominica and later used by the British Navy as a sloop of war, an act that may have stiffened French resolve to assist the rebel Americans (MBA p. 60).
18. GV, p. 50; MBA, p. 66.
19. GV, p. 50.
20. Adventures of Ships Owned by William Bingham 1777–1779 (Bingham Papers, HSP).
21. Francois Claude Amour, marquis de Bouillé (1739–1800) — The marquis de Bouillé was a distinguished career soldier, and a cousin of the Marquis de le Fayette. He had served in the Seven Years War, and his tour of duty in Martinique ran from May 1777 to March 1783. On his return to France he was appointed governor of the Three Bishoprics of Alsace and of Franche-Comte. He was opposed to the French Revolution and remained loyal to Louis XVI, as a result going into exile in Russia in 1791. He died in London in 1800.
22. GV, p. 64.
23. LODC, WB to Franklin, March 5, 1778.

24. LODC, WB to Commissioners in Paris, June 16, 1778.
25. LODC, Lovell to WB, March–May 1778.
26. LODC, WB to Franklin, April 13, 1779.
27. GV, p. 75.
28. LODC, Jay to Congress; RDC, p. 449.
29. RDC, p. 448.
30. LODC, Jay to Congress, December 25, 1779; RDC, p. 446.
31. GV, p. 78.
32. *Pilgrim* Affair, MBA, pp. 83–87, also see Appendix F.
33. LODC, Jay to Congress, December 22, 1779.
34. RDC, p. 449.
35. WB Memorial, see Appendix B of GV, p. 454; LODC, WB to Congress, June 29, 1779.
36. Letter from Bouillé to Congress, March 13, 1780.
37. SH, p. 247.

Chapter 8

Chapter 8, "Benjamin Franklin, an American in Paris," derives from BFM, GV, and Helen Auger's *The Secret War of Independence* (SWI).

1. GV, p. 42.
2. GV, p. 65; Brant II, p. 136.
3. BFM, p. 261.
4. BFM, p. 261, GV, p. 65.
5. BFM, pp. 261, 268, 269.
6. William Jackson (1759–1828) was born in Cumberland, England, in March 1759. His parents died suddenly, and neighbors arranged for him to immigrate to Charleston, South Carolina, to be brought up by Owen Roberts, a family friend, merchant, and soldier. Roberts (a veteran of the French and Indian War) introduced his ward to the colonial idea of the citizen soldier and the patriot cause.

In the summer of 1775, South Carolina joined the rebels. Roberts initially served as the major of the First Carolina Regiment, but was soon promoted to command the artillery regiment, the Fourth South Carolina. The young William Jackson followed him into the regiment as a cadet before his seventeenth birthday. By May 1776 William was commissioned as a second lieutenant, and saw action defending Charleston from a British attack.

The focus of the war moved northwards and Jackson developed his skills as junior officer and was twice promoted. As the French entered the war, the British again moved south. Jackson's commanding officer Charles C. Pinckney (later to be a signatory to the Declaration of Independence) persuaded Major General Benjamin Lincoln to appoint him as his aide.

William Jackson, now major, served with Lincoln in skirmishes that followed the American loss of Savannah and the bloody battle of Stono Ferry in 1779 and witnessed his guardian killed in action.

In 1780 the British besieged Lincoln at Charleston for 42 days and finally he was forced to surrender in May of that year. Jackson was among the Americans captured. In November he, Lincoln and others were exchanged. His aptitude in his staff role had not gone unnoticed, however, and he was assigned as secretary to George Washington's aide, Lieutenant Colonel John Laurens.

He and Laurens were sent to France to negotiate the shipment of war supplies. Laurens returned with supplies for the Yorktown campaign, while Jackson remained to negotiate (along with Benjamin Franklin and John Adams) with the Dutch government for further shipments.

Jackson returned to Philadelphia in 1782 and accepted Lincoln's offer to serve as assistant secretary of war (Lincoln having just been appointed secretary of war), to act as liaison between Congress and the Army. He was just 23 years old.

The tragic loss of his guardian closed off the business career that might otherwise been open to him, and he decided to develop his own business as a merchant. He returned briefly to Europe in 1783 but after a period of trade he travelled back to Philadelphia, his newly adopted home, to study law, and was admitted to the bar in 1788.

During his study, however, he applied for and won the position of secretary to the Constitutional Convention in 1787 and his signature appears on the Constitution in addition to the 39 delegates. After this he was selected by George Washington to be his secretary, becoming one the very first civil servants to the United States government.

He resigned in 1791, turning down Washington's offer of Adjutant General to the Army to further a career in business and law.

In 1793 Jackson was engaged by William Bingham to travel to Europe to negotiate the sale of his Maine lands. Armed with Bingham's letters of introduction, he was entertained by Lord Lansdowne (Earl of Shelburne), Dr, Joseph Priestley and Benjamin Vaughan. He presented himself to Francis Baring and made several visits to his county seat and met Sir Francis' eldest son Alexander, who was then the "principle assistant in Mr Hope's counting house."

Having become close to Thomas Pinckney, the American minister in London, and being armed with letters of introduction from Thomas Jefferson and George Washington, he travelled to Paris to attempt to sell Bingham's Maine land to the French government with the possibility of settlement. The French government's view was that its citizens were needed for the "Revolution" and it declined to pursue Bingham's offer.

Jackson returned to London for one last attempt on the House of Baring and, although unsuccessful, carried with him back to Philadelphia a letter of interest from Sir Francis to William Bingham. While he may not have made the deal with Hopes and Barings, he had laid the foundations for what would become the springboard for Barings Bank and in turn the financing of the Louisiana Purchase in 1803.

In 1795 he married Elizabeth, daughter of Thomas Willing (becoming William Bingham's brother-in-law), whose acquaintance he had made prior to his trip to Europe. This no doubt provided an element of security which enabled him to re-evaluate a public career, and in the same year he was appointed by George Washington to the position of surveyor of customs for the Port of Philadelphia.

A strong supporter of the Federalist Party, Jackson unfortunately lost his job in 1801 when Thomas Jefferson became president and with him a change of political orientation.

Major William Jackson returned to the law and for a time edited Philadelphia's *Political and Commercial Register*, a pro-federalist newspaper.

In 1824 he provided the official welcome for his friend and former comrade-in-arms, General Lafayette, to Philadelphia. He died in 1828 (ND, SCON, SSC).

7. Alexander Gillon (1741–1794) was born in Rotterdam in 1741. He entered commerce in London before settling in Charleston, South Carolina, in 1766. He was elected a representative for South Carolina to the second Continental Congress in 1775 and 1776. In 1775 he became a contractor to the Secret Committee, and in 1778 was created commodore of South Carolina's navy, and as such was sent to France to acquire naval vessels.

He left a trail of deceit and disaster behind him, and massive debts that Benjamin Franklin endeavored to repay. He attempted to make off with Franklin's final gift of 6 million livres, having persuaded William Jackson to join him in the venture, effectively kidnapping him in the process, before returning to Philadelphia in 1782.

He was elected to the Continental Congress in 1784, but did not attend. He was elected to serve in the Third Congress in March 1793, but died at his plantation in October 1794 (BDUS).

8. BFM, p. 269.
9. BFM, p. 270.
10. BFM, p. 271.

Chapter 9

Chapter 9,"Barings, Hopes and the Triple Alliance," draws on various sources, including BBO, BBZ, Marten G. Buist, *At Spes Non Fracta* (SNF), and SHE.

1. John Dunning (1731–1783) was born in Ashburton, Devon, the son of a lawyer to whom he was articled. He was admitted to the Middle Temple in 1750 at the age of 19 and called to the bar in 1756. His early years as a barrister were quite unremarkable; he spent several years without receiving a single brief!

In 1762 he was employed to draw up a defense of the British East India Company against the Dutch East India Company. His document was described at the time as "masterly" and provided him with "reputation and emolument." In 1763–1764 he distinguished himself as counsel on the side of John Wilkes, charged with sedition and obscene libel.

The case of *Leach v. Money* (June 1763) consolidated his reputation, and his practice increased to such an extent that in 1776 he is said to have been in receipt of £10,000 per annum.

In 1766 he was appointed recorder of Bristol, and in December 1767 solicitor general. He was elected MP for Calne in 1768; a seat secured for him by Lord Shelburne, and which he retained until elevated to the peerage in 1782, and he accepted the rich sinecure of chancellor of the Duchy of Lancaster.

John Dunning was without doubt one of the most influential lawyers and politicians of his age.

He married Elizabeth Baring, Francis Baring's sister, in 1780. They had a son, Richard Barré Dunning, born 1782, and he succeeded to the title as second Lord Ashburton on the death of his father in 1783. Richard died in 1823, at which time the title became extinct, but it was revived in 1835 by Alexander Baring (EB).

Thomas Fitzmaurice (1737–1805), who was created Earl of Kerry in 1723, married the daughter of Sir William Petty, from which union there was no son. The estates passed to his nephew John Fitzmaurice, who took the additional name of Petty in 1751 and was advanced to Earldom of Shelburne in 1753. His son William was born in Dublin in May 1737. He spent his childhood in the remotest parts of southern Ireland and had little formal education. With the help of a tutor he entered Christchurch College, Oxford, in 1755. He left in 1757 without taking a degree, and he was bought a commission into the Twentieth Regiment of foot guards by his father. He served in General Wolfe's regiment during the Seven Years War and distinguished himself at the Battle of Minden, being promoted in 1760 to the rank of colonel, and aide-de-camp to the King. He was elected to Parliament for the family seat of Chipping Wycombe the same year, but did not take his seat while serving the King (EB).

He took up his seat in the general election of 1761 but succeeded his father as Earl of Shelburne in the Irish Peerage, and as Baron Wycombe in the English Peerage. He served as president of the Board of Trade in Lord Bute's ministry, although his clear ambition for high office made him unpopular with his colleagues.

In 1763 George III dismissed Shelburne from his post as aide-de-camp because of his support for John Wilkes against the government in the North Briton affair. He took up his seat in the Irish Peerage and retired temporarily to his country estates.

In 1765 he married Lady Sophia Carteret, gaining the Lansdowne Estates (near Bath) as a result, and was appointed a major-general. He was offered the position of president of the Board of Trade in Rockingham's first ministry but turned it down because of his opposition to the taxation of the American colonists. He did, however, accept the post of secretary of state in Pitt's (Chatham's) ministry in 1766. His conciliatory policy towards America was thwarted by his colleagues and the King, and he was dismissed from office in 1768.

In 1771 Shelburne's wife Sophia died, and the following year he travelled extensively in France and Italy with his friend Isaac Barré. On his return he indulged his interests in the arts and sciences, employed Dr. Joseph Priestley as his librarian and archivist, was patron of Jeremy Bentham and engaged "Capability" Brown to landscape his estates.

Shelburne supported the Regulating Act for India in 1773 and in 1775 supported Chatham's motion to withdraw troops from Boston, Massachusetts. On Chatham's death in 1778 Shelburne took over the leadership of the Chathamites.

In 1779 he remarried, this time to Lady Louisa Fitzpatrick. In 1782 he accepted the post of secretary of state for the Home Department in Rockingham's second ministry (on the condition that the King recognize the United States). Rockingham died shortly after and Shelburne became prime minister, which led to the resignation of Charles James Fox and a number of Rockinghamites who would not serve under Shelburne.

Fox formed a strong coalition with Lord North, who opposed Shelburne's proposals for free trade and reform of the public service. Shelburne was forced to resign in 1783. When Pitt (the younger) became prime minister in 1784, Shelburne was not recalled, but was created Marquis of Lansdowne. Shelburne effectively bridged the period between the ministries of Pitts—elder and younger (EB).

Edmund Burke (1729–1797) was an English (Irish-born) radical, politician and writer, supporter of American colonialists and Parliamentary reform (EB).

Jeremy Bentham (1748–1832) was an English radical, economist, political theorist and writer. He was also a protégé of the second Earl Shelburne, and friend of Francis Baring and William Bingham (EB).

Joseph Priestley (1733–1804) was an English chemist, writer, companion, advisor and librarian to Earl Shelburne from 1772 to 1780, living at Bowood, where he "discovered" oxygen. He became acquainted with William Bingham in England and in Pennsylvania, where he retired in 1794. He was a long-time friend and associate of Benjamin Franklin (EB).

Benjamin Vaughan (1751–1835) was a Jamaican-born political economist, scientist, radical, printer, and publisher, a friend of Earl Shelburne and Benjamin Franklin, William Bingham and John Jay. He had significant involvement in the peace negotiations between Britain and America (EB, FA).

Dr. Richard Price (1723–1791) was an English liberal theologian, philosopher, supporter of American Colonial rights, and friend of Benjamin Franklin and William Bingham (EB).

2. SNF, p. 12.

Early history of Hope & Co.: John and Francis Baring started their partnership on Queen Street, Cheapside, in the city of London on January 1, 1763. On the very same day a year earlier John and Henry Hope joined with Thomas and Adrian Hope to form a new merchant and banking partnership to be known simply as Hope & Co. Unlike the Barings, though, the Hope family had already been successful merchants in Rotterdam and Amsterdam as far back as 1680. The roots of the family can be traced back to Scotland. Charles Hope of Hopetoun (ennobled in 1703 as the first Earl of Hopetoun) was a cousin to Archibald Hope of Amsterdam, who died in 1720. His will stipulated that his merchant house should be carried on by his sons Henry and John, with places reserved in the business for Isaac and Thomas, who were underage at the time. By 1734 the business was being run by Thomas Hope and a younger brother Adrian, and the title of the house became Thomas and Adrian Hope. Over the next 20 years the business emerged as one of Holland's most successful houses, built on a cautious and balanced approach to risk. Towards the end of the Seven Years War, Thomas and Adrian were joined in partnership by Thomas' son John and their American nephew Henry (Henry's father, also a Henry, had immigrated to Braintree, Boston, around 1730). Henry Hope's father had left for America 30 years earlier and maintained trade connections with the house in Amsterdam. They endeavored to trade with the French West Indies and France itself through the war, to the irritation of the British, and many cargoes and vessels were lost to the British Navy or privateers.

Young Henry was sent to England in 1735 at the age of 13 for his education, and in 1754 joined the house of Gurnell Hoare & Co. in London for his apprenticeship (SNF, pp. 3–17).

At the end of the Seven Years War Amsterdam was the financial hub of Europe, the center for credit and foreign exchange, and at the core of all this was the Exchange Bank. Hope's turnover with the Exchange Bank grew rapidly through the Seven Years War and by 1763 they had become pre-eminent. They were in a position to place the substantial British government loans that were required to fund the war with France.

Hope & Co. steered its way thought the financial crisis of 1763 (many did not) and under Henry Hope continued to expand its business with the Exchange Bank. While the firm continued to trade in commodities, it was the trade in money itself that was driving their growth.

Hope & Co. was at the forefront of the growth of international government loans, and as the volume of loans increased the volume of exchange dealing diminished.

The Dutch banking houses had cornered the market in foreign loans, and continued to do so beyond the end of the Seven Years War. British and French loans were issued in those countries since they already had reasonably sophisticated capital markets of their own, and the bonds of these loans could be sold there or in Holland. In the case of the "emerging markets," meaning Sweden, Russia, Poland, Austria, the German states, Spain and Portugal, without established capital markets, the loans would be issued in Holland and all interest and principle would be paid in guilders.

Hope & Co. brought together a state requiring loan finance with Dutch capitalists through the medium of what they termed "entrepreneurs" or loan contractors who would in turn have been engaged by a broker. The entrepreneurs themselves would also act as issuing houses themselves in the case of smaller loans, and the brokers might also subscribe to loans which they had helped to arrange (SNF, p. 24).

Despite Hope's heavy involvement in credit and foreign loans, it continued a broad spectrum of trade and speculation. As far as Henry Hope was concerned, exchange dealing, acceptance credit, and the issue of loans were all elements of the same mercantile business. All of these elements required an accurate assessment of the financial stability of their correspondents, whether they were merchant houses or governments. It was not possible to analyze balance sheets since such external information did not exist.

Hope's approach was to make assessments of "solidity" based outward signs; a luxurious or dissolute lifestyle rated negatively, evidence of a strong family life, prudence, honesty, and reliability were all positive indicators, as was evidence of proper bookkeeping and demonstrable knowledge of trade and the market. References were sought from other houses. All this information was recorded and updated if and when circumstances changed. In effect they produced their own Standard and Poor's credit rating for every account and the amount of credit advanced was determined from the book (SNF, p. 36).

Hope & Co. maintained the same standards that they expected from their correspondents, although their own aristocratic and sumptuous lifestyle was apparently quite acceptable. Their own bookkeeping was impeccable. The general ledgers were updated from the daybooks twice a month using the double entry method. The balance sheet and profit and loss account were derived from these at the end of the year and the profit or loss divided amongst the partners in the proportions determined in the partnership agreement. In normal circumstances a substantial proportion of the profit was retained and carried forward in the firm's capital.

Of the partners of the Hope & Co. firm established in 1763, Thomas died in 1779 and Adrian in 1781, leaving Henry and John, who were joined by Nicolas Baudin and John Williams Hope on July 4, 1782. John Hope died in 1784, and his sons Thomas, Adrian Elias and Henry Philip were minors. Nicolas Baudin had also expressed a wish to retire and there was now a real concern for the continuity of the business (SNF, p. 39).

To bolster the partnership Hope & Co. engaged a very capable trader, Robert Voute. Voute's background was with his father's brokerage firm, specializing in dyes, coffee and tea. It was Robert Voute's involvement that drew the relationship between Hope & Co. and John and Francis Baring & Co. from correspondents and occasional entrepreneurs to close commercial partners and friends.

3. SNF, p. 40.
4. SNF, p. 21.
5. COE, p. 81.
6. BBA, General Ledgers, 1773–1776.
7. SHE, p. 408.
8. SHE, p. 408.
9. BBO, p. 9; BBZ p. 37; Baring Mss (B) 17.

Charles and John Baring had already tried for Parliament. Charles tried unsuccessfully for Tiverton, and John, having failed for Honiton in 1774, acquired the seat of Exeter in 1776 (at a cost of £6,000), which he retained until he stood down in 1802.

Francis Baring was still running his business effectively on his own until, confident of some degree of security for himself and his family, he elevated his senior clerk James Mesturas to become a partner and admitted Charles Wall also as a partner. They were offered a salary of £900 per annum and a $\frac{1}{7}$ profit share.

10. BBZ, p. 33, January 1786, letter from Baring to Lansdowne.

Chapter 10

Chapter 10, "Bingham Returns to Philadelphia," draws from GV, LODC, and BFM.

1. GV, pp. 87, 88.

Philadelphia's political situation was also in turmoil; the state assembly had fallen to a radical faction, under the leadership of George Bryan and Charles Wilson Peale, who were opposed to the conservative group led by John Dickinson and Robert Morris. Fearing the influence of the College of Philadelphia and its trustees (including, of course, John Dickinson, Thomas Willing, and James Wilson), the Radicals revoked the college charter and confiscated its estates and endowments, transferring them to a new establishment under the control of the radical group. This was a move too far and the conservative establishment re-asserted itself in the city.

2. GV, p. 89.

3. Bingham's memorial to Congress, *Pilgrim* Affair, June 6, 1780, LODC, see Appendix F.

4. GV, p. 86; LODC, vol. 14, March 19, 1780, Samuel Huntington.

5. LODC, vol. 14, July 5, 1781, James Lovell to Robert Morris, MBA, p. 80.

6. GV, p. 90.

7. GV, p. 90.

8. Henry P. Johnstone, *The Correspondence and Affairs of John Jay*; GV, p. 91.

James Wilson (1742–1798) was probably one of the leading constitutional lawyers among the Founding Fathers. Scottish-born, he studied at St. Andrews, Edinburgh, but left without taking a degree. He came to America in 1765 and taught Latin (including to William Bingham) at the new Philadelphia College (now the University of Pennsylvania). He studied law under John Dickinson and set up a practice in Reading, Pennsylvania. In 1771 he married the heiress Rachel Bird. He became actively involved in revolutionary activities in Pennsylvania and was a delegate to the Continental Congress from 1775 to 1777. He voted for and signed the Declaration of Independence. He made many attempts to improve his personal wealth in land speculation and other activities, with variable success. He played a key role in the creation of the Bank of Pennsylvania, effectively the first American national bank. He represented Pennsylvania in the Confederation Congress and more effectively in the Constitutional Congress of 1787, where his role was second only to James Madison. He was frustrated not to be appointed first chief justice of the Supreme Court (John Jay was) by George Washington, but was appointed to the Supreme Court in 1790. Also in 1790 he became the first law professor and founder of the Law School at the College of Philadelphia.

His first wife died in 1786, and he married the 20-year-old Hannah Gray. His financial speculations finally overwhelmed him and he was imprisoned for debt in 1797, and again in North Carolina in 1798 where he died. He remained a Supreme Court justice and Penn law professor until his death (UPENN).

9. BFM, p. 289.

10. BFM, p. 293.

11. BFM, p. 293, letter from James Madison to Thomas Jefferson.

12. BFM, p. 294, letter from Benjamin Franklin to Congress.

Chapter 11

Chapter 11, "Mr. & Mrs. Bingham," draws on GV; Francois Jean Chastellux, *Travels in North America* (TNA); MBP.

1. GV, pp. 93, 94.

2. The Willing Mansion was considered at the time to be one of the grandest in Philadelphia before the Revolutionary War. Charles Willing and Anne Shippen had six surviving children, Thomas (born 1731) and five daughters: Anne, Mary, Elizabeth, Abigail and Margaret. Anne Married Tench Francis Jr., Mary married William Byrd III, Elizabeth married Samuel Powel and Margaret married brewer Robert Hare. Abigail never married.

John Adams dined with Judge Thomas Willing on October 11, 1774 just prior to the first Continental Congress and noted: "Dined at Mr. Willings, who is a Judge of the Supreme Court here, with the gentleman from Virginia, Maryland and New York. A most splendid feast again — turtle and everything else.... Mr. Willing is the most sociable, agreeable man of all."

During several months of the Revolutionary War General Washington took the former home of the Byrd family as his headquarters. This house was immediately adjacent to the Willing Mansion and separated by a garden. The teenage Anne Willing was a frequent guest of George and Martha Washington during that period.

Thomas Willing married Anne McCall and they had ten surviving children. In 1780 Anne (Nancy), the eldest was sixteen, Charles was fourteen, Elizabeth, twelve, Mary, ten, Dorothy, eight, George, six, Richard, five, Abigail, three, William Shippen, one.

3. GV, p. 94; MBP, p. 287.

4. Francois Jean Beauvoir Chevalier de Chastellux (1734–1788) joined the French army in 1747 at the age of 13. He was a prolific writer of essays and books on music, drama and politics. He was elected to the French Academy in recognition of these works. He joined the French Expeditionary force of Rochambeau as third in command. He travelled widely during his three years in America and his notes were published initially without his approval. The original candid text was very popular in Europe, and was probably the first description of post-colonial American society (*Source:* Independence National Historical Park).

He became acquainted with many important Americans of the period, and corresponded with, among others, Thomas Jefferson and George Washington.

William and Anne Bingham entertained him in Philadelphia and they were reacquainted in Paris in 1784.

5. TNA, pp. 224–226; MBP, p. 288.
6. GV, pp. 99–100; MBP, p. 288.
7. Gouverneur Morris (1752–1816) was born in Morrisania, New York, of a wealthy and aristocratic family. He had a classical education and studied law, completing his studies in 1771. In 1775 he was elected to the New York Provincial Congress. He was appointed a delegate from New York to the Continental Congress of 1778, but failed to be re-elected in 1779. He stayed on in Philadelphia to practice law and engage in mercantile affairs.

Robert Morris had no hesitation in choosing Gouverneur Morris as assistant superintendent of finance in 1781 (a post which he held until 1785). During this time Gouverneur enjoyed the hospitality of William and Anne Bingham and their social circle.

He was appointed a delegate from Pennsylvania to the Constitutional Convention in 1787, where he emerged as one of the leading figures, making 173 speeches. He acted as the scribe or "pen-man," and the actual drafting of the Constitution is his work.

Gouverneur Morris returned to New York but soon left for France on a commercial venture in partnership with Robert Morris. In 1790–1791 he undertook a diplomatic mission to negotiate an improvement in relations with Britain, which did not succeed. Washington appointed him minister to France, replacing Thomas Jefferson. He then travelled extensively in Europe before returning to the United States in 1799, where he served in the U.S. Senate.

He remained an ardent Federalist, was defeated in his bid for re-election in 1802 and retired to his estate at Morrisania. He married Ann Carey in 1809, and they had one son. He died in 1816 (SCON, p. 195; GV, p. 103).

8. GV, pp. 103, 491.
9. For details of Bingham's settlement from Congress, see MBA, p. 82.
10. GV, pp. 104–106.
11. GV, p. 108.
12. GV, p. 112.

Among the other directors were James Wilson, Thomas Fitzsimmons, and Samuel Inglis.

13. GV, pp. 106, 113–114.

Chapter 12

Chapter 12, "The Grand Tour," uses various sources, including GV and MBP.

1. GV, p. 119.
2. Gilmor Memoir, p. 17 (RGS).

Robert Gilmor (1748–1822) was born in 1748 at Paisley in Scotland. He travelled to America in 1767, at 19 years old, to sell an assortment of goods, He arrived at Oxford,

Maryland, and decided to stay on, engaging in business on the Eastern Shore of Maryland, where he stayed for ten years, marrying Louisa Airey in 1771.

During the Revolutionary War the British blockades of Charleston, Norfolk, the Delaware and New York dictated a move to Baltimore, which had been relatively unhindered by British naval activity. Gilmor's business prospered and he started a long-term commercial relationship with Willing, Morris & Co. in Philadelphia, which in turn brought him to the attention of William Bingham.

At the end of the war, in 1782, Bingham, Gilmor and Samuel Inglis set up the merchant house of Bingham, Inglis and Gilmor, based in Amsterdam, to re-establish the trade of Virginia and Maryland staple produce to Europe. Gilmor agreed to run the business, with Bingham and Inglis supplying four-fifths of the capital. Gilmor put up the remaining capital and sailed on November 27, 1782, for Amsterdam with his family, arriving January 12, 1783. Gilmor met John Adams, who gave him letters of introduction to the Dutch bank Willink (with whom Adams was negotiating loans for the United States government), thereby establishing an important trading link for Gilmor and Bingham that lasted for another half century.

Gilmor made rapid progress in the new enterprise, which was brought to an end by the unexpected and sudden death of Samuel Inglis at the end of 1783. His death concluded the partnership, but not before Hope & Co. and Francis Baring were added to the list of correspondents. William Bingham was in Europe by this time and formed a new partnership with Robert Gilmor: Robert Gilmor & Co. Gilmor returned to Baltimore and the new partnership survived the events of the next 15 years. Gilmor and Bingham developed a strong personal respect for each other, and an unbroken friendship right up to Bingham's death.

William Bingham attempted to draw Gilmor into his land speculations, but without great success, and Gilmor's continuing liquidity through the disasters of the 1790s probably kept Bingham afloat. By 1796 Bingham's share of the capital of Robert Gilmor & Co. was $500,000, a remarkable sum. Gilmor and Bingham expanded their shipping operations with Willing, Francis & Co. to South America and to China with the ships *Canton*, *Roebuck*, *Criterion* and *America* (which Bingham owned outright).

When Alexander Baring joined William Bingham in the Maine land purchases, he became impressed with Gilmor's ability, describing him as "by far the best merchant in the United States, and the family looks likely to last."

In 1799 the Gilmor and Bingham partnership was dissolved when Gilmor's sons Robert and William were old enough to join him, the new firm continuing under the name of Robert Gilmor and Sons. Bingham and Gilmor remained the closest of friends and continued shipping adventures together until 1802.

Such was Alexander Baring's trust in Gilmor, he left duplicate papers relating to the Louisiana Purchase in Baltimore with Gilmor with instructions to complete the deal in the event of any mishap befalling him.

William Bingham appointed Robert Gilmor as one of his executors, the others being Alexander Baring, Henry Baring, Thomas Mayne Willing and Charles Willing Hare.

Robert Gilmor died in 1822 at Beech Hill, Baltimore (RGM, RGS, GV).

Robert Gilmor Jr. (1774–1849) was the eldest son of Robert Gilmor, and an almost exact contemporary of Alexander Baring. He undertook a tour of the eastern states in 1797 in the company of an English gentleman, Sherlock, and wrote a description of their travels, providing a vivid account of the times and life in the Bingham household, in which he spent time with Alexander Baring.

Robert Gilmor Jr. took over the running of Robert Gilmor and Sons until his retirement in 1830, after which he became a major patron of the arts and philanthropist. In 1842 he provided assistance to Charles Dickens on his speaking tour of America (RGS, RGM, GV).

Samuel Inglis (1745–1783) was the second son of John Inglis (1708–1775, merchant, founder and trustee of College of Philadelphia) and Catherine McCall, born in Philadelphia of Scottish ancestry. He became a merchant in Norfolk, Virginia, and married Ann Aitchison (also of Scottish descent) in

1774. He returned to Philadelphia at the outbreak of the War of Independence and went into silent partnership with Willing, Morris & Co., while the city was occupied by the British and Robert Morris had been forced to leave. Inglis was able to act for Robert Morris in Philadelphia during the occupation.

Between 1779 and 1781 he fitted out eight privateers under letters of marque. In 1781 he subscribed to the Bank of North America and became a director. In 1782 he joined in partnership with Robert Gilmor and William Bingham, but died suddenly at the end of 1783, bringing the partnership to an end (GV, UPENN, www.inglis.uk.com).

3. GV, p. 115.
4. GV, p. 116.
5. GV, p. 120, Arthur Lee.
6. MBP, p. 289.
7. GV, p. 122, letter from James Wilson to WB, May 15, 1784.
8. MBP, p. 289.
9. GV, p. 122.
10. GV, p. 124.
11. BFM, p. 288.
12. MBP, p. 289; "Letter from an American Now Resident in London to a Member of Parliament on the Subject of the Restraining Proclamation, and Containing Strictures on Lord Sheffield's Pamphlet on the Commerce of the United States," William Bingham.
13. APS, Benjamin Vaughan Papers, p. 495.
14. MBP, p. 289; GV, p. 134.
15. GV, p. 137.
16. GV, p. 130.
17. MBP, p. 291.

Chastellux's candid digests of his travels, *Travels in North America, in the Years 1780, 1781, and 1782*, were not yet published, in fact the Marquis had intended these to be printed for the entertainment of his close friends. But they were published by an unscrupulous French printer and became the most popular travel guide of the time. Anne and William would be unaware at the time but in France they would already have a celebrity status.

18. TNA, p. 18.
19. GV, p. 152.
20. MBP, p. 290.
21. GV, p. 144.
22. MBP, p. 292.
23. MBP, p. 293.
24. GV, p. 136.
25. GV, p. 148.
26. GV, p. 149.
27. GV, p. 149.
28. GV, p. 152.
29. GV, p. 153.
30. MBP, p. 294; GV, p. 156.
31. GV, p. 156.

William Bingham also apparently made considerable sums speculating on the outcome of political events; in particular the naval battle between the French Count de Grasse and the British Admiral Rodney (the Battle of the Saints), upon which he opened a book taking odds against a British victory. It is said that Bingham was already aware through his contacts in Martinique that the French were already defeated.

Chapter 13

Chapter 13, "New Country, New Constitution," uses a number of sources, including GV, BFM, SCON, MBP, and W. A. Newman Dorman, *The Second Troop of Philadelphia Cavalry* (ND).

1. William Bingham sent his drawings back to Philadelphia via Anne's uncle Robert Hare to Thomas Willing, GV, p. 157; MBP, p. 296.

2. Bingham had been impressed with Manchester House in Portman Square. In 1761 the Portman family started to develop lands north of Oxford Street which were then open fields. Samuel Adams, a builder, acquired plots on the north of what is now the square and started work on the house but did not complete it. In 1776 George Montague, the fourth Duke of Manchester, bought the leasehold and work continued under architect Joshua Brown. The front façade had a characteristic Venetian window. Anne and William Bingham would have observed the building in its final stages before their return to America. The Bingham Mansion was broadly similar but somewhat larger. Manchester House was renamed Hertford House, and is now a museum housing the Wallace Collection. For a description of Bingham Mansion, see *John F.*

Watson's Annals of Philadelphia and Pennsylvania, 1857, vol. 1, chapter 56. http://www.usgwarchives.org/pa/philadelphia/watsontoc.html.

For more on the James Monroe story, see GV, p. 164.

3. BFM, p. 302.

Franklin now decided that Philadelphia needed the political equivalent of the Philosophical Society, and on February 9, 1787, formed the Society for Political Enquiries, for Mutual Improvement in the Knowledge of Government, and for the Advancement of Political Science. William Bingham and George Clymer were elected vice presidents. Franklin, of course, was president. Other members of the society, which met every two weeks in Franklin's house, included Thomas Paine, James Wilson, Robert Morris, Gouverneur Morris and Benjamin Rush.

4. GV, p. 166.
5. ND, p. 257.
6. GV, p. 169.
7. SCON, pp. 14–17.
8. Towards the end of 1786, in desperation a group of 600 disgruntled farmers led by former Captain Daniel Shays marched on Springfield, causing the Supreme Court to disband. In January of 1787, Shays and over 1,000 "insurgents" attacked the federal arsenal. The local militia suppressed the rebellion and Shays fled to Vermont. The rebellion focused the minds of the gentrified classes to the possibility of mob rule and encouraged the nomination of delegates to the Constitutional Convention (SCON).

9. GV, p. 172, WB to Richard Price, December 1, 1786, GV, p. 499.
10. MBM, p. 389; SCON, p. 23.
11. GV, p. 175, WB to Lansdowne, March 4, 1787, GV, p. 499, Shelburne Papers.
12. For details of the delegates to the convention, see SCON, pp. 32–37.
13. GV, pp. 177, 499, Thomson to WB, June 25, July 8, 1787.
14. GV, p. 199.
15. GV, pp. 200, 500, Hamilton Papers V, pp. 432–433, VI, p. 656.
16. GV, p. 201, Bingham's memorial to Hamilton, Wettereau's discovery, GV, pp. 202, 500.
17. GV, p. 202.
18. GV, p. 206.
19. GV, p. 208; MBP, p. 299.
20. GV, p. 209; MB, p. 391.
21. GV, pp. 21, 501.
22. GV, pp. 217, 502.

Brissot returned to France and assumed the position of leader of the Girondists, or "Brissotins." He came to a sticky end.

23. GV, p. 218.
24. GV, pp. 219, 502.

Chapter 14

Sources for chapter 14, "Property Fever," include GV, MB, and ALLIS.

1. GV, p. 164; MBM, p. 432.
2. GV, p. 178.
3. Ohio Company, GV, p. 180.
4. Lancaster Turnpike, GV, p. 236.
5. GV, p. 222; MBP, pp. 301–302. The Penn family had made a tactical withdrawal to England for a while after the War of Independence.
6. GV, p. 224; MBM, pp. 399–402.
7. MBM, p. 405.
8. MBM, pp. 411–412; GV, p. 227.
9. GV, p. 228; MBM, p. 414, Knox Papers.
10. Henry Knox (1750–1806) was born in Boston, Massachusetts, of Scottish and Irish ancestry. His father died when he was nine years old, and Henry left school at 12 to work in a bookstore to help support the family. He later opened his own bookstore at the age of 21. He married Lucy Flucker (from a Boston loyalist family, her father being secretary of the province) in 1774. His marriage to Lucy improved his social connection, but he never quite threw off the tradesman image despite his subsequent exploits. He joined the local militia in 1772, and was present at the Boston Massacre. He served as a member of the Boston Grenadier Guards at the Battle of Bunker Hill in 1775. George Washington noticed his ability and he soon became Chief of Artillery. He famously dragged 60 tons of captured artillery from Fort Ticonderoga to New York. He was at Washington's side through most of the war, reaching the rank of Major General. After the British defeat at Yorktown he was given the command of West Point and served as the senior officer of what was left

of the Continental Army until 1784. During this time Bingham and Knox became close friends through their time together in Congress. He was appointed secretary of war in 1785, a post he retained until he assumed the same role in Washington's first cabinet.

Knox retired from government in 1795, but had started to engage in various optimistic speculations, in particular the purchase with William Duer of vast tracts of land in the District of Maine. When Duer found himself in difficulties, Knox and William Bingham became partners as well as friends.

Knox left Philadelphia and removed himself and family to Thomaston, Maine, (where Lucy had inherited land) after his retirement to build himself a mansion in the style of the Binghams, which they called Montpelier.

Bingham saved Knox from financial disaster, and Montpelier was eventually completed, and the small town of Thomaston around it.

Henry and Lucy Knox had 13 children, but sadly only three survived to adulthood. Henry Knox died in 1806, mourned as a war hero but not as a property speculator. Lucy Knox died in 1824 (GV, General Henry Knox Museum).

11. GV, pp. 230, 506; ALLIS, pp. 93–95.
12. GV, p. 230.
13. GV, pp. 231–232; ALLIS, p. 674.
Maine Lands pamphlet, GV, p. 234; ALLIS, p. 278.
14. MBM, p. 418.
William Jackson travelled to Europe with Thomas Willing Francis (Tench Francis' son, Anne Willing Bingham's cousin)

7. SNF, p. 24.
8. GV, pp. 240, 241.
9. GV, pp. 249, 508; HSP, Bingham Papers, William Jackson to William Bingham, August 1793, Correspondence 1793.

Jackson wrote to Bingham on the July 25, 1793,"Mr. Hope is in London ... says he is interested in lots in the Federal City," which suggests that Hope & Co. were serious about speculative real estate investments in America. *Source:* HSP Bingham Papers, Correspondence 1793.

William Jackson to William Bingham, September 27, 1793 (HSP, Bingham Papers, Correspondence 1793).

An invitation to dine with "Mr. Pitt" suggests not only that Jackson had intelligence on American affairs that the prime minister was keen to tap into, but that he was respected in his own right, probably because of his close relationship with George Washington.

10. Gouverneur Morris and Major Jackson did not get on, and words were exchanged. Morris complained to Congress about Jackson's attacks on him. Gouverneur Morris had quickly adopted the French style and was part of a complicated love affair involving Madame Adelaide de Flahaut, Monsieur de Flahaut, Lord Lansdowne's son and Charles Maurice de Talleyrand. Major Jackson did not approve of this behavior in a representative of the United States government.

11. SNF, pp. 49, 50; BBZ, p. 54.
12. MBM, p. 419.
13. GV, p. 260; ALLIS, p. 383.
14. MBM, p. 419.
15. FB to WB, August 31, 1795; ALLIS, pp. 592–594.

Chapter 15

The sources for chapter 15, "Sir Francis Baring Bart," include BBZ, SHE, SNF, MB, and ALLIS.

1. BBZ, pp. 39–40.
2. BBZ, p. 39; NP, May 1793.
3. BBZ, p. 51, Public Characters of 1805, London 1805, p. 34.
4. SNF, p. 42.
5. SNF, p. 41.
6. SNF, pp. 44, 45.

Chapter 16

Chapter 16, "Bingham and Baring Strike a Deal," draws from a number of sources, including BBZ, GV, MB, ALLIS, and SNF.

1. BBZ, p. 61.
2. An American lawyer, politician and diplomat, Rufus King (1755–1827) was born in Scarborough, Massachusetts. He read law at Harvard, but his education was interrupted in 1778 by militia service in the Rev-

olutionary War, becoming a major at the Battle of Rhode Island. He completed his legal studies and was admitted to the bar in 1780. He was elected to the Massachusetts State Assembly in 1783, and was elected a representative to the Continental Congress from 1784 to 1787 (serving with William Bingham), and to the Constitutional Convention in 1787. He moved to New York and was elected to the New York state legislature in 1788, and then was a U.S. senator from New York from 1789 to 1796.

In 1796 he was sent to London by President Washington as minister to the Court of St. James, replacing Thomas Pinckney, where he served until 1803, through the administrations of John Adams and Thomas Jefferson. King and Bingham maintained a correspondence through this period. King inevitably became a correspondent of Francis Baring and Lord Lansdowne.

Rufus King came to trust Francis Baring, and subsequently Alexander Baring, and considered them close personal friends, and in particular friends of the United States. This trust soon resulted in Baring's activities extending from supplying muskets to negotiating U.S. bonds and finally to the Louisiana Purchase and the agency of the United States.

William Bingham resumed his friendship with King when he returned to Britain in 1802; it was Francis Baring that wrote to King on the death of William Bingham in 1804.

Rufus King returned to the United States and served as U.S. senator for New York from 1813 to 1825. He served as American minister again briefly between 1825 and 1826. Rufus King died on April 27, 1827 (BBZ, GV, CH).

3. BBZ, p. 62, Rufus King to Baring, October 6, 1798, Rufus King Papers, vol. 39, f. 62.

4. GV, pp. 268, 269; MBM, p. 421, Papers of Henry Knox.

5. GV, p. 276.

6. GV, p. 269; MBP, p. 301.

7. GV, p. 269.

8. GV, p. 271; ALLIS, Cobb to WB, January 11, 1796.

9. SNF, p. 53; BBZ, p. 63.

10. Charles Baring Jr. (1774–1865) was the second son of Charles Baring (1742–1829), Francis Baring's younger brother. Charles' mother Margaret Gould had inherited the Lew Trenchard Estates in Cornwall, England on the death of her brother Edward. The estates passed in due course to Charles' brother William (on the condition that he change his name to Baring-Gould).

Charles travelled to Charleston, South Carolina, sometime around 1790 to seek a mercantile future there. Francis Baring had established correspondents in Charleston in 1784 or 1785, although it is not known whether Charles was acting for John and Francis Baring & Co. He was unlikely to have been working with his father Charles, who appears to have been in continuous difficulties at the time.

When Alexander Baring travelled to America in late 1795, early 1796 the two cousins (and Alexander Baring's brother Henry) met up in Philadelphia. Alexander Baring subsequently met Charles again in Charleston in 1797. Charles Baring appears as a shareholder of the Bank of Pennsylvania at this time.

In 1797 Charles Baring married Susan Heyward (born in England around 1765), the young widow of wealthy rice planter James Heyward (brother of Thomas Heyward, signer of the Declaration of Independence) of Charleston.

Alexander Baring reported to his father in a letter dated February 13, 1799:

"Charles Baring does not talk of returning or establishing himself in London — he is doing well," and on May 7, 1799, again to his father: "I have heard nothing of the project of sending Cole from Exeter to join Charles Baring."

(John and Charles Baring were in partnership with a Mr. Cole, and the Cole mentioned by Alexander is perhaps a son.)

Susan had inherited several plantations from James Heyward and theirs was a comfortable and prosperous existence.

Around 1829 Charles and Susan purchased 400 acres at the settlement Flat Rock, in western North Carolina, on which they built a summer home, Mountain Lodge, built in the style of an English country estate, with deer park and forest. They started a trend that many other Charlestonians were to follow.

Charles Baring continued to acquire land

at Flat Rock, eventually owning 3,000 acres which he later sold to aspiring Charleston second home owners.

In 1836 Charles and Susan Baring built an Anglican Church, in rural English style, St. John in the Wilderness at Flat Rock.

Susan died around 1844 and her plantations reverted to the Heyward family. Charles had by this time purchased substantial tracts of land in his own right and continued as a plantation owner. In 1850 the Baring plantation extended to over 4,500 acres, 1,600 under cultivation, and included 140 slaves.

Charles remarried at the age of 70, Constance Dent (1816–1891), born in Charleston. They had one child, Alexander, born 1848. Charles and Constance moved to Flat Rock permanently in 1860.

Charles Baring Jr. died in 1865 at the age of 91 (LODC, The Village of Flat Rock, BBA, www.south-carolina-plantations.com)

11. GV, p. 273.
12. BBZ, p. 46.
13. MBM, p. 422.
14. MBM, p. 423.
15. GV, pp. 276–277; ALLIS, p. 658, AB to Hope & Co., May 16, 1796.
16. GV, p. 277.
17. William Duer had made substantial losses on his Ohio Land Company speculation.
18. Jay Treaty, GV, p. 279.

The Jay Treaty:

While Jackson was in Europe, relations between Britain and the United States started to deteriorate again, partly because of the unfinished business arising from the Treaty of Paris, and partly because of the pro-French stance taken by the Republicans, in particular James Madison and Thomas Jefferson. Britain was at war with France again, this time fairly half-heartedly, but its naval blockade was hurting the neutral nations, one of which America had now become. Merchants of all political persuasions were indignant at British treatment of their vessels and their crews, although since many were actively breaking the embargo, the British behavior may well have been justified.

Madison proposed a series of economic retaliatory measures, including an embargo, which were not well received, and by the spring of 1794 war against Britain seemed probable. Hamilton and the Federalist leaders proposed measures to normalize relations; the Republicans remained belligerent but failed to support measures to rearm. In particular they proposed that the president send a special envoy to Britain to attempt reconciliation. John Jay was chosen for the mission after Robert Morris turned it down, and William Bingham and Thomas Fitzsimmons were nominated to bring the merchant community into line, and denounce the Republican retaliation measures.

Despite the support that Bingham and Fitzsimmons were able to rally the Republican measures were passed by the House, but tied in the Senate. Vice president John Adams, using his casting vote from the chair, defeated the motion, and by doing so probably averted war with Britain. How relations with France would fare was another matter (GV, pp. 255, 256).

John Jay left for England on May 12, 1794.

William Bingham wrote to Lord Lansdowne with the news from Congress and impressed on him the importance of a successful treaty. In February 1795 the Pennsylvania Assembly met to propose a new senator to Congress to replace Robert Morris, now retiring. Thomas Fitzsimmons and Speaker William Bingham were proposed as Federalists against three Republicans, including Peter Muhlenberg. Bingham won the vote to become the fourth senator to represent Pennsylvania (GV, pp. 263, 510).

Jay spent several difficult months in negotiation with British foreign secretary Lord Grenville, not helped by the anti–British sentiment in America and in France from new minister James Madison. In early 1795 John Jay sent the treaty arrangements he had been able to make back to President Washington.

Jay and Grenville actually made substantive agreements on a number of issues; the British agreed to vacate the western forts, and in return the United States gave Britain most favored nation trading status and guaranteed pre-war debts to British merchants.

It was certainly not what Washington had hoped for, and, and most definitely not what the pro-French Jeffersonians were expecting, and it would take four months before he could summon the courage to put it before Congress.

President Washington convened the Fourth Congress in June, bringing the date forward from December to debate the "Jay Treaty."

The treaty was debated for 16 days, and although Jay had produced a pragmatic and realistic solution it became the first issue to split the politics of America's emerging parties.

In the end the Senate approved the treaty by the required two-thirds majority. Jay and Hamilton (for his part in drafting the terms), even Washington himself, were vilified as monarchists betraying the Revolution.

Washington passed the bill into law, but the Republicans in the House made a further attempt to kill the treaty almost a year later by denying the appropriations to enable it. Only the oratory of Fisher Ames finally overcame the Republican resistance, and the Jay Treaty was finally put into effect, ensuring peaceful and profitable relations with Britain, at least for another ten years. The Jay Treaty came into effect in April 1796 (GV, p. 279).

Alexander Baring had been there to witness the coming of age of the United States Congress.

The old order, however, was changing; Washington had declared his intention not to run for a third term in office, triggering, as Fisher Ames put it, "a signal, like dropping a hat, for the party racers to start" (GV, p. 293).

19. GV, p. 283, AB to Hope & Co., February 26, 1796.

20. GV, pp. 284–289; ALLIS, p. 654.

21. MBM, p. 429.

Louis-Marie, Vicomte de Noailles (1756–1804) was a French aristocrat and brother-in-law to the Marquis de Lafayette who served with Rochambeau's French expeditionary force. He attended Bingham's wedding ball in 1780 with Rochambeau, Lafayette and the Comte de Damas before returning to the campaign in Newport, Rhode Island.

He returned to France and was elected to the Estates-General in 1789, but left for the United States as the French Revolution took hold. He took up residence with Anne and William Bingham at the Mansion House, where Alexander Baring described him as a "necessary family appendage." He joined Bingham and Alexander Baring on the Maine trip and became a lifelong and close friend. He had salvaged some of his fortune and became an active trader and speculator. He never returned to France; instead he accepted another commission under Rochambeau (the son of his former commander) in Santo Domingo, where he held Mole St. Nicholas against a British siege for five months, before running the blockade and escaping to Cuba. He engaged the British frigate *Hazard*, using his near-perfect English to draw close enough to board and capture the vessel as a prize. He took *Hazard* into Cuba but died there from wounds sustained in the skirmish on January 9, 1804 (EB, GV).

22. GV, p. 286.
23. GV, p. 287.
24. MBM, p. 429.
25. ALLIS, AB to *Hope & Co.*, September 1796.

Chapter 17

Chapter 17, "Barings and Bingham, American Consolidation," is drawn from GV, MB, ALLIS, BBZ, BBO, and BBA.

1. GV, p. 318; MBM, p. 425.
2. GV, p. 320; MBM, p. 425, WB to Knox, March 7, April 23, 1797.
3. Henry Philip Hope (1774–1839) was the second son of John Hope (1737–1784). In 1794 he fled Amsterdam for Germany with his brothers Thomas and Adrian.

In 1797 he travelled to America and toured the eastern states with Alexander Baring. He remained a partner of Hope & Co. but spent much of his life travelling. He had inherited great wealth from his father, and in due course inherited the art collection which Henry Hope had taken to London in 1794.

Henry Philip continued to collect art and gems, including one that has become known as the cursed Hope Diamond. This had been known as the French Blue, part of the French crown jewels, and was worn on occasion by Louis XVI. It was stolen while he and Marie

Antoinette were incarcerated during the French Revolution. It reappeared in the possession of London diamond merchant Daniel Eliason in 1812, 20 years after the theft and beyond the statute of limitations on the theft. The diamond may have been acquired by the British royal family, but no records exist to substantiate that. It appeared in a published catalogue of Henry Philip Hope's gem collection just before his death in 1839.

It passed through many hands before being acquired by New York diamond merchant Harry Winston, who donated it to the Smithsonian Institution in 1958, where it now forms part of the National Gem Collection. It is estimated to be worth $350 million.

4. GV, p. 322; ALLIS, pp. 919–935.
5. GV, p. 322.
6. GV, 322, FB endorsed a letter from AB to FB, May 31, June 1, 1797; MBP, p. 318; BBZ, p. 65.
7. GV, p. 323.
8. GV, pp. 295, 512.
9. GV, p. 300; Papers of Thomas Jefferson, LOC June 15, 1797.
10. ALLIS, p. 842.
11. William Bingham became acquainted with Talleyrand in 1797; they seemed to have mutual interest in money. Bingham was able to put their relationship to good use in Paris in 1803.

Charles Maurice de Talleyrand-Perigord (1754–1838) was born into an aristocratic family in Paris. A limp prevented military service and he entered the church. He was ordained in 1779 and with the help of family influence the distinctly irreligious Talleyrand was appointed Bishop of Autun in 1789.

He was sent to England in 1792 as an unofficial envoy to attempt to avoid war with Britain. He failed in this and was expelled by prime minister William Pitt, travelled to the United States and lived effectively in exile from France until 1796.

He involved himself in various speculations and developed a close relationship with Alexander Hamilton and, for a while, with William Bingham, to whom Lord Lansdowne had directed him, as was his habit with influential French émigrés. He returned to France in 1796 and became foreign minister in the new Directory. He allied himself with Napoleon Bonaparte and kept his position after the 1799 coup.

He was involved with the Quasi-War with the United States, demanding bribes in exchange for his cooperation. He negotiated on behalf of Napoleon in the disposal of the Louisiana tract.

He continued as foreign minister of France through the reigns of Napoleon Bonaparte, Louis XVIII, Charles X and Louis-Philippe, before becoming prime minister in 1815 and French minister to Britain from 1830 to 1834. He died in 1838.

12. GV, pp. 334–336.
13. GV, p. 337.
14. GV, p. 339.

F.D. Roosevelt could have used those words 143 years later.

15. GV, p, 340; Rufus King Papers II, pp. 979, 980, King to WB, December 8, 1798.
16. GV, p. 341.
17. Colonel William Stephens Smith, GV, p. 517.
18. GV, p. 346.
19. BBZ, p. 62; Rufus King Papers, Barings to Rufus King, July 20, 1797.

Chapter 18

Chapter 18, "The Death of Anne Bingham and a Turning Point," is drawn from GV, MB, ALLIS, BBZ, BBO, and BBA.

1. GV, p. 348; SHE, p. 422.
2. GV, p. 350.
3. BBZ, pp. 54, 43.

Alexander Baring was still employed, technically at least, by Hope & Co., with Peter Labouchere managing the day-to-day affairs of the business from London. Labouchere had become attracted to Francis Baring's daughter Dorothy while in London, and had suggested to Henry Hope that should he and Dorothy marry perhaps a partnership in Hope & Co. would be appropriate. He inquired of Francis Baring whether he might approve of a marriage to Dorothy should he become a partner in Hopes. Both Baring and Hope agreed and in time he became a partner in Hope & Co. and husband to Dorothy Baring.

4. BBO, p. 15.

5. BBZ, p. 67; Baring Mss (B) DEP 3 III, AB to FB, January 20, 1799.

Oliver Woolcott, Treasury secretary, had fixed the interest on his subscription offer rather than taking soundings first on the minimum interest that might be offered to complete subscription. Francis Baring also felt that Woolcott should entrust all the loan activity at the London end to him.

6. BBZ, p. 69, FB to WB, November 12, 1800 (Northampton Papers).

7. GV, pp. 383–394.

8. GV, p. 394; BBA, AB to FB, May 7, 1799, "troubles in Mr. Bingham's family...."

9. GV, pp. 394–398.

Before this could happen though, Senate had some unfinished and largely irrelevant business to complete. Envoy Governor Davie had returned from France with a convention that had been signed on September 30 of the previous year, which was little more than a commercial understanding, since no progress had been made on the substantive issues. Europe's political climate had moved on in the previous two years, with Britain close to making peace with France, at least in the short term. The Federalist pugilists attempted to block even these proposals, but the Senate saw sense, and not wishing to be the only power at war with France, approved the convention (treaty) on February 3, 1801.

10. GV, p. 404.

11. GV, p. 410; BBA, AB to FB, March 29, 1801.

12. BBA, AB to FB, May 12, 1801; GV, p. 412.

13. GV, p. 413.

14. BBA, AB to FB, January 20, 1799; GV, p. 415.

15. BBA, AB to FB, May 7, 1799, AB to FB, April 17, 1800.

16. BBA, AB to FB, January 1801.

17. GV, pp. 414, 526; Thomas Willing Francis had travelled to Europe with William Jackson in 1792–1793.

18. William Bingham wrote to Willing & Francis, on August 3, 1801, with instructions regarding his ships *America* and *Canton*.

"It would be expedient to have them sold on arrival.... I should rather take $18,000 for the former ... as for the Canton, she is a very unwieldy vessel ... calculated for the East India or China trade, in which too many adventurers are engaged.... I think £32,000–$40,000 can be obtained for her, but if this price cannot be obtained, the only recourse which will remain is to fit her out on a voyage to Batavia for a cargo of coffee from thence to proceed to Europe with orders to Francis Baring by touching in the channel.

"I hope the cargo of this vessel from Calcutta will arrive to a good market. I shall write in a future letter and give particular directions relative to the apportionment of my share of the proceeds. Considering the embarrassment of the European trade during the present year, it is probable that many of the articles which compose her cargo may be scarce and in great demand. Mr Baring will be happy to give you particular information on this subject of which you may avail yourselves....

"With my most ardent wishes for the success of your establishment" (WL).

Chapter 19

This chapter, "The Louisiana Purchase," draws on several sources, including BBZ, GV, and Thomas Fleming, *The Louisiana Purchase* (LPF).

1. BBZ, p. 49.

2. Proposed partnership in Hope & Co., SNF, p. 56.

3. Comte de Tilly, GV, pp. 368–380.

Jacques Alexandre, the Comte de Tilly (or so he claimed), was one of a series of French aristocratic émigrés who introduced themselves to William Bingham. A friend of the "necessary appendage" Noaillles, the 36-year-old arrived in 1796. He charmed William and particularly Anne with his stories of the French court, claiming to have been a page boy to Marie Antoinette. They soon became alarmed at the passion with which he appeared to court the 15-year-old Maria Matilda, but before any action could be taken Maria crept from the Mansion House and eloped with the handsome Comte and they were married that night.

William Bingham dispatched search parties to recover his daughter and she was "rescued" by the gallant Alexander Baring. The marriage was annulled and Tilly was paid off in exchange for his immediate and permanent departure from the country.

Sadly for Maria Matilda this was only the first of several attempts to relieve her of the Bingham inheritance by marriage.

4. GV, p. 419; MBP, pp. 320–323.
5. GV, p. 417; ALLIS, p, 1115, Richards to Hope & Co., June 7, 1801.
6. LPF, p. 8.
7. LPF, pp. 4, 8, 9.
8. GV, p. 420, WB to Rufus King, January 3, 1803.
9. LPF, p. 26; GV, p. 421.
10. Francois Barbe-Marbois (1745–1837) was born in Metz. He was appointed secretary of the French legation to the United States in Philadelphia, where he stayed until 1785, when he was transferred to Santa Domingo. He returned to France in 1789. Suspected of being a royalist, he was arrested and transported to French Guiana in 1797, and then the island of Oleron. In 1799 he was freed by Napoleon Bonaparte, returned to France and appointed Treasury minister.

He negotiated the Louisiana Purchase (with Talleyrand) in 1803. He continued to hold high office through the restoration of Louis XVIII, and was appointed minister of justice by the Duc de Richelieu in 1815 (The Avalon Project; Yale Law School, *http:// avalon.law.yale.edu/19th_century/louis2. asp*); LPF, p. 114.

11. BBZ, p. 71.
12. U.S. National Archives and Records Administration; Wayne T. De Cesar and Susan Page, "Jefferson Buys Louisiana Territory, and the Nation Moves Westward," *Prologue* 35, no. 1 (Spring 2003).
13. BBZ, p. 71.
14. SNF, p. 60.
15. LPF, p. 130.
16. GV, 424, WB to Cobb, October 15, 1803; ALLIS, pp. 1169, 1172.
17. GV, p. 426.
18. WB's will, GV, p. 427; also see chapter 21, "Epilogue." GV, p. 428, Rufus King Papers IV, p. 384, March 1, 1804.
19. Benjamin Rush autobiography, pp. 268, 269; GV, p. 429.

Chapter 20

1. In 1813 president John Quincy Adams wrote that "the Presidency, the capital and the country had been governed by William Bingham and his family connections."

Source: Maine League of Historical Societies and Museums, Doris A. Isaacson, ed., *Maine: A Guide "Down East"* (Rockland, Maine: Courier Gazette, 1970), p. 381

Chapter 21

This final chapter, "Epilogue," is based on GV, BBZ, BBO, and MBP.

1. GV, p. 427; MBP, p. 434, Philadelphia County Wills, no. 1365.
2. GV, p. 432.
3. GV, p. 428, FB to King, Rufus King Papers IV, p. 384, March 1, 1804.
4. GV, pp. 440, 441. For more information on the Powel House, see Appendix C, Heritage Locations.
5. GV, p. 432.
6. GV, p. 437.
7. BBZ, p. 48.
8. BBZ, p. 51; BBO p. 21; *Gentleman's Magazine*, 1810, p. 293.
9. SNF, p. 56.
10. SNF, p. 64.
11. SNF, p. 68.
12. SNF, p. 69.
13. Henry Philip Hope, see note 3, chapter 17.
14. BBZ, p. 74.
15. BBZ p. 86.
16. GV, pp. 433, 435.
17. GV, p. 435.
18. GV, p. 441.

Appendix D

1. MBM.
2. George Washington to Gilbert Stuart, April 11, 1796.
3. White House Historical Association, *The White House, An Historic Guide* (Washington, D.C.: White House Historical Association, 1971), p. 35.
4. Reid Goldsborough, "The Draped Bust Coins, Anne Bingham's Life," 2008. http://home.comcast.net/~reidgold/draped _busts/intro.html
5. Emily T. Cooperman, ed., *The Country Seats of the United States, William Rus-*

sell Birch (Philadelphia: University of Pennsylvania Press, 2009), pp. 3, 4, 12.

6. Thomas Jefferson to Anne Willing Bingham, February 7, 1787, Anne Willing Bingham to Thomas Jefferson, June 1, 1787.

Source: Letters of Thomas Jefferson: 1743–1826 (RR).

7. Thomas Jefferson to Anne Willing Bingham, March 11, 1788.

Bibliography

Archive and Manuscript Sources

American Philosophical Society, Philadelphia
The Baring Archive, London
City of Westminster Archives, London
Devon Record Office, Exeter and Plymouth
Hampshire Archives and Local Studies Centre, Winchester, Hampshire
Harvard Business School Library, Boston
Historical Society of Pennsylvania, Philadelphia
Independence National Historical Park Library, Philadelphia
James Madison University, Harrisonburg, Virginia
Lewisham Local Studies Centre, London
Library of Congress, Washington
The Lilly Library, Indiana University, Bloomington, Indiana
The Library Company, Philadelphia
Maryland Historical Society, Baltimore
Massachusetts Historical Society, Boston
UK National Archives, Kew, London
U.S. National Archives, Washington
New Jersey Historical Society, Newark
Smithsonian Institute, Washington
University of Delaware Library, Newark, Delaware
University of Pennsylvania Archives, Philadelphia
Whitehouse Historical Society, Washington
Wiltshire Heritage Museum and Library, Devizes, Wiltshire
Winterthur Library, Delaware

Internet Sources

Internet URLs often change over time; these are accurate at the time of writing.
Adams Family Papers—Massachusetts Historical Society, *http://www.masshist.org/digitaladams/aea/*
American Heritage, *http://www.americanheritage.com/*
American Philosophical Society, *http://www.amphilsoc.org/*
American Revolution, the Preservation Society for the American Revolution, *http://www.americanrev.org/*
Ancestry.com — genealogy source, *www.ancestry.com*
The Baring Archive, *http://www.baringarchive.org.uk*

Biographical Directory of the United States Congress, *http://bioguide.congress.gov/bio search/biosearch.asp*
Central Intelligence Agency, *https://www.cia.gov/index.html*
Colonial Hall.com — Biographies of the United States Founding Fathers, *http://colonial-hall.com/index_t1.php*
Cotton-spinning in Northampton: Edward Cave's Mill, Northampton Past and Present, Volume 9, No. 7, 1996-7, *http://www.northamptonshirerecordsociety.org.uk/nrsNpp.html*
The Draped Bust Coins, *http://home.comcast.net/~reidgold/draped_busts/intro.htm*
Famous Americans—virtual American biographies, *http://www.famousamericans.net/*
The Papers of Benjamin Franklin, *http://www.yale.edu/franklinpapers/index.html*
Historical Society of Pennsylvania, *http://www.hsp.org/*
Independence National Historical Park Library, *www.nps.gov/inde/library-and-archives.htm*
The Papers of Rufus King—New York Historical Society, *http://dlib.nyu.edu/finding aids/html/nyhs/king.html*
General Henry Knox Museum, *http://www.generalknoxmuseum.org/*
Library Company of Philadelphia, *http://www.librarycompany.org/*
Library of Congress—American Memory Project, Law Library of Congress, *http://lcweb2.loc.gov/ammem/index.html*
A Century of Lawmaking—U.S. Congressional Documents and Debates, Law Library of Congress, *http://memory.loc.gov/ammem/amlaw/lawhome.html*
Documents from the Continental Congress and the Constitutional Convention, Law Library of Congress, *http://memory.loc.gov/ammem/collections/continental/*
Letters of Delegates to Congress, 1774–1789, Law Library of Congress, *http://memory.loc.gov/ammem/amlaw/lwdg.html*
Journals of the Continental Congress, Law Library of Congress, *http://memory.loc.gov/ammem/amlaw/lwjc.html*
Indiana University Library — Guide to the Collections of the Lilly Library, *http://www.indiana.edu/~liblilly/overview/history_in.shtml*
Independence National Historical Park, *http://www.nps.gov/inde/*
National Parks Service — Signers of the United States Constitution, *http://www.nps.gov/history/history/online_books/constitution/constitution.htm*
The Pennsylvania USGENWEB project, *http://www.usgwarchives.org/pa/philadelphia/watsontoc.htm*
University of Pennsylvania archives, *http://www.archives.upenn.edu/*
The Peerage.com — genealogical survey of the peerage of Britain, *www.thepeerage.com*
Philadelphia architects and buildings, *http://www.philadelphiabuildings.org/pab/index.cfm*
Source of United States political biography, *http://politicalgraveyard.com/index.html*
From Revolution to Reconstruction—a hypertext on American history from the colonial period until modern times, University of Groningen, *http://www.let.rug.nl/usa/index.htm*
Soldier Statesmen of the U.S. Constitution, United States Army Center of Military History, *http://www.history.army.mil/books/RevWar/ss/ss-fm.htm*
Supplying Washington's Army, United States Army Center of Military History, *http://www.history.army.mil/books/RevWar/risch/risch-fm.htm*
Teaching American History, Ashbrook Center for Public Affairs, Ashland University, Ohio, *http://teachingamericanhistory.org/*
James C. Samuel Touchet's Florida Plantation, 1771, Tequesta XXXV, Historical Museum of Southern Florida, *http://hmsf.org/publications/tequesta-1971–1980.htm*.
UK genealogy archives, *www.uk-genealogy.org.uk*

UK National Archives, *http://www.archives.gov/*
U.S. History.org, the Independence Hall Association in Philadelphia, *http://www.ushistory.org/index.html*
United States military history online — United States Army Center of Military History, *http://www.history.army.mil*
U.S. National Archives Library Information Center, *http://www.archives.gov/research/alic/index.html*
United States Department of State, *http://www.state.gov/*
United States Supreme Court index of cases, *http://supreme.justia.com/index.html*
University of Virginia Library, *http://www2.lib.virginia.edu/etext/index.html*
Virtuology education project, *http://www.virtualology.com/*
Winterthur Library, the Bingham Papers at the Winterthur Museum and Country Estate, Delaware, *http://www.winterthur.org/about/library.asp?sub=whats_new*

Printed Sources

Alberts, Robert C. *The Golden Voyage: The Life and Times of William Bingham, 1752–1804*. Boston: Houghton Mifflin, 1969.
Allen, G.W. *The Naval History of the American Revolution*, 2 vols. Boston: Russell and Russell, 1913.
Allis, Frederick S. *William Bingham's Maine Lands, 1790–1820*. 2 vols. Boston: Colonial Society of Massachusetts, 1954.
Ashton, T. S. *An Economic History of England: The Eighteenth Century*. London: Routledge, 2005.
Auger, Helen. *The Secret War of Independence*. New York: Duell, Sloan and Pearce, 1955.
Bingham, William. *A Description of the Situation, Climate, Soil and Productions of Certain Tracts of Land in the District of Maine and Commonwealth of Massachusetts*. Philadelphia, 1793.
_____. *A Letter from an American Now Resident in London, to a Member of Parliament ... on the Commerce of the United States*. Philadelphia, 1784.
Brant, Irving. *James Madison, the Nationalist, 1780–1787*. Indianapolis: Bobbs-Merrill, 1948.
Brown, Margaret L. "Mr. & Mrs. William Bingham of Philadelphia, Rulers of the Republican Court." *Pennsylvania Magazine of History and Biography* 61, no. 3 (July 1937): 286–324.
_____. "William Bingham, Agent of the Continental Congress in Martinique." *Pennsylvania Magazine of History and Biography* 61 (Jan. 1937): 54–87.
_____. William Bingham, Eighteenth Century Magnate. Pennsylvania Magazine of History and Biography 61, no. 4 (Oct. 1937): 387–434.
Buist, Marten G. *At Spes Non Fracta*. Amsterdam: Bank Mees & Hope, 1974.
Cerami, Charles A. *Jefferson's Great Gamble*. Naperville, IL: Source Books Inc., 2003.
Chastellux, Francois Jean. *Travels in North America, 1780, 1781, 1782*. London, 1787.
Christie, I. R. *Crisis of Empire, Great Britain and the American Colonies 1754–1783*. New York: W. W. Norton, 1966.
Clark, William Bell. *Lambert Wickes: Sea Raider and Diplomat*. New Haven, CT: Yale University Press, 1932.
Conway, Stephen. *War, State and Society in Mid-Eighteenth Century Britain and Ireland*. New York: Oxford University Press, 2006.
Cooke, Alistair. *America*. London: Weidenfeld & Nicholson, 2002.

Cooperman, Emily T., ed. *The Country Seats of the United States, William Russell Birch.* Philadelphia: University of Pennsylvania Press, 2009.
Deane, Silas. *The Papers of Silas Deane.* Collections of the New York Historical Society: New York, 1887–1891.
De Cesar, Wayne T., and Susan Page. "Jefferson Buys Louisiana Territory, and the Nation Moves Westward." *Prologue* 35, no. 1 (Spring 2003).
Ferguson, Niall. *Empire: How Britain Made the Modern World.* London: Penguin, 2003.
Ferris, Robert G., and James H. Charleton. *The Signers of the Constitution.* Flagstaff, AZ: Interpretive Publications Inc., 2001.
Fitzmaurice, George Lord Edmund. *Life of William, Earl of Shelburne, Afterwards First Marquess of Lansdowne.* 2 vols. London: Macmillan, 1912.
Fitzpatrick, John C., ed. *The Writings of George Washington.* 39 vols. Washington, D.C.: Government Printing Office, 1931–1944.
Fleming, Thomas. *The Louisiana Purchase.* Hoboken, NJ: John Wiley, 2003.
Gardiner, Michael. *The Gardiner Family History.* London: Library of the Society of Genealogists.
Gilmor, Robert. *Memoir or sketch of the history of Robert Gilmor as derived from his books and papers in the possession of his eldest son, and from the conversations with his father and mother on the subject at various times.* Baltimore: privately printed, 1840.
_____. *Memorandums Made in a Tour of the Eastern United States in 1797.* Boston: Bulletins of the Boston Public Libraries, 1893.
Haymer, Philip May, George C. Rogers, and David R. Chestnut, eds. *The Papers of Henry Laurens.* Columbia: University of South Carolina Press, 1972.
Hidy, R. W. *The House of Baring in American Trade and Finance.* Cambridge, MA: Harvard University Press, 1949.
Howard, James I. *Seth Harding: A Naval Picture of the Revolution.* New Haven, CT: Yale University Press, 1930.
Jackson, Joseph. "Washington in Philadelphia," a paper read to the Historical Society of Pennsylvania on March 14, 1932, Philadelphia, *Pennsylvania Magazine of History and Biography* 56, 1932,
Johnson, Paul. *A History of the American People.* London: Weidenfeld & Nicolson, 1997.
King, Charles R., ed., *The Life and Correspondence of Rufus King.* 6 vols. New York: Putnam, 1894–1900.
Laurens, Henry. *The Papers of Henry Laurens.* Laurens Papers Project, Department of History, Columbia: University of South Carolina.
Maine League of Historical Societies and Museums. Doris A. Isaacson, ed. *Maine: A Guide "Down East."* Rockland, ME: Courier Gazette, 1970.
Morgan, Edmund S. *Benjamin Franklin.* New Haven, CT: Yale University Press, 2002.
Newman Dorman, W. A. "The Second Troop of Philadelphia Cavalry." *Pennsylvania Magazine of History and Biography* 45, July 1921, pp. 257–291; vol. 46, January 1922, pp. 57–77, April 1922, pp. 154–172; vol. 49, January 1925, pp. 75–94.
Oberholzer, Ellis Paxton. *Robert Morris: Patriot and Financier.* New York: Macmillan, 1903.
Orbell, John. *Baring Brothers & Co, a History to 1939.* London: Baring Brothers, 1985.
Owen, Roger. *Lord Cromer.* New York: Oxford University Press, 2005.
Rush, Benjamin. *Autobiography.* George W. Corner, ed. Philadelphia: Princeton University Press, 1948.
Sawtelle, William Otis. *William Bingham of Philadelphia and His Maine Lands* Philadelphia: Genealogical Society of Pennsylvania, 1926.
Trevelyan, G. M. *A Shortened History of England.* London: Penguin Books, 1942.
Wharton, Francis, ed. *The Revolutionary Diplomatic Correspondence of the United States.* 6 vols., Washington, D.C.: Government Printing Office, 1889.

White House Historical Association. *The White House, An Historic Guide*. Washington, D.C.: White House Historical Association, 1971.
Wright, Robert K., Jr., and Morris K. MacGregor, Jr. *Soldier-Statesmen of the Constitution*. Center of Military History, United States Army, Washington, D.C., 1987.
Young, Eleanor. *Forgotten Patriot: Robert Morris*. New York: Macmillan, 1950.
Ziegler, Philip. *The Sixth Great Power, Barings 1762–1929*. London: Collins, 1988.

Index

Page numbers in **_bold italics_** indicate a biographical sketch.
Page numbers in _italics_ indicate an illustration.

ABN AMRO 167
Adams, Abigail (wife of John Adams) 95, 99, 110, 190
Adams, Miss Abigail (Nabby) 95, 96, 110, 143
Adams, John 29, 36, 63, 79, 80, 81, 90, 92, 96, 99, 110, 130, 137–140, 144, 148, 156, 170, 171, 216–218
Adams, John Quincy 64, 95, 227
Adams, Samuel 28, 63
Adlum, John 114
Administration of Justice Act 31
American Philosophical Society 17, 102, 184
American War of Independence 1, 2, 37, 72, 75, 79, 91, 112, 118, 170, 206, 219
Ames, Fisher 130, 195
Annapolis Convention 105
Argout, Capt.-Gen. d' 51, 52, 54, 92
Arnold, Maj. Gen. Benedict 77, 92
Articles of Confederation 65, 93, 104
Ashburton, 1st Lord of the First Creation _see_ Dunning, John
Ashburton, 1st Lord of the Second Creation _see_ Baring, Alexander
Ashburton, 2nd Lord of the Second Creation _see_ Baring, William Bingham
Ashburton, Lady Ann Louisa (wife of Alexander Baring) _see_ Bingham, Ann Louisa
Ashburton, Harriet (Lady Montagu; wife of William Bingham Baring) 192

Bache, Benjamin Franklin 62, 139
Baker-Holroyd, John (1st Earl of Sheffield) 93
Bancroft, Dr Edward **_210_**, 216

Bank, Mees & Hope NV 167
Bank of North America 87, 88, 90, 91, 111, 146, 204, 205, 219
Bank of Pennsylvania 79, 82, 83, 86, 146, 205, 216
Bank of the United States 111, 146, 171
Barbe-Marbois, Francois 159, 160, **_227_**
Baring, Alexander (Lord Ashburton; Francis Baring's son) 118, 121–123, _124_, 125–136, 141–143, 146–152, 154–163, 164–169, 172, 2–3, 204, 218, 222
Baring, Ann Louisa (wife of Alexander Baring _see_ Bingham, Anne Louisa
Baring, Anne Eugenia (daughter of Alexander Baring) 178
Baring, Charles (son of Johann Baring) 6, 7, 9, 127, **_201_**, 202, 203
Baring, Charles, Jr. (son of Charles Baring) 127, 131, 136, 151, **_222_**, 223
Baring, Dorothy (daughter of Francis Baring) 171
Baring, Edward Charles (1st Lord Revelstoke; son of Henry Baring) 1, 169
Baring, Elizabeth (Lady Ashburton; daughter of Johann Baring; wife of John Dunning) 6, 73, **_203_**, 213
Baring, Elizabeth (wife of Johann Baring) _see_ Vowler, Elizabeth
Baring, Evelyn (1st Earl of Cromer; son of Henry Baring) 193
Baring, Francis (son of Johann Baring) 6–9, _10_, 11–14, 68, 72, 118–125, 131, 153, 160, 161, 173, 199, 201, 202, 213, 215
Baring, Francis Thornhill (1st Baron Northbrook) 192
Baring, Franz (Johann Baring's father) 5, 199, 201

Index

Baring, George (Francis Baring's son) 11, 118, 131, 146, 151
Baring, Harriet (Francis Baring's wife) *see* Herring, Harriet
Baring, Henry (Francis Baring's son) 11, 118, 127, 131, 151, 154, 163–166, 218
Baring, Henry Bingham (William Bingham's grandson; Henry Baring's son) 178
Baring, Johann (Francis Baring's father) 5, 6, 199, 200, *202*
Baring, John (Johann Baring's son) 6, 8, 14, 200–203
Baring, Maria Matilda (wife of Henry Baring) *see* Bingham, Maria Matilda
Baring, Thomas (1st Earl Northbrook) 192
Baring, Thomas (son of Francis Baring) 118, 166
Baring, Thomas Vowler (son of Johann Baring) 6, 200–203
Baring, William (son of Francis Baring) 118, 131, 146, 151
Baring, William Bingham (2nd Lord Ashburton; William Bingham's grandson; Alexander Baring's son) 146, 192
Baring Brothers & Co 1, 167, 171
Barre, Isaac 27, 68, 72, 73, *206*
Barry, Capt. John 47
Beaumarchais, Pierre Augustin Caron de 38, 55, 63, 72, 139, *208*
Bellevue, Blackpoint, New Jersey 113, 185
Benezet, Hannah (wife of John Benezet; William Bingham's sister) *see* Bingham, Hannah
Benezet, John (William Bingham's brother-in-law) 55, 79, 85
Bentham, Jeremy 80, 94, 213, *214*
Biddle, Edward 34
Bingham, Ann Louisa (William Bingham's daughter; wife of Alexander Baring) 91, 97, 131, 147, 141, 150–154, 163–166, 170, 171
Bingham, Anne (wife of William Bingham; Thomas Willing's daughter) 82, 83, *84*, 85, 90–96, 101, 111, 115, 123, 131, 151, 163, 171, 187–191
Bingham, Lady Anne (wife of Lord Lucan) 100, 187
Bingham, Hannah (William Bingham's sister) 85
Bingham, James (William Bingham's brother) 21, 85
Bingham, John (William Bingham's brother) 21, 85
Bingham, Maria Matilda (William Bingham's daughter; wife of Henry Baring) 92, 97, 131, 150–153, 163–164, 226
Bingham, Mary (Molly) Stamper (William Bingham's mother) *see* Stamper, Mary (Molly)
Bingham, William 2, 18, *19*, 20–36, 40–50, 54, 58–62, 72, 78–82, 85–87, 90–102, 112–117, 124–137, 149 —164, 170, 187–191, 205, 209, 210, 214, 217
Bingham, William (William Bingham's father) 18
Bingham, William, Jr. (William Bingham's son) 148, 151, 152, 164, 165
Bingham Estate 164, 195
Bingham, Inglis & Co. 90, 120
Birch, William Russell 190
Blackwell, Hannah Bingham Benezet (wife of Robert Blackwell; William Bingham's sister) *see* Bingham, Hannah
Bonaparte, Lucien 157
Bonaparte, Napoleon 138, 139, 145, 156, 159, 173, 225, 227
Bonvouloir, Archard de 38, 39
Boston Massacre 29
Boston Port Act 31
Boston Tea Party 30, 72
Bouille, Gen. Francois Claude Amour 56–59, 78, 83, 94, 99, *210*
Bowood Estate 74, 94, 121, 154, 186, 214
Brissot, Jean-Pierre 110, 220
Bulteel, Louisa Emily 193
Burke, Edmund ' 70, 72, *214*
Burr, Aaron 148, 149
Byrd, William, III 14

Cabot, Sen. George 140
Canaan Company 91, 112
Carmichael, William 59
Carpenters Hall 32, 111, 184
Chapman, Capt. John 51
Chastellux, Gen. Marquis de 83, 95, *217*
Chatham, Earl of *see* Pitt, William, the Elder
Cheapside 5, *7*, 8, 11, 185, 214
China Trade 113, 206
Christ Church, Philadelphia 82, 109, 111, 206
City Tavern, Philadelphia *33*, 34, 78, 87, 88, 106, 184
Clymer, George 78, 107
Cobb, Gen. David 123, 126, 128, 131, 136, 155, 161, 163
Cobbett, William 139

Index

Cock, Edmund 5, 200
Codman, John 126
Coercive Acts 31, 32, 34, 36, 72; *see also* Intolerable Acts
College of Philadelphia (later the University of Pennsylvania) 16, 18, 41, 109, 206, 216
Committee of Secret Correspondence 35, 37–43, 50, 52, 209
USS *Confederacy* 58, 59, 61, 77, 79
Constitutional Convention 106, 108, 115, 211
Continental Army 35, 37, 39, 41–43, 53, 65, 103, 107, 221
Cornwallis, General Charles 67, 73, 87, 88
Courcey, Gov. de 51, 54

Damas, Comte de 85, 224
Davie, William Richardson 145, 226
Deane, Silas 35, 39, 40, 52, 54, 60–63, 92, 93, 205, *208*
Declaration of Independence 35, 52, 216
Democratic Republican Party 107, 130, 138, 140, 144, 148, 156, 223
De Smeth 161
Devonshire Bank 72, 202
Devonshire Square 119, *120*, 122, 152, 166, 185
Devonshire, Duchess of (Georgiana) 187
Dexter, Samuel 148
Dickinson, John 18, 28, 35–37, 216
Disraeli, Benjamin 119, 168
Draped Bust Coin *190*
Duer, Col. William 112–115, 127, 172
Duer Panic 119
Dumas, Charles 37, *207*
Dunning, John (1st Lord Ashburton of the First Creation; Francis Baring's brother-in-law) 68, 203, *212*

East India Company 30, 31, 68, 71–73, 131, 146, 171, 212
Elsworth, Oliver 145

Federalist Party 85, 104, 108, 138, 140, 144, 145, 156, 171, 212
Fenwick, John 18
First Continental Congress 12, 34
Fitzmaurice, Willam Petty (later 2nd Earl of Shelburne; 1st Marquess of Lansdowne) 68, 73, 75, 80, 90, 93, 94, 99, 106, 118, 121, 164, 163, 170, 173, 188, 203, 207, *213*
Fitzsimmons, Thomas 93, 107, 217, 223

Flete Estate 1, 186
Fox, Charles James 130, 213
Francis, Tench, Jr. 79, 88, 152, 216
Francis, Thomas Willing (son of Tench Francis) 152, 226
Franklin, Benjamin 17, 18, 34, 37–42, 57, 62–68, 80, 81, 86, 88, 90, 102–105, 201, 205
Franklin, William Temple 62, 166
French Revolution 131, 156

Gage, Gen. 31, 35
Gallatin, Albert 129, 149, 160, 173
Galloway, Joseph 32
George II (King of England, 1727–1760) 26
George III (King of England, 1760–1820) 26, 34, 72, 73, 172, 213
Gillon, Alexander 66, 67, *212*
Gilmor, Robert 90, 92, 99, 114, 118, 127, 152, 155, 156, 164, *217*
Gilmor, Robert & Co. 95
Gilmor, Robert, Jr. 113, *218*
Gould, Edward 202, 222
Gould, Margaret 202, 222
Graaf, Johannes de 54
Grafton, Duke of 28
Grange 167, *168*, 172, 186
Great Northwest Ordinance 26, 106, 112
Great Proclamation 26
Greenleaf, James 135
Grenville, George (British Prime Minister) 26, 27, 31

Hallock, William 43
Hamilton, Alexander 99, 105–110, 114, 135, 141, 148, 156, 170, 171, 205
Hamilton Economics 108
Hancock, John 34, 104
Harding, Capt. Seth 59
Hare, Charles Willing 152, 164, 218
Hare, Robert 91, 216
Harrison, Benjamin 36
Harrison, Richard 52, 55, 209
Henry, Patrick 145
Herring, Harriet (wife of Francis Baring) 11, 154, 166
Herring, Thomas (Archbishop of Canterbury) 11
Herring, William (Harriet Herring's father) 11
Hertford House 186, 219
Historical Society of Pennsylvania 184
Hodge, William 54, 62, 209, 210

Hope, Adrian 70, 214
Hope, Henry *69*, 70, 95, 119–122, 125, 127, 128, 130, 153, 160, 167, 170, 214, 215
Hope, Henry Philip 122, 136, 167, 215, **224**
Hope, Thomas 70, 119, 122, 167, 214
Hope & Co. 2, 70, 71, 95, 119–121, 128, 136, 137, 146, 151, 159, 167, 170, **214**, 215
Hope Diamond 167, 224
USS *Hornet* 43, 46
Hortalez, Roderigue et Cie 34, 54, 55, 57, 72, 208
Humphreys, David 125
Huntington, Samuel 60, 83, 194

Inglis, Samuel 90, 95, 217, **218**, 219
Intolerable Acts *see* Coercive Acts
Izard, Ralph 64, 65

Jackson, Elizabeth (wife of Maj. William Jackson) *see* Willing, Elizabeth
Jackson, Maj. William 65, *66*, 67, 96–98, 103, 109, 115, 121, 122, 125, 146, 172, **211**, 221
Jay, John 36, 59–63, 78, 85, 36, 58–63, 78, 85, 94, 98, 110, 223
Jay, Sarah 58, 85
Jay Treaty 123, 130, 138, **223**
Jefferson, Thomas 34, 36, 40, 62, 63, 79–81, 95–98, 107, 110, 121, 135, 137, 140, 146, 148, 156, 160–163, 170, 187–191, 212, 217
John and Charles Baring & Co. 8, 11, 68, 71
John and Francis Baring & Co. 1, 8, 9 68, 71, 75, 94, 143, 146, 151, 152, 203, 214, 215

Kennebec Tract 127, 128, 165, 185
King, Rufus 125, 141, 154, 163, 170, 221, 222
Knox, Gen. Henry 107, 114, 115, 123, 126, 128, 136, 141, 146, 158, 164, 172, **220**, 221
Knox, Lucy Flucker 115, 122

Labouchere, Peter Cesar 119, 123, 166, 167, 225
Lafayette, Marquis Marie Joseph du Motier de 85, 97, 204, 208, 212, 224
Lancaster Turnpike Company 113
Langdon, John 35
Lansdown House, Philadelphia *113*, 131, 154, 164, 185, 188
Lansdowne, Lord *see* Fitzmaurice, William Petty (later 2nd Earl Shelburne)

Lansdowne House (formerly Shelburne House, London) *74*, 94
Lansdowne Portrait 188, *189*
Larkbeare House 186
Laurens, Henry 65, 79, 81, 90, 93, 201
Laurens, John 65–67, 96, 201, 211
Lazzarini, Francois 110
Leclerc, Gen. Charles Victor Emmanuel 158
Lee, Dr. Arthur 38, 40, 62, 63, 86, 92, **207**
Lee, Richard Henry 36, 62, 63, 208
Lee, William 64, 65
Lee Manor, Lewisham 153, *154*, 186
Le Maitre, Adrien 52, 209
Lewis, Mordecai 113, 114
USS *Lexington* 46, 47, 209
Library Company 110, 184
Library Hall 184
Lincoln, Levi 149
Liston, Sir Robert 34, 36
Livingston, Philip 35
Livingston, Robert (American Minister to France) 80, 86, 98, 158, 160
Longleat Estate 168
Louis XVI (King of France, 1754–1791) 38, 63, 65, 72, 96, 121, 208
Louisiana Purchase 2, *159*, 160, 161, 167, 170, 173, 218
Lovell, James 36, 58, 78
Lucan, Lady *see* Bingham, Lady Anne
Luzerne, Chevalier de la 83, 90

Madison, Dolley (wife of James Madison) 188
Madison, James 63, 81, 99, 105, 109, 128, 134, 149, 157–161, 163, 171, 173, 223
Maine Lands 115, 125, 126, 128, *133*, 212
Manchester Square *102*, 186
Manchester Trade 71
Mansion House, Philadelphia 101, *102*, 110, 113, 128, 131, 140, 152, 164, 184, 217, 219
Marshall, John 99, 138, 148
Massachusetts Bay Regulating Act 31
McCall, Anne (wife of Thomas Willing) 17
McHenry, James 148
McKean, Thomas 35, 88, 109
Membland Estate 1, 186
Mesturas, James 75, 118
Mifflin, Thomas 32, 109
Mildmay, Anne Eugenia Baring (wife of Humphrey St. John Mildmay; daughter of Alexander Baring) *see* Baring, Anne Eugenia

Index

Mildmay, Henry Bingham (Alexander Baring's grandson) 1, 2, 169
Mildmay, Humphrey St. John 178
Mincing Lane 119, 185
Molasses Act 25, 27
Monroe, James *101, 158–160, 220*
Montpelier, Maine 115, *132*, 134, 185, 221
Morris, Gouverneur 85, 120, 121, *217*, 221
Morris, Robert 2, 14, *15*, 17, 17, 35, 37, 39–42, 53, 55, 63, 77, 78, 80, 82, 85–91, 94, 106, 108, 112, 113, 121, 135, 173, *204*, 205, 209, 216
Morris, Robert, Sr. 204, 205
Murray, David (2nd Earl of Mansfield; Viscount Stormont) 56
Murray, William Vans 144, 145

USS *Nancy* 46, 47
Navigation Act 24, 28, 42
Nelson, Admiral Horatio 144
New York Restraining Act 27
Nicholson, John 135
Nixson, Thomas 166
Noailles, Vicomte Louis de 85, 131, 134, *224*, 226
Non Importation Agreement 22, 29
North, Lord Frederick 28, 31, 72, 73, 89, 213, 224

Ohio Company 112, 114
Oswald, Richard 80
Otis, James 25, 27, 28
Ouverture, Toussaint L' 156, 158

Paice, Nathaniel 8, 9, *201*
Paine, Thomas 36, 40, 63
Penn, John 92, 113
Penobscot Tract 128, 129, 136, 165, 185
Pichon, Louis Andre 144, 158
Pilgrim Affair 60, 78
Pinckney, Charles 148, 211
Pinckney, Thomas (American Minister to London) 138, 139, 212, 222
Pitt, William the Elder (Earl of Chatham) 28, 213
Pitt, William the Younger 73, 76, 93, 108, 118, 144, 171, 207, 221
Pontiac Rebellion 26
Powel, Elizabeth Willing (wife of Samuel Powel; Anne Bingham's aunt) 83, 143
Powel, Samuel 14, 109, *204*, 216
Powel House 165, 184, 204
Prejent, Coctiny de 56

Price, Richard 56, 80, 92, 94, *214*
Priestley, Dr. Joseph 70, 80, 94, 212–*214*

Quartering Act 31
Quasi-war with France 145, 156, 225

Read, Jacob 145
USS *Reprisal* 46–53, 62, 209, 210
Republican Court 110, 171
Revelstoke, 1st Lord *see* Baring, Edward Charles
Revenue Act 27, 29
Revere, Paul 32
Reynolds, Sir Joshua 98, 190
Richards, John 131, 132, 137, 155
Richelieu, Duc de (Prime Minister of France) 2, 167
Rochambeau, Gen. Jean Baptise (Comte de) 83, 87, 217, 224
Rockingham (2nd Marquis) *see* Watson-Wentworth, Charles
Ross, James 145
Rothschilds 167, 171
Royal Bank of Scotland 167
Royal Exchange Assurance 68, 73
Rush, Dr. Benjamin 34, 79, 103, 163, 164

Second Continental Congress 51, 212
Secret Committee 35, 37, 39, 41, 43, 52, 53
Seven Years War 5, 24, 26, 35, 70, 71, 157, 170, 214, 215
HMS *Shark* 49, 50, 51, 53, 61, 209
Shays Rebellion 104
Sheffield, John, Lord *see* Baker-Holroyd, John
Shelburne, 2nd Earl *see* Fitzmaurice, William Petty
Sherman, Roger 36
Shippen, Anne (wife of Charles Willing) 14, 204, 216
Shippen, Edward 14, 204
Shippen, Joseph 14, 204
Short, John 202, 203
Smith, Abigail Adams (wife of William Stephens Smith; daughter of John Adams) *see* Adams, Abigail
Smith, Col. William Stephens 110, 141
"Sons of Liberty" 27, 29, 207
Spencer, Lady Diana 193
Stamp Act 27, 35, 205, 207
Stamper, John (William Bingham's father-in-law) 18, 27, 72
Stamper, Mary (Molly; William Bingham's mother) 18, 77, 82, 88

Stamper Bingham Blackwell Mansion 18, 25
Stockton, Richard 145
Stone, Richard 68, 70
Stormont, Viscount David Murray *see* Murray, David
Stratton Park 152, *155*, 167, 186, 212
Stuart, Gilbert 98, 188
Stuart, John (3rd Earl of Bute) 207
Sugar Act 26
Swinton, Holland 166

Talleyrand, 139, 141, 144, 145, 156, 159, 173, 221, ***225***, 227
Tea Act 28, 29, 30, 72
Thynnne, Henry Frederick (3rd Marquis of Bath) 192
Tilly, Comte de 154, 165, ***226***
Tilly, Maria Matilda (wife of the Comte de Tilly; William Bingham's daughter) *see* Bingham, Maria Matilda
Touchet, Samuel 7, 8, 71, 73, ***200***–202
Townshend, Charles 27, 201, 207
Townshend Duties 27, 28, 30, 201
Treaty of Amiens 157
Treaty of Amity and Commerce 62, 64
Treaty of Ildefonso 157
Treaty of Mortefontaine 156, 157
Treaty of Paris 81, 89, 93, 113, 121

Vaughan, Benjamin 70, 94, 105, 212, ***214***
Vergennes, Comte de Charles Gravier 38, 56, 63–66, 79–81, 87, 139, ***208***
Vogels, Rebecca 5, 199
Voute, Robert 215
Vowler, Elizabeth (daughter of John Vowler; wife of Johann Baring) 5, 6, 8, 200
Vowler, John 5, 6, ***200***

Wall, Charles 75, 118, 146, 166
Wallace Collection 186, 219
Walpole, Robert 26
Ward, Samuel 35
Washington, George 26, 35, 41, 53, 55, 57, 65, 67, 73, 77, 78, 83, 87, 90, 96, 99, 106, 110, 115, 120, 123, 135, 138, 141, 145, 147, 188, 190, 221, 224
Washington City 114, 148, 149, 151
USS *Wasp* 46, 47
Watson-Wentworth, Charles (later 2nd Marquess of Rockingham) 3, 9, 27, 73, 213
Webster-Ashburton Treaty 185
Welgelegen 119, 185
Wentworth, Paul 210
West, Benjamin 98, 190
Wharton, Thomas 21, 22, 35, 40
Wickes, Capt. Lambert 46, 48, 50–52, 54, ***209***
Wickes, Richard 47
Wilkes, John ***207***, 213
Willing, Abigail (daughter of Thomas Willing; Anne Willing's sister) 131, 164
Willing, Anne (daughter of Thomas Willing; wife of William Bingham) *see* Bingham, Anne
Willing, Charles 14, 16, 187, 204, 216
Willing, Elizabeth (daughter of Thomas Willing; wife of Major William Jackson) 116, 117, 123, 212
Willing, Francis & Co. 147, 152
Willing, Morris & Co. 14, 17, 34, 39, 41–45, 55, 72, 82, 95, 205
Willing, Thomas 14, *16*, 17, 39, 41, 45, 78, 82, 87, 88, 97, 107, 110, 116, 123, 146, 147, 150, 152, 163, 165, 168, 204, 216
Willing, Thomas Mayne (son of Thomas Willing) 152, 164, 218
Willing Mansion 82
Willinks 79, 127, 161
Wilson, James 21, 34, 78, 83, 87, 90, 91, 112, ***216***
Wolfe, Gen. 24, 206, 213
Woolcott, Oliver 226

"XYZ" Affair 140

Yorktown, seige of 67, 73, 87, 220

www.ingramcontent.com/pod-product-compliance
Lightning Source LLC
Chambersburg PA
CBHW051219300426
44116CB00006B/634